New Femininities in Digital, Physical and Sporting Cultures

Series Editors
Kim Toffoletti
School of Humanities and Social Sciences
Deakin University
Melbourne, VIC, Australia

Jessica Francombe-Webb
Department for Health
University of Bath
Bath, UK

Holly Thorpe
School of Health
University of Waikato
Hamilton, New Zealand

Aarti Ratna
Leeds, UK

Palgrave's New Femininities in Digital, Physical and Sporting Cultures series is dedicated to exploring emerging forms and expressions of femininity, feminist activism and politics in an increasingly global, consumer and digital world. Books in this series focus on the latest conceptual, methodological and theoretical developments in feminist thinking about bodies, movement, physicality, leisure and technology to understand and problematize new framings of feminine embodiment. Globally inclusive, and featuring established and emerging scholars from multi-disciplinary fields, the series is characterized by an interest in advancing research and scholarship concerning women's experiences of physical culture in a variety of cultural contexts.

Jorge Knijnik • Gabriela Garton
Editors

Women's Football in Latin America

Social Challenges and Historical
Perspectives Vol 2. Hispanic Countries

Editors
Jorge Knijnik
School of Education
Western Sydney University
Penrith, NSW, Australia

Gabriela Garton
World Players Association
Melbourne, VIC, Australia

ISSN 2522-0330   ISSN 2522-0349   (electronic)
New Femininities in Digital, Physical and Sporting Cultures

ISBN 978-3-031-09126-1   ISBN 978-3-031-09127-8   (eBook)
https://doi.org/10.1007/978-3-031-09127-8

This Palgrave Macmillan imprint is published by the registered company Springer Nature Switzerland AG.
The registered company address is: Gewerbestrasse 11, 6330 Cham, Switzerland

Jorge dedicates this book to his treasured parents Carlos and Olga; I will forever cherish our family's car trips across South America when I took in bits of the continent's diverse cultures, and, most of all, I learned how to love South American hermanos y hermanas.
Gabriela dedicates this book to her husband Cristian; thank you for your support and company as we moved across the world to follow my footballing and academic dreams; I'm looking forward to sharing many more adventures with you in the years to come, including this new experience called parenthood.

Foreword

This book is the story of a marginalised community trying to deconstruct, reshape, and take ownership of the most engrained and influential popular expression in Latin America: *fútbol*, which is full of myths. It is more than a space to socialise. It is, in many ways, a form of living with specific codes and ideals. Since the nineteenth century, football has been used as a political arena, whether to discuss politics or as a place to seek political support. Nevertheless, this platform historically has been played and led by men.

Being a core part of the Latin American cultural life, this activity also has played a role in educating new generations and transmitting values and social expectations. Masculinity and femininity have been clearly shaped and reproduced by football all over the region, including the role of women in and out of the sport. As Brenda Elsey, the author of *Futbolera*, stated: 'misogyny and homophobia constitute a significant part of sexism facing women's football'. Furthermore, since the 1980s, the sport has had to endure the stereotype of being a 'breeding ground' of lesbianism, with all the bullying and consequences that affect girls and women who dare to practice it. Yet, as all the authors in this book argue, progress is being achieved on many grounds led by women, particularly players as agents of change.

While writing these lines, players are fighting for equal investments, salaries and conditions in developed countries. For example, in the

United States, a historic settlement between the US Women's National Team players and the US Soccer Federation has been reached. This agreement includes, among other things, a payment of $24 million and a promise that players on the women's and men's teams will be paid at an equal rate going forward, contingent on the negotiation of the next collective bargaining agreement (CBA). In Australia, a new 2021 CBA has positioned the W-League as one of the most progressive in the world. Sweden also has developed the same conditions and compensation for men's and women's national teams. New Zeeland, Denmark, and other countries are on similar paths.

Unfortunately, this is not the case in Latin America, which is not there yet. Collective agreements are almost nonexistent and rarely consider the voice of the players. Nevertheless, there is hope. As will be seen in the course of this book, there are major milestones and turning points underway for women's rights: Argentina with the semi-professionalisation of the sport; Chile with a landmark law passed in Congress that mandates the execution of contracts for women players in the national league; in Mexico the *Liga MX Femenil* has become a benchmark in terms of visibility and growth of the industry; and so on.

This book should facilitate the readers' understanding of how the historical power dynamics have set the rhythm for progress in women's football in Latin America, as well as the current challenges it faces. Notably, it helps to unveil some of the barriers beyond the recurrent arguments and myths that contend that there is 'simply' insufficient interest, relegating women's football to an inferior version of the 'true' game.

The book's chapters make a remarkable contribution to a perception of how women and organised movements have shaped football in the last decade and how the sport has served to dismantle other myths about the role of women in the social and political sphere. The authors invite everyone to rethink and deconstruct what it means to be a woman soccer player. What does it mean to be a professional in the region? What constitutes a fan? Undoubtedly, what is here will help readers understand why the most *'footballised'* region in the world has not been able to unleash the full potential of women at local and international levels they deserve in the sport.

A new framework is needed that allows for gender equality, visibility, recognition and investment. Here, academia has a tremendous role to play in advancing women's football, recognising the history, struggles and bravery of its community and questioning the current system that makes the barriers to the development of women's football a nearly insurmountable task. National and international institutions that govern football at various levels are responsible. The 2020 FIFPro's 'Raising Our Game' report on women's football showed the unequal treatment governing bodies give to the game and players, especially outside Europe and other industrialised countries. It is true; the sport is growing but at very unique paces. This book allows one to reflect on the historical burden, and the current challenges players face in Latin America as a way to think of a future with more opportunities for the next generations.

Vice President, FIFPro   Camila García Pérez
Director, Chile's National Association
of Female Football Players (ANJUFF)

Acknowledgements

This book, as a collaborative initiative of producing and disseminating original practices and research, is in debt to numerous people who have exchanged ideas and dreams with the authors and facilitated our work 'from behind the scenes'. Therefore, we would like to convey our appreciation and gratitude to many of them who were incredible sources of inspiration and support.

Initially, to all chapter authors and contributors in this book; their patience during the numerous steps of the peer review and editing processes, as well as their belief in our work were terrific; without their efforts and high level of expertise this book would never have seen the light of day. Extra kudos to them for producing brilliant research in academic English all through a pandemic that severely hit most of their South American countries.

We are truly thankful to Associate Professor Kim Toffoletti, Dr. Jessica Framcombe-Webb, Professor Holly Thorpe, and Dr Aarti Ranta—the wonderful Palgrave Macmillan editors of the New Femininities in Digital, Physical and Sporting Cultures book series. Since the inception of our book proposal their collegiality, confidence, as well as intellectual input to this project were outstanding; after working with them, there is no doubt that we will publish feminist books only under their guidance.

We are also indebted to the amazing crew at Palgrave Macmillan who helped achieve the best outcome we could ever dream of for this book; in addition, we thank Dr. Marcella Meneguello for her diligent efforts with the formatting and editing of the book's initial draft.

In addition, we would like to express our gratitude to the Institute for Culture & Society at Western Sydney University, in particular to Professor Brett Neilson, for providing the preliminary funding to support the book proposal. To Dr. Jamie Cleland for his input when this book was only a dream; to the *Centro Esportivo Virtual* (CEV) and to the *Associacion Lationoamerica de Estudios Socioculturales del Deporte* (ALESDE) for their support in disseminating the original trilingual call for papers that resulted in more than 70 potential contributions. Finally, we are grateful to all the external reviewers who gave their time and extensive know-how to improve all manuscripts submitted for this book.

Last, but certainly not least, we would like to acknowledge the *guerreras*—past, present and future—who have fought and continue to fight for a better and more equal sport and world. This book would not have been possible without you. Thank you for telling your stories and letting us fight by your side, on and off the pitch.

Jorge Knijnik
Gabriela Garton

Contents

Notes on Contributors

Eliana Aguilar Aguilar is a Bolivian professor and a researcher; she has a bachelor's degree in Psychology from the Universidad Católica Boliviana (La Paz, Bolivia). She is a therapist for women victims of violence, children and adolescents at risk. Her research interests include gender violence, football and family relationships from a gender perspective.

Ana Alcazár-Campos is a full Professor in the Department of Social Work and Social Services at the University of Granada (Spain). In addition, she is a member of the Group of Research: 'Otras. Perspectivas Feministas en Investigación Social' at the University of Granada. Her research interests include the analysis of public policies from a gender perspective, specifically those related to gender violence; the interaction between feminisms; and social intervention.

Miguel Cornejo Améstica is a full Professor in the Department of Physical Education in the School of Education at Universidad de Concepción (Chile). He was initially trained as a physical education teacher and received his PhD degree in Physical Activity and Sports Sciences at Université Joseph Fourier (Grenoble, France). He was the inaugural president of the Latin American Sociology of Sports Association (ALESDE, 2008–2014).

Jimena Aon has been an activist with *La Nuestra Fútbol Feminista* (Buenos Aires) since 2014. She is currently a shoe manufacturer. During the 1990s she fought neoliberalism in Dario Santillan Popular Front. She has studied Popular Education at the Universidad Madres de Plaza de Mayo (Argentine, 2001) where she formulated workshops in territorial social movements. She joined La Nuestra in 2014, where she can put into practice the knowledge acquired on her journey.

Gabriela Ardila Biela is a historian with a master's degree in interdisciplinary Latin-American studies from the Freie Universtät (Berlin). She is currently a doctoral candidate at the University of Hamburg where she is examining the historic path of female football in Colombia. Her work focuses on feminist and anticolonial historiographic research methodologies.

Mark Biram is a PhD candidate at the University of Bristol in the United Kingdom. He holds a master's in Latin American Interdisciplinary Studies from the University of Newcastle (UK). His PhD project is an ethnographic study emphasising players' perspectives on Women's Club Football in Brazil and Colombia. The project is supported by a University of Bristol scholarship and has been supported financially by the Society of Latin American Studies (SLAS) and the Bristol–Brazil fund.

Belén Bramanti has a bachelor's and teaching degrees in Physical Education. He is an educator and an activist with *La Nuestra Futbol Feminista* (Buenos Aires) in a political space that he deems to be an inexhaustible source of learning, challenges and where he founded the *abrazo de una manada*.

Claudia Pedraza Bucio is a researcher and Professor at the La Salle University in Mexico City. She holds a PhD in political and social sciences (National Autonomous University of Mexico). Her research interests are focused on gender, communication and sports issues. She worked as a sport journalist for websites like *Diosas Olímpicas*, *Buen Toque* and *Provincia*.

Felipe Canan is a Senior Lecturer in the Physical Education department at the University of the State of Amazonas (UEA/Brazil). He holds a PhD in physical education from the State University of Maringa (UEM/Brazil). He is a researcher on the fields of sports politics and sports pedagogy.

Isela Guadalupe Ramos Carranza is a full-time Research Professor in the School of Educational Sciences of the University of Colima (Mexico). She holds a PhD in physical culture from the Autonomous University of Nuevo León and a bachelor's of physical education and sport from the University of Colima. She is a member of the Mexican National System of Researchers and of the Academic Group UCOL85, 'Education and Movement'.

Carlos Matus Castillo is a Professor in the Departamento de Ciencias del Deporte y Acondicionamiento Físico at the Universidad Católica de la Santísima Concepción in Chile. He is a teacher of physical education and has a master's degree in physical education from the Universidad de Concepción (Chile); a master's in motor skills and education, and PhD in physical activity and sport from the University of Barcelona and INEFC (Spain). He is a researcher around physical education and sport from the social sciences. He is a recipient of a Chilean Research Council (ANID) Grant for Early Career Researchers and is currently examining gender topics in Physical Education and Initial Teacher Training.

Rosa López de D'Amico has a PhD and is Full Professor at the Universidad Pedagógica Experimetal Libertador (Venezuela) and the Coordinator of the Research Center: Estudios en Educación Física, Salud, Deporte, Recreación y Danza (EDUFISADRED), Maracay, Venezuela. She is the president of the International Society for Comparative Physical Education and Sport (ISCPES) and has edited, among others, *Women and Sport in Latin America* (Routledge, 2016*) and Sport in Latin America: Policy, Organization, Management* (Routledge, 2016).

Carolina Paz Cabello Escudero is a sociologist from the Universidad de Valparaíso, Chile. She has a master's in Economic and Social History from the Pontificia Universidad Católica de Valparaíso and is a PhD candidate in history from the same university. Additionally, Carolina has a diploma in 'Culture, Memory and Heritage' UV, a diploma in 'Gender and Sport' UBA, and a specialisation course in 'Sports Management' at the Chilean Olympic Committee and 'Sports and Society' at CLACSO. She is a researcher at ASIFUCH, CESDE, 'Formiga, Hacía una economía política del fútbol chileno' and 'Archivo Fútbol Femenino'; a member of the study group 'Sport, Culture and Society' at CLACSO. Also, she is a director of Santiago Wanderers of Valparaíso and a feminist activist, sports communicator and amateur female football player.

María José Figueroa is an activist with *La Nuestra Fútbol Feminista* (Buenos Aires) and an undergraduate sports student at the Universidad de Avellaneda. She is a feminist, a football player and a Football Technical Director. She considers *La Nuestra* a space for co-learning and personal growth.

Gabriela Garton has a bachelor's degree in Hispanic Studies from Rice University and a master's degree in Sociology of Culture and Cultural Sociology from the National University of San Martin. She has a PhD in Social Sciences from the University of Buenos Aires. Gabriela is also a doctoral fellow with the Argentine National Council for Scientific Research (CONICET) and currently is a visiting scholar at the Sport and Exercise Science Department at Victoria University in Melbourne. She also is involved in research projects related to football, gender and sports in general at both Victoria University and the Gino Germani Research Institute.

Julia Hang has a degree in sociology and her PhD in social science from the University of La Plata (UNLP), Argentina, where she is also a Professor of Classical Social Theory II. She received a postdoctoral fellowship from the National Scientific and Technical Research Council (CONICET). Julia studies sports, gender and politics in Argentinian sports clubs.

Matthew Hawkins has a PhD in anthropology from Carleton University, Ottawa, Ontario, where he is also an instructor (faculty) in the Department of Sociology and Anthropology. Matthew studies Argentinian football clubs in the formation of the urban space, as well as football fandom as a site of social politics.

Nemesia Hijós has a bachelor's degree in social anthropology from the Universidad de Buenos Aires (UBA), a master's degree in anthropology from the Institute of Economic and Social Development (IDES)—Institute for High Social Studies (IDAES)—of the Universidad Nacional de San Martín (UNSAM); she has a PhD in social sciences from the University of Buenos Aires (UBA), where she also serves as an Assistant Professor. In addition, she is a recipient of a doctoral fellowship from the Argentine National Council for Scientific Research (CONICET). Nemesia is a member of research groups related to football, politics, management, gender and social studies of sports at the Gino Germani Research Institute (IIGG).

Jorge Knijnik is a Brazilian-Australian academic currently working as an Associate Professor at Western Sydney University (Australia), where he is a researcher in the Institute for Culture & Society and the Centre for Educational Research. Dr. Knijnik embarked on his doctoral studies at Universidade de São Paulo (Brazil) where he developed an original interpretation of women's and gender issues in football, as well as human rights violations. In 2010, he was presented with the prestigious 'building the gender equity' award by UNICEF, the Brazilian Research Council and the UN-Women for his research work promoting gender equity within educational settings. He has authored/edited, among others: *Tales of South American Football: Passion, Glory and Revolution* (Fair Play Publishing, 2023); *Australianas: Cultura, Educação e Esporte do outro lado do mundo* (Fontoura, 2021); *The World Cup Chronicles: 31 Days that Rocked Brazil* (Fair Play Publishing, 2018); *Embodied Masculinities in the Global Sport* (FIT, 2015); *Gender and Equestrian Sports: Riding Around the World* (Springer, 2013); *Genero e Esporte: masculinidades e feminilidades* (Apicuri, 2010); *A mulher brasileira e o esporte: Seu corpo, sua historia* (Mackenzie, 2003).

Paula Korsakas has a bachelor degree in sports sciences and a master's degree in sport pedagogy from the University of São Paulo (USP/Brazil) and is a PhD candidate at Universidade Estadual de Campinas (UNICAMP/Brazil). She is also an international coach developer, sport consultant and activist for the right to play sports and gender equality. She met *La Nuestra Futbol Feminista* in 2019 and was the facilitator of the Community of Practice on Popular Education, Feminism and Football in 2020.

Sophie Legros is a PhD candidate in International Development at the London School of Economics. She is currently doing fieldwork in Medellin, Colombia, using mixed methods to research changes and continuities in gender norms and their intersections with women's economic empowerment, gender inequalit and development outcomes. She has extensive experience as a practitioner in sport for development in 20 countries worldwide.

Emilio Gerzaín Manzo Lozano is a full-time Research Professor in the School of Educational Sciences and a member of the Academic Group UCOL85, 'Education and Movement', at the University of Colima (Mexico). He was initially trained as an elementary school teacher and has received a bachelor's in hearing and language, a master's in linguistics, and a PhD in modern literature, with a specialty in hermeneutics and orality. His research interests are physical culture and sport, pedagogy and didactics of physical culture.

Juliana Roman Lozano has been an activist with *La Nuestra Fútbol Feminista* (Buenos Aires) since 2010. She is a Colombian, a feminist and a football player. She is also a migrant woman who, since a very young age, has been travelling around the world. She is a documentary filmmaker, a National football technical director and an anthropology student. In 2020 she was part of the only all-women coaching team for Huracán, a First Division football club during Argentina's first professional womens championship. She considers *La Nuestra* as her place in the world; there her battles are voiced and her strength for militancy, learning and knowledge is nurtured.

Verónica Moreira is a Professor at the University of Buenos Aires (UBA) in Argentina, where she earned a PhD in social sciences. She also has completed a (research) master's in social anthropology (IDES-IDAES/UNSAM) and a bachelor's degree in anthropology (UBA). She is a researcher at the Argentine National Council for Scientific Research (CONICET). For several years, she has coordinated research groups related to football, politics, sports in general and body techniques at the Gino Germani Research Institute (IIGG).

Giovanna Xavier de Moura is a PhD candidate in the Department of Physical Education at the State University of Maringa (UEM/Brazil). She is a lecturer in the Physical Education Department at Ingá University Centre (Uningá, Brazil). She is a researcher in the Research Group on Public Policies of Sports and Leisure. Her interests are focused on studying gender relationships in sport, rugby and sport policies.

Sarah Oxford is a researcher at the School of Public Health and Preventative Medicine, Monash University, Australia. Her work examines the intersections of gender, sexuality, race and class, with a specific focus in sport for development. Sarah completed her PhD in 2018 at Victoria University, receiving a citation for the Vice Chancellor's Award for Excellence in Research and Research Training. Sarah's research has been published widely in peer-reviewed journals and scholarly books.

Magali Perez Riedel received her PhD in communication from the Universidad Nacional de La Plata, Argentina. Her areas of study are digital communication, discrimination, queer studies and representations of LGBTQ people. Magalí is the author of 'Gender and Sexual Diversity' in the blog *Boquitas Pintadas* (2014) and the editor of *Trans, Out, and in the Public Eye: Representations of Transgender People on Television and Film* (Peter Lang).

Ana Margarita Salas de la Hoz is from Santa Marta, Colombia. An early researcher, she is pursuing studies in anthropology and is the author of the article 'Women's Football: A Goal against Machismo. A Global and Local Perspective on Processes of Violence and Gender Inequality'.

An activist, youth leader and student-athlete herself, she plays for the Magdalena regional team selection.

Ciria Margarita Salazar is a full-time Research Professor in the School of Educational Sciences of the University of Colima (Mexico). She is a member of the Mexican National System of Researchers, a member of the Academic Group UCOL85, 'Education and Movement'. She holds a PhD and a master's in physical and artistic education from the University of Extremadura, and a master's in social sciences from the University of Colima.

Mónica Santino is an activist with *La Nuestra Fútbol Feminista* (Buenos Aires). She is a physical education teacher, a sports journalist, a football technical director, and a former football player. She has worked in several women's football community clubs, and she plays an active part in the Argentinian Homossexual Community (1989–1996). She played football for the All Boys in the Argentinean Football Federation (AFA) tournaments (1995–2000).

Pablo Ariel Scharagrodsky is a lecturer and a researcher in the School of Education at the Universidad de Quilmes (UNQ/Argentine), where he is the cocirector of the research group, 'Discourse, Practices and Institutions in Education'. He has earned a PhD in social sciences and humanities from the Universidad Nacional de Quilmes (UNQ/ Argentine). He has also completed a master's (research) in social sciences with a major in education (FLACSO, Argentina) and a bachelor's degree (teaching) at the Universidad Nacional de La Plata (UNLP/Argentine). His research interests are history of education, feminist pedagogies and gender studies. He has published, among others, *The Changing Face of the Sport: Anglophonic Perspectives* (1970–2010), coedited with Cesar Torres (Editorial Prometeo, 2019), and *Women on the Move* (Editorial Prometeo, 2016).

Fernando Augusto Starepravo is an Associate Professor in the Department of Physical Education at the State University of Maringa (UEM/Brazil). He holds a PhD in physical education from the

Universidade Federal do Paraná. He is the leader of the Research Group on Public Policies of Sports and Leisure. His research focuses on sports policies for various social groups.

Enriqueta Tato has been a physical education teacher since 2012, a sign language interpreter (Villasoles, 2013–2015), a ASAM (2015–2017), a feminist activist, a football player until 2017, and a physical trainer and runner. She is a teacher and has played for several football clubs—Racing, Huracán, Boca and San Lorenzo, with whom she disputed the Libertadores Cup in 2012. In 2020 she was part of the only all-women coaching team for Huracán, a first division football club during the first professional women's championship in Argentina. She has been part of La Nuestra's coaching team since 2013. She oversees the training sessions for the youth and adult categories and of the planning for all categories.

Giovanni Alejandro Pérez Uriarte is a PhD candidate in contemporary and modern history at the Instituto de Investigaciones Dr. José María Luis Mora (Mexico). He received a master's degree in history and a bachelor's degree in Latin American studies from the Universidad Nacional Autónoma de México. His research interests are the social and cultural history of football in Latin America. He is a researcher of the Research Group of History of Physical Education and Sports in Mexico.

Lesbia Verenzuela is an Associate Professor (PhD) at the Universidad Nacional Experimental Politécnica de las Fuerzas Armadas (UNEFA), Campus Cagua, Venezuela. She is a researcher in the Research Centre: Estudios en Educación Física, Salud, Deporte, Recreación y Danza (EDUFISADRED) in Maracay, Venezuela.

List of Diagrams

List of Tables

1

Introduction

Jorge Knijnik and Gabriela Garton

Football is ubiquitous. The omnipresence of the 'world game' across the continents, however, does not mean that its cultures are homogeneous. On the contrary, diverse people take the game, adjust it to their social contexts and create a range of footballing cultures that are distinct and unique in the various regions where the sport is played.

For these reasons, Jayne Caudwell (2011), in her major work about women's football in Europe, emphasises the importance of more local gender analysis within football to continue to build feminist momentum within the game. Caudwell's points are critical to understanding today's female participation in football in Latin America, and how it represents, or does not, an act of gender resistance both in the sport and beyond.

J. Knijnik (✉)
School of Education, Western Sydney University, Penrith, NSW, Australia
e-mail: J.Knijnik@westernsydney.edu.au

G. Garton
World Players Association, Melbourne, Australia

© The Author(s), under exclusive license to Springer Nature Switzerland AG 2022
J. Knijnik, G. Garton (eds.), *Women's Football in Latin America*, New Femininities in Digital, Physical and Sporting Cultures,
https://doi.org/10.1007/978-3-031-09127-8_1

1

The publication of the two volumes of the *Women's Football in Latin America: Social Challenges and Historical Perspectives*, a book-length collection within Palgrave's New Femininities in Digital, Physical and Sporting Cultures series, is thus both timely and relevant for global gender research. It indicates that new forms of gender expression, performance and feminist activism that have been influenced by, but also impacted neoliberal ideologies around the world, have found a complex and paradoxical social terrain in South American football.

As shown by the amazing, and many times surprising, narratives of both volumes of the collection (volume 1, *Brazil*, and this volume, *Hispanic Countries*), the gendered contexts where South American football drama reveals itself is undoubtedly linked with the global gender (dis)order, changes and tensions that have been described and analysed in the other volumes of the '*New Femininities*' series. This link becomes clearer when initially looking into the fertility of the new feminist research methodologies applied by researchers in both the Brazilian and the Hispanic Countries volumes: (1) from oral and documentary historical analysis that connect the sporting femininities of the nineteenth and early twentieth centuries to those of the twenty-first century, and (2) from local ethnographies to policy studies that enhance one's understanding of the social constraints, where it tries to stay afoot, as well as employing digital tools to further comprehension of the mediatic forces that shape women's football in South America. All the analytical tools displayed in the *Women's Football in Latin America* collection reveal and offer novel ways to investigate the diverse range of physical cultures emerging in this post-feminist era.

Another relevant feature of both volumes of this collection is the multidisciplinary application of its contents. The array of disciplines within the social sciences and humanities—from philosophy to sociology, from media studies to sports pedagogies and sport for development approaches—are a sound indication of the relevant overlapping that need to be carefully considered when researching women's football in the contemporary moment. Moreover, new data (e.g., women's indigenous football in South America) that appear in the volumes reinforce the necessity for more refined studies that acknowledge the relevance of the native population in the construction of the gender order within local and global sporting and physical cultures; they are central for advancing ongoing debates around new femininities in sports and physical cultures.

Therefore, and following Caudwell's insights on sustaining the drive of football feminism in Latin America, this Hispanic Countries volume of the *Women's Football in Latin America* collection aims to bring to the international English readership a variety of high-quality research on Latin American women's football that has emerged during the past decade, with a focus on the Spanish-speaking countries. With chapters written by researchers and practitioners with a profound knowledge of the diverse contexts in which women's football is played and lived across Latin America, they look at the social and historical meanings of the embodied representations of gender differences that have been deeply embedded in the history of Latin American women and football.

The authors report on how, in a variety of ways, Latin American women have found spaces in-between, amid severe *macho* structures, to establish and play their football. Moreover, the studies in this volume show that these patriarchal configurations are embedded by intersectional inequalities of race, geography and social class. The researchers bring evidence to demonstrate that these intersectional oppressions act together to reinforce each other, making the work of denouncing, untangling and overcoming them a craft that requires ongoing theoretical and analytical fine-tuning efforts to unveil the various levels of oppression that girls and women face within these macho structures of football in Latin America.

The volume has been structured around three sections. The first, 'Football: The Final Feminist Battleground in Latin America', presents four studies that directly demonstrate how football became a major front for feminist struggle in Latin America. In the first chapter, Gabriela Garton, Nemesia Hijós and Verónica Moreira, after showing what the Argentinean women's players withstood during the last decades—harsh conditions when trying to play the game—and how they overcame these obstacles, discuss the players' feminist-inspired self-organisation that finally delivered better, but far from perfect, circumstances for the players to achieve their sporting goals. Next, Matthew Hawkins and Julia Hang discuss the socio-historical processes where the feminist agenda has intertwined with female athletes' demands, resulting in the creation of a feminist football political movement in Argentina.

In the following chapter, Claudia Pedraza Bucio presents an in-depth study of women's football supporters in Mexico, pointing out once again how distinct waves of feminism have affected the political struggle for space and respect within the football context of the *barras*. Wrapping up this section, the team from *La Nuestra Fútbol Feminista*—Enriqueta Tato, Jimena Aon, Juliana Roman Lozano, Maria Belén Bramanti, María José Figueroa, Mónica Santino and Paula Korsakas—analyse the history of their Community of Practice in Popular Education, Feminism and Football. They discuss their trajectory within a Buenos Aires *villa* (i.e., a shantytown) and the challenges faced to sustain educational momentum during the COVID-19 pandemic.

A relevant point to note in this section is how authors of various chapters employ the critical work of Brazilian educationalist Paulo Freire. They go beyond the mere denunciation of the harsh conditions of the social and material oppressions lived by the communities they work with; these authors and football activists are inspired by Freire to support their groups, within dissimilar contexts, to go through the consciousness process as described by Freire, not only to denounce the current unsustainable practices and unequal conditions but also to announce a better reality: the Freirean untested feasibility—a world where another and more equitable football is possible.

After this influential first section, what follows is '*Mujeres Futbolistas*: Experiences and Achievements', a section that looks at a range of achievements and conquests of *mujeres futbolistas* (women footballers) across Latin America. In its first chapter, Sophie Legros, Sarah Oxford and Ana Margarita Salas de la Hoz discuss how Colombian women have been affected by the political power and policies that have restricted their access to sporting practices, specifically football. Moreover, their analysis also shows the intersectional factors that permeate footballing's gender relationships in the country—for example, either furthering or hindering sporting opportunities for women according to their social class. Next, Eliana Aguilar Aguilar and Ana Alcazár Campos bring the football trajectories of the *karimachus*, Bolivian women who dared to challenge the country's strict unwritten gender rules to play football, to the reader; their in-depth look at these women's life journeys within football is a clear portrait of how the sport can be a turning point in the struggle against deep-rooted prejudices within Bolivian society.

Venezuelan women's football is the topic of the next chapter. Using a well-developed argument, Rosa López de D´Amico and Lesbia Verenzuela show the path that women took from invisibility to being acknowledged as footballers by the football authorities in the country; thus, they demonstrate how politics and power intertwine with women's football in that country and how the game once again empowers women towards freedom of movement and action. This fight is also reflected in the following chapter, where Mark Biram tells the interesting story of the JC Sport Girls, a female-only Peruvian club, that, despite being able to represent their country in several major international tournaments, has not been able to secure funding from their federation to further their football activities. In this text, the author also demonstrates the limitations of CONMEBOL policies directed to support women's football on the continent.

Next, Ciria Margarita Salazar, Isela Guadalupe Ramos Carranza and Emilio Gerzaín Manzo Lozano affirm the relevance of semi-amateur football practices among well-educated women in Mexico. The authors argue that by playing football, these academic women have not only found individual freedom and satisfaction but also legitimised female bodies and all their potential within a highly patriarchal society. Women's football in Chile closes out this section, as Miguel Cornejo Amestica, Carlos Matus Castillo and Carolina Paz Cabello Escudero outline the achievements of Chilean women in football over the past two decades and discuss the sexist barriers they encountered and overcame to achieve more egalitarian conditions within the sport. What draws readers' attention in this section is clearly the existing link between all these experiences; although some took place in the North (Mexico) or more in the South of the continent (Chile), they are all deeply marked by gender oppression and by the progressive consciousness of women and how they had to fight for their right to play football.

The third section, 'Latin American Conversations: *pasado, presente y futuro*', examines the past ('pasado') record of women's football on the continent, the changes that are currently ('presente') in place and contemplating on what the future ('futuro') holds for the sport. Pablo Ariel

Scharagrodsky and Magali Perez Riedel start the section with an intriguing historiography of how media coverage of women's football during early twentieth-century Argentina was shaping the feminine ideals that would prevail in the next decades. The authors argue that, at the end of the day, such standards would delay women's participation in football in the years to come. Next, Giovanni Alejandro Pérez Uriarte presents an exquisite study on Alicia Vargas, a pioneer Mexican footballer. By using her story as a case study, the author presents a comprehensive portrait of the evolution of women's football in Mexico within a rigid, male-controlled structure.

In the next chapter, readers will be able to get a comprehensive view on the historical developments of women's football in Colombia since the late 1940s, as well as an understanding of the machinery behind their erasure from the country's footballing historiography. Gabriela Ardila Biela, the author, incorporates the voices of many Colombian players who have helped build this history while challenging the gender binaries within Colombian society. In the following chapter, Fernando Augusto Starepravo, Giovanna Xavier de Moura and Felipe Canan offer an original interpretation of the new CONMEBOL initiatives to support women's football in South America. As the authors present the data and the outcomes of these policies, they pose the intriguing question of whether CONMEBOL's new regulations can be seen as the 'saviour' of women's football on the continent, comparing it to the initiatives of Title IX legislation in the United States. Jorge Knijnik and Gabriela Garton close the section and the book with a range of considerations on what is to come in women's football on the continent and what the role of social researchers should be to sustain this feminist moment within the sport and beyond.

The chapters of this book were written by popular educators, coaches, historians, teachers and players—in summary, people who are on a football field daily, struggling for change even during the COVID-19 pandemic. Throughout the conversations we had with the authors while preparing to write the stories presented here, many questions were asked as to whether the writing in the language of the coloniser (English) would advance, or not, the feminist football cause. Finally, a consensus was reached; as a language, football could also be interpreted as a coloniser's cultural product; however—and the chapters of this volume are evidence of this—football can also be used and adjusted to serve one's own purposes. This is made clear across this volume's outstanding, and many times startling, accounts. The stories undeniably will provide a comprehensive insight into Latin American women's football, from historical advances to previous and current social challenges, to anyone who reads them.

Additionally, the chapters' writers will be rewarded if their narratives can be pedagogically used to instruct and encourage people around the globe to keep struggling for gender and social justice across Latin American countries. As shown in every single chapter, the football field is certainly one of the vital spaces in Latin America that can be used to build a fairer gender order in countries that are so diverse but share a strict patriarchal order. The authors' hope is that this volume can join the many actions already under way to support a new gender order in Latin America.

Reference

Caudwell, J. (2011). Gender, feminism and football studies. *Soccer & Society, 12*(3), 330–344.

Part I

Football: The Final Feminist Battleground in Latin America

2

No nos callamos más: A Turning Point in Women's Football and Women's Rights in Argentina

Gabriela Garton, Nemesia Hijós, and Verónica Moreira

Introduction

After 12 years without qualifying for a World Cup, in 2018 the Argentine women's national football team secured the chance to compete in the sport's most prestigious competition. Qualifying for the 2019 Women's

_____

G. Garton (✉)
Gino Germani Research Institute, University of Buenos Aires,
Buenos Aires, Argentina
e-mail: gabygarton@gmail.com

N. Hijós
Gino Germani Research Institute, University of Buenos Aires,
Buenos Aires, Argentina

Faculty of Health Sciences, National University of Mar del Plata,
Mar del Plata, Argentina

CONICET, Buenos Aires, Argentina
e-mail: nemesiahijos@gmail.com

© The Author(s), under exclusive license to Springer Nature Switzerland AG 2022
J. Knijnik, G. Garton (eds.), *Women's Football in Latin America*, New Femininities in
Digital, Physical and Sporting Cultures,
https://doi.org/10.1007/978-3-031-09127-8_2

World Cup (WWC) in France, as well as the squad's performance in the tournament, were the team's most significant sporting achievements, although these were also accompanied by other collective triumphs off the pitch. This team played a key role in raising awareness about their sport and in the eventual (semi-) professionalisation of women's football in Argentina. Within the context of the massive growth of women's movements both nationally and globally, these players, along with many others from teams throughout all of Argentina, began to question and challenge their historic marginalisation from the country's most popular sport.

The objective is to analyse this process of change through the theoretical lens of Paulo Freire's (2017) notion of '*conscientização*', complemented by Nancy Fraser's (1998) discussion of the dual aspects of social justice claims and her understanding of gender as a two-sided category. This chapter begins with a brief discussion of the history of women's football in the broader context of sports in Argentina. Although some examples of the earliest evidence of women playing football are mentioned, the focus is more on the sport in its last years of 'amateurism'—although this period can be better described as '*marronismo*' (literally 'brownism' or 'illegal professionalism').

Later, the events and context leading up to the (semi-) professionalisation of the women's first division in 2019 are considered to understand the relationship between this political decision and the organisation and mobilisation of Argentine female footballers, in an attempt to improve their physical conditions—demands from earlier years that had gone unheard of and unattended to—in a context marked by massive demands for the expansion of the rights of women and malcontent genders in various areas of society.

V. Moreira
Gino Germani Research Institute, University of Buenos Aires,
Buenos Aires, Argentina

CONICET, Buenos Aires, Argentina
e-mail: vmoreira@sociales.uba.ar

'Conscientização' and Social Justice on an Uneven Football Pitch

To analyse the concept of change as a dialectic process, an interaction between dominant and subordinate groups, we use Brazilian educator Freire's (2017) notion of '*conscientização*' (critical consciousness)—the idea of 'learning to perceive social, political, and economic contradictions, and to take action against the oppressive elements of reality' (p. 9). According to Freire, as conscious beings, people 'exist in a dialectical relationship between the determination of limits and their own freedom' (p. 72) because of their awareness of themselves and the world. This concept of limits and people's awareness of the situations that restrict them, labelled by Freire as 'limit-situations', is key in understanding social change. By recognizing limit-situations as encumbrances rather than 'insurmountable barriers', people can challenge these limits through 'limit-acts' and attempt to overcome them, thus creating a new reality with new limit-situations

Nevertheless, it is important to note that at the same time people are restricted and denied by limit-situations; others benefit either directly or indirectly from these conditions. Freire calls what lies beyond these limit-situations 'untested feasibility', which for oppressed groups represents the hope of liberation. For the groups who benefit from the existing limit-situation, however, 'untested feasibility' represents a threat, and thus they fight to maintain the status quo. This concept of 'untested feasibility' was utilised by Jorge Knijnik (2012) to analyse Brazilian female footballers' struggle for autonomy and recognition in a country where, like Argentina, football has historically been considered a 'man's sport'.

As one tries to understand the processes of social change, we turn to Fraser's (1998) discussion of social justice as two-sided, requiring claims for both redistribution and recognition. Although these are often considered separately, Fraser argues that in today's context, neither is sufficient on its own, but rather issues of maldistribution and misrecognition are interconnected. Fraser's definition of the category of *gender* is useful to understand the relevance of these two aspects of justice when considering women's sports, which are also two-sided. On the one hand, gender is a basic principle that organises society's economic structure, defining the 'fundamental division' between paid 'productive' or unpaid 'reproductive' labour, this second type mainly is assigned to women. Within the first labour category, there is also a division between manufacturing and professional occupations, which are higher-paid and male-dominated, and lower-paid hospitality and domestic service occupations, which are female-dominated. Thus, the resulting economic structure creates forms of distributive injustice specifically related to gender.

In terms of recognition, gender also serves as a marker of status by which norms are constructed that privilege traits related to masculinity while those considered 'feminine' are devalued and disparaged. The consequences of this androcentrism, however, go beyond being looked down on. When these norms are institutionalised, according to Fraser:

> … [W]omen suffer gender-specific status injuries, including sexual assault and domestic violence; objectifying and demeaning stereotypical depictions in the media; harassment and disparagement in everyday life; and exclusion or marginalization [sic] in public spheres and deliberative bodies. (1998, p. 2)

This text examines how Argentine women's players experience both kinds of injustice and then considers both aspects of their claims for change.

Methodology

This chapter is part of a larger study on women's football in Argentina that aims to consider power and gender relationships in the traditionally male-dominated context of sport. The data analysed here stems from auto/ethnographic field work undertaken by the first author towards the completion of her doctoral dissertation. The research was carried out between July 2015 and December 2019 during which time Garton studied the women's team of Club *Deportivo Universidad Abierta Interamericana de Urquiza* (UAI Urquiza, originally from Villa Lynch, Argentina) as well as Argentina's women's national team . While researching the players of these teams, the first author also played as a goalkeeper for both squads and thus used the auto/ethnographic technique of participant observation, which was also complemented by semi-structured interviews.

By employing the ethnographic perspective proposed by Rosana Guber (2001) to conceive of ethnography as an approach, method and text, we attempt to comprehend the experiences and discourses of female footballers and the leaders within the institutions that regulate the sport. This methodological instrument helps one understand the meanings, practices and imaginaries significant to interlocutors by living and experiencing them 'in the flesh' (Guber, 2001). When describing the technique of participant observation, considered almost synonymous with ethnographic field work, Guber (2001) draws a parallel between learning a game by playing, an image which in the social study of sport appears to be quite relevant, and learning about a culture by living and experiencing it.

As a player who was not 'native' to Argentine football—born in the United States to an Argentine mother—the first author took on a kind of hybrid positionality in the field as both an insider as a lifelong footballer and an outsider because of both her upbringing and her status as a researcher (Merriam, 1998; Pang, 2019). Throughout her field work she was able to begin to understand and embody the experiences of playing elite women's football in Argentina: the frustrations, disappointments, celebrations and joys as well as the logics, values, morals and relationships that organize the social space. Inevitably, she also participated in the power struggles between players and the institutions which organise and manage their practice, including the leadership of clubs and the Argentine Football Association (AFA))—observing and experiencing firsthand the situations described in later sections of this chapter.

Women and Football: Playing on a Minefield

In Argentina, as in the rest of South America, football has historically been dominated by men—narrated, governed and played by them (Archetti, 1994; Alabarces, 2008). Since the sport's arrival to Argentina from England in the mid-1800s, women—as players, fans, administrators, journalists and officials—have been almost entirely ignored in football's social imaginary. As football began to be structured as the country's national sport, it also became a constructor of masculinities, and the media played a central role in the creation of a football narrative, which formed a national and masculine identity (Archetti, 1995). Thus, the presence of women in football threatened this masculine narrative that remained under construction.

Nevertheless, the exclusion of women from the nation's traditional football narrative does not imply their actual nor absolute absence from the sport. There is evidence of women's teams as early as the first decades of the twentieth century (Elsey & Nadel, 2019), and in 1971 the first Argentine women's national team participated in an international tournament organised in Mexico independently from the Fédération Internationale de Football Association (FIFA). Football's international governing body would not begin to recognise women under its label until the late 1980s, finally organising the first official Women's World Cup in China in 1991 (Williams, 2007).

That same year, Argentina created its first women's league sanctioned by AFA. This would appear to be coincidental, but rather it was a response from AFA to FIFA's global strategy to institutionalise women's football. Through the promise of financial support for the development of the sport in the form of an annual stipend, FIFA generated an incentive for its member associations to create women's national teams and official domestic leagues.

The first edition of the women's league of AFA had eight teams that, according to 'Las Pioneras'[1] (The Pioneers), already competed in unofficial tournaments organised by the Argentine Women's Football Association (AAFF). Nils Altuna is credited with the creation of AAFF, which already had support from private sponsors to cover the operational costs of its competitions (Pujol, 2018, 2019; Garton, 2019). The pre-

---

[1] '*Las Pioneras del Fútbol Femenino*' (the 'Pioneers of Women's Football' is a group created by former goalkeeper Lucila Sandoval who competed in the AFA women's league from the early 1990s until her retirement in 2015. The group was founded in 2016 on Facebook and would later generate face-to-face gatherings of former players and the organisation of events for both 'Pioneers' and current players. The recent creation of the Pioneers has resulted in recognition from AFA and clubs, like Racing de Avellaneda, for the players who made up the first women's national team, which competed in the non-FIFA sanctioned 1971 World Cup in Mexico. It has also served to reunite the players who played from the 1970s through to the 1990s as well as to offer a reference point for contemporary players while establishing a history of women's football in Argentina.

AFA stage of women's football is marked by an amateurism without aspirations of professionalisation, whether because of its apparent impossibility, the lack of institutional support or the desire not to lose the pleasurable and ludic nature inherent to unofficial competition (Janson, 2008; Pujol, 2019).

The phrase used as a title by Adolfina Janson (2008) for her book, 'That game which made you happy has ended', refers to this time of 'amateur sport for pleasure' in which the games were not as regulated and players felt a certain sense of belonging through encounters on neighbourhood pitches as well as through the typical post-match gatherings among friends. According to Janson, the creation of AFA's league and the institutionalisation of the practice represented the end of the concept of 'playing for fun' or 'playing for the sake of the game'. This shift may or may not have been as Janson described; however, the foundation of the league did establish a distinction: the creation of a recognised, regulated, institutionalised and competitive league for women.

Far from a professional competition, from 1991 until 2019, the league was classified as amateur, although the level of amateurism varied not only among the various clubs but also over time. In the last stage, between 2013 and 2019, though for a few clubs before this period as well, it would be more precise to classify the discipline's status as '*marronismo*' (literally translated as 'brownism'), rather than amateurism. *Marronismo* is a concept developed by social historian Julio Frydenberg (2011) in his work on men's football's beginnings in the early decades of the 1900s in Argentina, prior to the professionalisation of the sport. It describes practices utilised by clubs as strategies to attract and retain the most talented players of the working classes with financial incentives, which would cast progressively more doubt on the amateur regulation in place at that time.

These practices included payments hidden in the form of stipends and bonuses for winning whereas some players were offered work through the contacts of club administrators. Private businesses as well as public offices would offer part-time work obtained through connections, and these positions often had little to no requirement for attendance or had 'undemanding' duties (Frydenberg, 2011). These strategies are comparable to some used by women's football teams prior to the (semi-)

professionalisation of AFA's women's first division in 2019, though some clubs continue to employ these practices to varying degrees.

Although FIFA's first Women's World Cup (WWC) was organised in 1991, Argentina's first FIFA-sanctioned international competition was the 1995 *Sudamericano Femenino* (Women's South American Championship) held in January in Minas Gerais, Brazil. Of the 10 member federations associated with the South American Football Confederation (CONMEBOL), only five national teams participated in this tournament—Argentina, Bolivia, Brazil, Chile and Ecuador. Despite a second-place finish, Argentina did not qualify for the 1995 WWC in Sweden; only Brazil represented South America in that edition. Then, in 1998, the third *Sudamericano Femenino* was held in the coastal city of Mar del Plata, Argentina. Even though the competition was organised in Argentina, the Argentine players remember receiving little to no support from their association:

> They [AFA] do it because they have to do it. One example was when the National Team went to play in Mar del Plata. They took them 15 days before the tournament. They had to play a friendly against a local team to train, but they couldn't play because the field maintenance staff would not let them enter because he didn't want to let them, because the pitch was damp and he didn't want them to ruin the grass, and no one could do anything about it. The girls got back on the bus, and they had to go back. Neither the president of the Argentine delegation nor anybody could do anything about it. There isn't support from AFA; that's the reality. (Interview of a former Argentine women's national team player cited in Janson, 2008)

With another second-place finish, Argentina would face Mexico in a play-off to qualify for the 1999 WWC in the United States, which resulted in a victory for the Central American team, thus qualifying for its first World Cup. In an interview with the first author, an former player of the Argentine women's national team, Carla,[2] told her that, following the 1998 *Sudamericano*, the team played a few friendlies in 2000, but then did not train or play again until late 2002 in preparation for the next *Sudamericano* in 2003. Carla explained that, at that time, the national

---

[2] The player's real name has been changed to maintain her anonymity.

team only trained sporadically; the weeks they did train, they would do so in the city of Buenos Aires twice a week at the National Centre for High Performance Sport (CENARD), where the majority of elite athletes who represent Argentina in their respective sports prepare for international competitions. Only after the players were able to qualify for the team's first WWC in 2003—the *Sudamericano* was held at the beginning of the same year for qualification—would AFA allow the women's team to train at its national training centre in Ezeiza in the Buenos Aires Province.

Later in the interview, Carla explained that when the team was not preparing for travel or for a competition, the players who had to travel to the Capital from other provinces for training received a stipend covering only a one-way bus ticket and had to find their own accommodations to stay in the city during the week. They had barely the minimum in official attire, using mostly hand-me-downs from the men's and boys' teams, which can be seen in the prematch photographs of the team in which players are wearing uniforms many sizes too large.

Even 15 years later, during the 2018 *Copa América Femenina* (Women's Copa America), AFA continued providing the women's team with hand-me-downs and outdated attire that the men were no longer using. Garton (2019) recalls that throughout the tournament, her teammates remarked on multiple occasions that they were 'ashamed' or 'embarrassed' to be wearing that clothing; they felt both uncomfortable because the clothing was a poor fit and neglected by the federation because some of the clothing was up to 10 years old, even though the coaching staff was equipped with the latest gear.

Not only was the women's team in the early 2000s poorly equipped in terms of resources and clothing but also in terms of personnel. Carla explained that their team 'physician' was actually a physiotherapist, and the squad had the bare minimum for a coaching staff with only a head coach, assistant coach and a strength and conditioning coach. The team's only contact with AFA's administration was through the president of the women's football committee who would give them their stipend after the last training session of each week. According to Carla, many of the players would stay with family members if they could while only one player received funding from her state government to cover her housing costs, '*but the rest of us just wandered*'.

That generation of footballers made history in 2006 when the team won the *Sudamericano* held for the second time in Mar del Plata. It remains the only occasion that Brazil was not crowned champion of the continent. There were hopes for things to improve for female footballers in Argentina following the team's performance and the achievement of qualifying for the two most prestigious competitions in the sport: both the 2007 WWC in China and the 2008 Beijing Olympic Games. In spite of these accomplishments, the team still felt unrecognised and unappreciated by AFA with little hope for the situation of the women's national team to improve.

Following the China WWC, a group of players tried to fight for better conditions, more recognition and support from AFA. Nevertheless, Carla explained in her interview that their efforts were squashed as she and seven other players, the most outspoken in the struggle, were left off the team roster for the next year's Olympics—the first and only time Argentina has qualified for that competition. The coaching staff told the players that they had been excluded from the team for reasons related to their '*on-pitch performance*', but one of those players had been the highest scorer over both legs of the 2008 Argentine domestic league. When the first author asked whether Carla and her teammates had made some sort of complaint or demand while with the national team, the former player laughed and explained:

> *Carla*: Oof, you're walking on a minefield, on a field truly covered in mines. The truth is that we really suffered, we really suffered [...] with respect to demanding, to the fight, that was always there. If we did it, they would drop us, and no one would find out. There was no external support. It was very difficult to demand or ask for things.

When Garton (2019) had her first encounter with the national team in 2011 and later in 2015, the situation had not changed much from Carla's experiences. The stipend had improved minimally (to 50 pesos per day in 2011 and then to 150 pesos per day in 2015, both sums approximately equivalent to $10 U.S.), and the players' accommodations in

Buenos Aires were now provided by AFA. The team always trained on the pitches at the national team's training complex in Ezeiza, but the support from the association was still almost nonexistent. In 2011, there were players whose boots (football footwear) had been sown to keep from ripping further because they could not afford to purchase a new footwear.

In conversations on the bus to and from AFA's football training complex, her new teammates explained that neither their clubs—except for Boca Juniors that would give its women players one pair per year—nor AFA provided boots. As in previous years, there was no continuity nor plans for the team's future; if Argentina did not have an official international competition, the national team would not train and would not play in any friendlies. In the 2015 Pan-American Games in Toronto, Argentina finished in last place. After the last match of the tournament, the players, including the first author, met with the president of the women's football committee at the time, Salvador Stumbo, and explained that they needed more support and continuity in the form of international competition to truly compete with the best teams in the world. The administrator's response was that they '*had to win something that mattered*'. Following that meeting and on return to Argentina, the women's national team was left without a coaching staff until mid-2017.

Despite the lack of response from AFA, the players' meeting with Stumbo evidenced the beginning of their process of *conscientização*, because they became aware of their situation and recognised the possibility of another reality beyond that limit-situation (Freire, 2017). From that moment onwards, the *conscientização* process never stopped. The following describes the continuation of this process and the progress to collective and individual action by both the national team and local league players starting in 2017 through the 2019 WWC.

'We want to be heard': Conscientisation and Collective Action

In 2017, women's football attained unprecedented levels of attention in Argentina, which, even for those who follow the sport's development closely, took everyone by surprise. It began to receive media coverage when the women's national team announced its first ever strike in September of that year, condemning the structural sexism of the sporting industry by exposing the poor conditions in which the players were expected to prepare for international competition ('*La Selección de fútbol*', 2017; Lichinizer, 2017).

The team wrote an open letter to the president of AFA's Women's Football Committee, Ricardo Pinela, in which they asked for more support and improvements in order to receive treatment similar to that experienced by their male peers. The athletes positioned themselves as protagonists prepared to fight for their rights: respectable stipends, attire and footwear in correct sizes, adequate training conditions, along with a long-term plan for training and development. The strike lasted until training resumed in February 2018 in preparation for the Copa America, although no agreement was reached between the administration and players.

Without any major modifications in the work and training conditions nor changes in the lack of television broadcasting of the team's matches (they were streamed live on Facebook), in April the national team travelled to Chile to play in the 2018 *Copa América Femenina* with only a few weeks of preparation as a complete squad. Between 2015 and 2018, a few changes had occurred in the team, notably, some of the key players had gone overseas to play in the United States, Spain and China. The first author was no longer the only player exposed to diverse realities in women's football; these other players experienced firsthand what it meant to play in 'professional' conditions with adequate medical staff, training and match facilities, clothing, gear, coaching, nutritional support and financial compensation. They had seen beyond the limit-situation (Freire, 2017) they had played and lived in for most of their lives; they had seen the possibility of a different reality while recognising the limits constraining them not as insurmountable barriers but rather as hindrances to be overcome.

Therefore, during the 2018 Copa America, the players organised meetings in the hotel first among the team and then with women's football committee president Ricardo Pinela, communicating not only their desire for better conditions but also their willingness to sacrifice the possibility of representing their country, recognising this as a potential risk to speaking out. There were also external factors that influenced the players' decision to take a stand, particularly the growth of feminist and women's movements in Argentina and the rest of South America (Natalucci & Rey, 2018).

The players used this moment of international competition to raise awareness about the team's claims, and prior to the second-phase match against Colombia, they posed with their right hands behind their ears, as a reference to a well-known pop-culture figure in Argentina, Topo Gigio.[3] The image travelled around the world and exceeded the coverage received by the previous year's strike. On social media and in interviews with the media, the players criticised the lack of support from AFA, reinforcing the cultural conception of football in Argentina as a space governed by and for men. These demonstrations served more than ever as a source of pressure so club administrators would begin to pay more attention to the sport, and AFA would begin to discuss the urgent need for a paradigm shift.

Following the third-place finish in the 2018 Copa América and the historic WWC qualifier playoff match against Panama in November of the same year, which had a record-breaking attendance of 11,500 people at Arsenal Fútbol Club's stadium, the players' struggle gained even more

---

[3] Topo Gigio is a mouse puppet in a children's show on Italian television who first appeared on Argentine television during the 1970s. This character was emulated in April of 2001 by the Argentine footballer Juan Román Riquelme as a celebration after scoring for Boca Juniors against his team's major rival, River Plate. This gesture also carried a political and economic significance: the player was fighting for a better personal contract with the club. With his hands behind his ears, he incorporated Topo Gigio as a sign of protest in Argentine football. In 2018, 17 years later, this same gesture was used by Soledad Jaimes in her celebration following her second goal in Argentina's match against Bolivia during the Copa América in 2018. It was after the forward's demonstration that this gesture was taken and expanded by the entire team as a way to ask to be heard—an emblem of collective struggle (Hijós, 2018).

exposure.[4] On the local stage, the case of Macarena Sánchez—the former UAI Urquiza striker who, asserting her position as a worker, sued the club after she was released mid-season in January 2019—took the discussion of women in football to another level (Wrack, 2019).

The pressure of their (individual) exposure and the precarious conditions faced by the players (as a collective) had worldwide repercussions and led to AFA's president, Claudio 'Chiqui' Tapia, alongside Sergio Marchi, general secretary of the Argentine players association, Futbolistas Argentinos Agremiados (FAA), announcing the creation of the Women's Professional Football League in March, just two months after Sánchez had implicated AFA in the lawsuit against her former club.

The announcement of the professionalisation of the league, with a few vague points, arrived at an opportune time: three months before the WWC in France as an institutional response to social pressures and the organisation of the players (Garton et al., 2021). Tapia's discourse at this event also hearkened back to his speech at the opening ceremony of the 2017 edition of the women's league, his first year as president of AFA. In that initial event, two years prior to the professionalisation of women's football, he had declared himself the 'president of gender equality' while highlighting his administration's plans to develop the women's game (Garton, 2019).

As pointed out by Fraser (1998), claims for social justice are typically divided into two main types: material claims for redistribution and symbolic claims for recognition, even though these are frequently seen as unrelated. In Argentina, however, the players' demands were, perhaps inadvertently, a combination of these, demanding both greater recognition through media exposure and broadcasting of matches, and redistribution of resources for better conditions for training and competition.

The players' struggle to improve their material conditions and to be recognised in a country where football is the main sport (Alabarces, 2008) can be set in a context of a series of demands that began to grow immensely and attract major media attention following the first '*NiUnaMenos*' ('NotOneWomanLess') protest in 2015, which since then has taken place

---

[4] For more, see Hang and Hijós (2018).

annually to condemn gender violence.[5] The year 2019 was characterised by the creation of commissions, secretaries and sub-secretaries of gender and diversity in football clubs and by the resignification of preexisting spaces to debate violence, rethink masculinities and hierarchies and generate alliances, which transversally implemented a gender perspective in these institutions.

Julia Hang (2018) observed that collective organisation allows for the construction—both from the institution of Argentine clubs and external activism—of spaces dedicated to the establishment of gender policies, which exposes the scarce participation of women and dissident genders in these organisations. According to data collected by the Feminist Football Coordinator (July 2019), the executive committees of clubs associated with AFA are composed of only 6.1% women and 93.9% men. This organisation argues that, in order to guarantee equity and the development of women's football beyond the pitch, it is necessary to ensure the entry of women into AFA—so that it will no longer be an 'old boys' club'—as well as in every space where decisions are made.

This was the period in which feminisms and social movements began to see football as a territory to be conquered (Hang, 2020). Through various strategies, they supported and propelled the demands of the players, in conditions of inequality, subordination and oppression (Hang, 2020). It was a significant moment in which some historically marginalised groups were able to recognise their daily experiences of discrimination and abuse as a product of a much wider system of power (Freire, 2017). With varying backgrounds and convictions about feminism, the players organised themselves, raised their voices and articulated their claims along with those of other sectors.

---

[5] Another significant event in the feminist and women's movements has been 8M (March 8th), which commemorates International Women's Day, and since 2017 has called for an international women's strike with the main objective of achieving equal labour conditions. The third strike was unique in that it incorporated dissident sexualities and nonbinary gender identities for the first time. At the same time, throughout this period, there was an ongoing fight for the legalisation of abortion led by the National Campaign for the Right to Legal, Safe, and Free Abortion (whose debates are constructed on those of the National Women's Encounters in 2003 and 2004). The year 2018 was particularly significant because of the debates generated in the National Congress and the massive demonstrations in support of the law for the Voluntary Interruption of Pregnancy.

Unlike what had occurred in the past, when, as Carla said, there was 'no external support' and 'it was very difficult to demand or ask for things', these footballers were backed by feminist groups, political parties, the media and diverse sectors of civil society (Hang & Moreira, 2020). Thus, the sport grew into a scene for expression, discovery and empowerment in the fight against the patriarchy and androcentric logic.

Freire's (2017) concept of *conscientização* is useful to consider the process leading to the Argentine national team's public protests, after decades of struggling against but also tolerating negligence from the governing bodies of their sport. As Freire (2017) explains, this process of *conscientização* can occur when the oppressed recognise that they are not in a 'closed world' with no way out, but rather they exist in a socially 'limiting situation' that can be transformed. Seeing beyond these limiting situations, which in large part was related to the support and change generated by the feminist movements in Latin America described in the preceding, has been key in the events leading up to the professionalisation of women's football in Argentina.

Semi-professionalisation as a Response to the Players' Fight

What constitutes professionalisation? As part of the agreement between FAA and AFA (March, 2019), each team in the *Primera A Femenina* (i.e., Women's First Division) must have a minimum of eight contracted players. These eight contracts are financed by the association, but if the club desires to offer more than the minimum—both in terms of salary and the total number of contracts—the difference must be financed by the club. It is important to note that not all clubs have committed themselves—and/or have the same material conditions—to advance the development of women's football. So, can one really talk about the professionalisation of the sport when there remains a minimal percentage of players with contracts while others still have to pay to play?[6] Various groups and lead-

---

[6] This can be through a membership fees or covering the costs of matches in the form of transport, referees, police and an ambulance.

ers have criticised the announcement of professionalisation by AFA's president and labelled this measure as 'semi-professionalisation'. According to a survey carried out in June 2021 by '*Pibas con Pelotas*' (literally 'Girls with Balls'), a media outlet dedicated to women's sports, of the 19 teams in the women's first division, only 53% of players are contracted (293 out of 542).

Even though there are currently more protections granted to players with the incorporation of professional contracts and access to the rights already established by the same collective bargaining agreement used by men's football (e.g., the right to a wage and access to medical and legal services provided by the players' association) some practices of *marronismo* remain, along with the reproductions of precarity (Garton, 2019). In the case of Club UAI Urquiza, football is still not the only source of income for the majority of players, given that the minimum wage established in the contracts is not sufficient to cover their cost of living, and many still depend on the club for part-time employment and/or housing. The *marronismo* of the pre-professional period persists, sustaining the dependence of the players on the club and maintaining the precarity of their situation as elite athletes, especially for those who are not contracted (Garton, 2019).

Nevertheless, UAI Urquiza represents an exception to the rule in the women's league as one of the few teams with more contracted players than the minimum of eight.[7] Only Boca Juniors, River Plate and San Lorenzo currently have their entire squad on contracts, and it is certainly important to note that these are among the wealthiest clubs not only in Argentina but also in the rest of South America. The rest of the first division clubs face the difficult decision of which players will be offered contracts and which will remain amateurs.

Even contracted players, however, still experience certain forms of precarity. For example, the average length of the contracts is only one year,

---

[7] Unlike the experiences of most female first-division players, UAI Urquiza's women's team has access to the same facilities as the men and also has a full coaching staff with a head, assistant and strength and conditioning coach, along with the same goalkeeper coach who works with the men's senior, reserve and youth teams. As well as a complete coaching staff, there is always a physiotherapist present at all training sessions and matches, the team has access to a physician on match days and a certified sport nutritionist has been working with the team on a weekly basis since 2018.

which does not offer long-term stability. Also, many players were unable to negotiate an exit clause into their contracts if they desired to leave the club—either to a club in another country or in the same league—before the contract's end. In spite of these difficulties, the players mainly expressed feelings of gratitude and positive emotion in regard to 'achieving the dream of signing a professional contract', a common caption underneath the social media posts of many players who signed contracts at various clubs.

In her study of female professional Australian rules football (AFLW) players, Adele Pavlidis (2020) observed similar attitudes among the athletes to rationalise their low pay and poor conditions: 'Gratitude and generosity are entangled in relations of power. Marginalised groups, in this case women entering into AFLW, relate to the conditions of their precarity through positivity and optimism. It is their hope to flourish and experience social and personal power through experiences of adversity'; however, 'bones break, passion does not pay the bills, and positivity does not assure success' (Pavlidis, 2020, p. 5). As in the case of the AFLW players, female footballers in Argentina work in a precarious space, their continuity as professionals is not guaranteed and can be disrupted or ended by injury, a change of coach or a drop in form.

Their work is undervalued in a space where the men's game remains not only the priority but also the standard. It is not insignificant that the minimum wage of the women's first division is equivalent to that of the men's fifth division (Primera D), which was historically an amateur division. As discussed by Fraser (1998), when it comes to issues of gender, maldistribution and misrecognition are intimately related. For female players, their financial status is affected by their social status as women; thus, both injustices must be remedied through redistribution as well as recognition.

The arrival of professionalism did not generate modifications in regard to the expectations or requirements of clubs in terms of the conditions of the practice. If a club desires to offer more or less resources to its women's team, this decision is left to each institution's leadership. In the smallest clubs, the discipline remains predominantly amateur, or *marrón*, with claims about late payments or lack of pay for contracted players, inadequate spaces for training—some teams only have access to a pitch one or two times per week, insufficient for a professional competition—and the absence of medical staff or physiotherapists to care for players. Furthermore, since most of the team is not contracted, players have to find other work to survive, which can often generate conflicts with training times and midweek matches.

During the first year of professionalism, the league's players protested against the administration of a club in the southern part of Greater Buenos Aires for the mistreatment of its players. In a meeting with other players around the league, which was attended by the first author, a player from this club shared her experiences of abuse at the club. She explained how, among other things, the eight contracted players were forced to go to the bank accompanied by a club administrator to withdraw their monthly wages in cash and give the money to said administrator, which would later be distributed as a stipend throughout the entire team.

Even though the contracted players did not disagree with the concept of redistributing their wages to teammates, when the players added up their 'stipends', they never equalled the total amount paid by AFA for the eight contracts. When they asked the club about this discrepancy, the administration responded that the difference covered the costs of the discipline—although the team's captain stated that she was often asked to personally pay for the ambulance and/or police presence for matches, since the club knew that her partner 'had a well-paid job'. At the meeting, the player expressed her fear about speaking up about what was happening at her club because the administration also threatened to drop the sport entirely or cut players if they ever shared what happened at the club with anyone outside the institution.

Although this could be considered an extreme example, similar experiences have been shared among members of *Futbolistas Unidas Argentinas* (i.e., Argentine Women's Footballers United), a group composed of first and second division players. This group was formed in 2019 to discuss problems faced by footballers in AFA's women's leagues, including the quality of their club's facilities, the conditions of their practice and even cases of sexual abuse and harassment. The mere formation of this group, however, is an indicator of the growing '*conscientização*' (Freire, 2017) of Argentine women's players: their social awareness started with dialogue and struggle within the national team, and then spread its impact to the domestic league. Local players had seen what collective action had achieved for the national team as well as the response it generated from the media and AFA; they were aware of the untested feasibility (Freire, 2017; Knijnik, 2012), which lies beyond the current limit-situation of an only semi-professionalised first division.

In prior seasons, most players would have endured mistreatment from their club with a mentality of 'gratitude' because they had been conditioned to the discipline and silencing, which has oppressed women historically (Barrancos, 2010), especially considering the experiences of Carla's generation. The authors do not intend to romanticise nor exaggerate the players' agency nor the ability to generate change in a space that historically has excluded and marginalised them; however, a turning point has occurred and players are aware that they do have more revolutionary power as a collective, with the support of feminist groups (e.g., the Coordinadora Sin Fronteras de Fútbol Feminista),[8] as well as feminist journalists and media outlets, which promote sorority and the questioning of traditional ways of conceiving football, contemplating how to build a feminist and popular sport, far from the logic of male fanaticism (Pierini & Hang, 2019).

Final Reflections

Football, metaphor for war, at times becomes real war.
—Eduardo Galeano, Football in Sun and Shadow

---

[8] The Coordinadora de Hinchas is an organised group of supporters from various Argentinian clubs to defend the associationist model of sports clubs in the face of the project to transform them into Public Limited Companies during the presidency of Mauricio Macri (2015–2019). With the expansion of feminist movements in the region, this collective began to problematise as well gender issues in a separate department. At the same time, self-organisations and commissions emerged to work on the implementation of a gender perspective in institutions. This was the impetus for the creation of the *Coordinadora Sin Fronteras de Fútbol Feminista*, an organisation that brings together supporters, members, managers, coaches, but also female football players. The role of these organisations promoted the awareness of women players, and challenged them politically in the fight against inequalities for the visibility of women and diversity in sports.

Similar to other cultural practices, football is a battlefield where disputes unravel to install and deconstruct legitimate meanings. The official history has led one to believe that football is a sport played, narrated, enjoyed and governed by men. The experiences of the national team, players in AFA's women's league and the pioneers of the 1971 unofficial World Cup, along with women from the first decades of the last century, allow for the telling of a different story: a story of play and enjoyment that has been silenced for many years. According to Carmen Rial (2013) in the Brazilian context, this mechanism meant a clean and even expulsion of women from the narratives of the 'fatherland'.

The story told today is one of rebellion, in which fights to break down strongholds on an unequal pitch continue and where power reinvents itself to maintain hegemony. The political decision to professionalise women's football in Argentina was a response to the collective action taking place on and off the pitch, in the intimacy of a group of footballers in collaboration with a broader social movement that supported them. In this context, the demands of the players' strike in September 2017 became legitimate claims in 2018 after the national team achieved significant sporting results: third place in the Copa América and World Cup qualification for the first time in 12 years.

In March 2019, the announcement to professionalise the league offered legitimacy to female footballers but also produced new inequalities. The new league did not disassemble a structure characterised by abuse, silencing and discipline, rather these mechanisms still exist. Nonetheless, unlike previous generations who protested in solitude, today when players say '*no nos callamos más*' ('we will never again be silent'), their words are echoed not only by other footballers but also by a multitude of women in Argentina and the rest of South America who continue to fight collectively for equity both on and off the field of play.

References

Alabarces, P. (2008). *Fútbol y Patria: el Fútbol y las Narrativas de la Nación en la Argentina*. Prometeo Libros.

Archetti, E. (1994). Masculinity and football: The formation of national identity in Argentina. In R. Giulianotti & J. M. Williams (Eds.), *Game without frontiers: football, identity and modernity* (pp. 225–243). Arena..

Archetti, E. (1995). Estilo y virtudes masculinas en El Gráfico: la creación del imaginario del fútbol argentino. *Desarrollo Económico, 35*(139), 419–442.

Barrancos, D. (2010). *Mujeres en la Sociedad Argentina: Una Historia de Cinco Siglos*. Sudamericana.

Elsey, B., & Nadel, J. (2019). *Futbolera. A history of women and sports in Latin America*. University of Texas Press.

Fraser, N. (1998). *Social justice in the age of identity politics: Redistribution, recognition, participation*. WZB Discussion Paper, No. FS I 98–108, Wissenschaftszentrum Berlin für Sozialforschung (WZB), Berlin.

Freire, P. (2017). *Pedagogy of the oppressed*. Penguin Modern Classics.

Frydenberg, J. (2011). *Historia Social del Fútbol: Del Amateurismo a la Profesionalización*. Siglo Veintiuno Editores.

Garton, G. (2019). *Guerreras: Fútbol, Mujeres y Poder*. Capital Intelectual.

Garton, G., Hijós, N., & Alabarces, P. (2021). Playing for change: (Semi-)professionalization, social policy, and power struggles in Argentine women's football. *Soccer & Society*. https://doi.org/10.1080/14660970.2021.1952692

Guber, R. (2001). *La Etnografía: Método, Campo y Reflexividad*. Grupo Editorial Norma.

Hang, J. (2018, December). *Política y género en el deporte. Apuntes introductorios en torno al área de género en un club de fútbol platense*. Paper presented at the X Jornadas de Sociología de la Universidad Nacional de La Plata, Argentina.

Hang, J. (2020). Feministas y triperas. Mujeres y política en el área de género del club Gimnasia y Esgrima La Plata. *Debates en Sociología, 50*, 67–90. https://doi.org/10.18800/debatesensociologia.202001.003

Hang, J., & Hijós, N. (2018, November). Ese juego que las hace felices. *Revista Anfibia*. http://revistaanfibia.com/ensayo/juego-que-las-hace-felices/

Hang, J., & Moreira, V. (2020). Deporte, género y feminismos: rupturas, negociaciones y agencias en un campo desigual. *Revista Ensambles, 12*, 2–9. http://www.revistaensambles.com.ar/ojs-2.4.1/index.php/ensambles/article/view/209/pdf_26

Hijós, N. (2018, April 12). Selección Argentina: la vuelta del Topo Gigio en el reclamo del fútbol femenino. *La Izquierda Diario*. http://www.laizquierdadiario.com/Seleccion-Argentina-la-vuelta-del-Topo-Gigio-en-el-reclamo-del-futbol-femenino

Janson, A. (2008). *Se Acabó Este Juego que te Hacía Feliz. Nuestro Fútbol Femenino* (desde su ingreso a la AFA en 1990, hasta el Mundial de Estados Unidos en 2003). Aurelia Rivera.

Knijnik, J. (2012). Visions of gender justice: Untested feasibility on the football fields of Brazil. *Journal of Sport & Social Issues, 37*(1), 8–30. https://journals.sagepub.com/doi/abs/10.1177/0193723512455924

La Selección de Fútbol Femenino Está de Paro: Qué le Piden las Chicas a la AFA. (2017, September, 21). *Clarín*. https://www.clarin.com/deportes/futbol/seleccion-futbol-femenino-paro-piden-chicas-afa_0_r1jSFK-sW.html

Lichinizer, D. (2017, September 25). Un reclamo de la selección argentina de fútbol femenino desnuda una cuenta pendiente de la AFA. *Infobae*. https://www.infobae.com/deportes-2/2017/09/25/un-reclamo-de-la-seleccion-argentina-de-futbol-femenino-desnuda-una-cuenta-pendiente-de-la-afa/

Merriam, S. B. (1998). *Qualitative research and case study applications in education*. Jossey-Bass.

Natalucci, A., & Rey, J. (2018). ¿Una nueva oleada feminista? Agendas de género, repertorios de acción y colectivos de mujeres (Argentina, 2015–2018). *Revista de estudios políticos y estratégicos, 6*(2), 14–34.

Pang, B. (2019). Ethnographic method. In P. Liampatting (Ed.), *Handbook of research methods in health social sciences* (pp. 443–456). Springer.

Pavlidis, A. (2020). Being grateful: Materialising 'success' in women's contact sport. *Emotion, Space and Society, 35*. https://doi.org/10.1016/j.emospa.2020.100673

Pierini, M., & Hang, J. (2019, November 5). Fútbol femenino: entre la cultura del aguante y la sororidad. *La tinta*. https://latinta.com.ar/2019/11/futbol-femenino-entre-cultura-aguante-sororidad/

Pujol, A. (2018, May 11). El día que Argentina jugó su primer Mundial de fútbol femenino. *Página/12*. https://www.pagina12.com.ar/114143-el-dia-que-argentina-jugo-su-primer-mundial-de-futbol-femeni

Pujol, A. (2019). *¡Qué Jugadora! Un Siglo de Fútbol Femenino en la Argentina*. Ariel.

Rial, C. (2013). El invisible (y victorioso) fútbol practicado por mujeres en Brasil. *Nueva Sociedad, 248*, 114–126.

Williams, J. (2007). *A beautiful game. International perspectives on women's football*. Berg.

Wrack, S. (2019, February 7). Macarena Sánchez: The Argentinian who is suing her club and federation. *The Guardian*. https://www.theguardian.com/football/blog/2019/feb/07/macarena-sanchez-legal-action-against-uai-urquiza-and-argentinian-football-federation

3

'Our football is joy, it's dissident, and it's feminist!': *La Coordinadora Sin Fronteras de Fútbol Feminista* and Women's Fight for the Right to Football in Argentina

Matthew Hawkins and Julia Hang

Introduction: Fresh Air, a New Way of Living Feminism

When you see the photos of the demonstration from above, the rectangle of the *cancha* [football pitch], La Coordi and all the *pibas* [girls[1]] around you, you get a sense of the passion that we bring. Beyond our feminist

---

[1] *Piba* refers to young women. *Pibe*, the masculine form, historically refers to young men and in the Argentine football imaginary, masculine players with a creative rebellious style of play (Archetti, 2008). To call themselves "*las pibas*" may be understood as a resignification of a historically masculine concept.

M. Hawkins (✉)
Carleton University, Ottawa, ON, Canada
e-mail: matthew.hawkins@carleton.ca

J. Hang
Argentine National Council for Scientific Research (CONICET) and the University of La Plata, La Plata, Argentina

J. Knijnik, G. Garton (eds.), *Women's Football in Latin America*, New Femininities in Digital, Physical and Sporting Cultures,
https://doi.org/10.1007/978-3-031-09127-8_3

35

activism, what really brought us together to go to the marches was football. Football brought us together; it's what we love and where most of us started our activism in the group.

—Caro, representative of *San Lorenzo Feminista*

Aerial images revealing a small *canchita* (an informal field) at the steps of Argentina's National Congress carved out of the mass of demonstrators participating in the protests on February 19, 2020, is one of the indelible images of the progression of Argentina's feminist movement in its campaign towards the right to safe, legal and accessible abortions. Over the course of the day-long demonstrations, matches took place between teams of women playing in *picaditos aborteros*,[2] a form of participation in protests that has become common place at marches and demonstrations by Argentina's feminist movement. Women, lesbians, transgender and nonbinary people organized into shifts by La Coordinadora Sin Fronteras de Fútbol Feminista (Coordinator of Feminist Football Without Borders, referred to as La Coordi by its members) arrived 24 hours before the demonstration to create and defend the space on the pavement.[3]

The ongoing claiming of space for football in prominent locations within feminist demonstrations has marked La Coordi as a significant organisation alongside established feminist groups in Argentina. The story of the *canchitas* draws one's attention to the creative tensions emergent in the proposal of a feminist football. This chapter unpacks the formation of La Coordinadora Sin Fronteras de Fútbol Feminista, as well as La Coordi's roots in women's activism over decades, to create, promote and nourish a space to play and be supporters of football and, in turn, expand on the significance of feminist football in contemporary Argentina. Giving attention to the contradictions and tensions consistently explored and debated by the activist members of feminist football reveals its contributions to a more equal and just football culture, as well as to an increasingly popular feminist movement.

---

[2] A *picadito* is a regional term for an informal game of football organized in an informal space, often among friends. *Picadito abortero* has become the name for the semi-organised games of football played during feminist and pro-abortion marches and demonstrations in Argentina.

[3] The plurality of identities that constitute *La Coordinadora Sin Fronteras de Fútbol Feminista* should be noted.

In recent history, Argentina's feminist movement has regained significant momentum and a prominent place in national politics, as well as being a symbolic referent for feminist movements across Latin America and the world. Following the femicide of Chiara Paez, the hashtag slogan #NiUnaMenos was created to convene hundreds of thousands of people across Argentina to protest femicide and gender-based violence on June 3, 2015. In addition, in support of Argentina's campaign for legal, safe and free abortions, the *pañuelo verde* (green bandana) became an iconic symbol for women's rights across the region. The movements have also expanded the horizons of feminist politics, recognising the rights and inclusion of transgender and nonbinary people as central components of ending patriarchy in society. A feminist football has emerged within the context of a reinvigorated feminist social movement, creating a powerful dialogue between feminism and football politics and practices.

This chapter is based on ethnographic data from marches and workshops, as well as interviews with Caro and Nadia, constituent members of La Coordi from San Lorenzo Feminista, and Mónica Santino, a leader in the movement.[4] Feminist football connects the right to play and participate with the notion of football as a human right and opposes the patriarchal formation of the sport that has long excluded women, transgender and nonbinary people. Further, as Mónica Santino described, feminist football is also, 'fresh air, a new way of living feminism'. Feminist football articulates a recognition that football can be a feminist practice and issue.

To make football feminist, activists have developed a praxis that entangles their passion for football with a sisterhood that arises from shared experiences of exclusion from the sport. In doing so, activists in *La Coordi*

---

[4] For this project Caro and Nadia were interviewed as members and organizers within San Lorenzo Feminista and represent San Lorenzo Feminista within the broader structure of *La Coordi*. Monica Santino, also interviewed for this project, is a life-long footballer and football coach, and organiser of the Club La Nuestra Fútbol Feminista in the popular neighbourhood Villa 31, an important institution that has advanced the inclusion of girls and young women in football since 2007. Santino has been an activist within the LGBTQ+ community, serving as president of the Comunidad Homosexual Argentina (Argentine Homosexual Community) from 1994 to 1996. The researchers have engaged with gender-based activists within the Club de Gimnasia y Esgrima La Plata, as well as events organised by San Lorenzo Feminista and La Coordi between 2019 and 2021.

are constructing a new form of feminist football folklore, explored in this chapter, which includes practices of *picaditos*, *canchitas* and *cancioneros feministas* against what they consider patriarchal football.

Recent Feminist Movements in Argentina: To Put Many of the Things That Happen to Women into Words

Argentina's feminist movement reinvigorated its presence on the streets following the first #NiUnaMenos demonstrations in 2015, which had crystallised the grassroots responses against femicides into a national movement. The demonstrations marked a turning point in the feminist movement as a rearticulation of historic feminist demands on social issues by an expanded plurality of sectors of society by developing new forms of legitimacy, popular support and transversality within feminist politics. Although centred on the issue of femicide and violent masculinity, the #NiUnaMenos mobilisations represented a 'heterogenous and polyphonic' feminism with a strong emphasis on horizontal organisation and tactics that required the taking-over and sharing of public space among diverse constituent collectives (Natalucci & Rey, 2018).

Social media networks also expanded the public visibility of feminist social demands, adding to the plurality of voices putting feminist demands onto the political agenda, and for activists to connect their occupation of the streets with the occupation of other public areas in cities across the country. Some authors characterize the novelty of this 'fourth wave of feminism' as its ability to take feminism to places previously deemed unthinkable' (Barrancos, 2014; Natalucci & Rey, 2018). From Mónica's perspective, previous iterations of feminism had formed a distant relationship with football, more broadly reflecting a distancing between Argentina's academic feminism and popular culture in Argentina. For example mainstream feminism had categorized cumbia villera, a popular music culture in Argentina as misogynist without reflecting on women's experiences of enjoyment and even empowerment (Silba & Spataro, 2017). Similarly, the world of football, which in Argentina has been structured as a space 'by men and for men' (Alvarez Litke, 2018; Hijós, 2018) had been largely ignored within dominant feminist politics as a site for constructive contestation. In part, the fourth wave of feminism in Argentina has seen greater recognition and engagement with sites of popular culture (e.g., football) as integral parts of a growing diversity in the lives of women, transgender and nonbinary people.

In recent years, political debates on the legalisation of abortion provided opportunities to mobilise the feminist movement in massive demonstrations. On March 5, 2018, the National Campaign for Legal, Safe and Free Abortion presented the Law for Voluntary Interruption of Pregnancy (i.e., the Law for IVE in its Spanish acronym) for the seventh time to Argentina's Chamber of Deputies of the National Congress, which it passed on June 14 of that year. The Chamber of Senators, however, voted down the legislation on August 9, 2018. Following this setback, participation in the feminist movement continued to develop and influenced the 2019 election victory of President Alberto Fernandez and Vice President Cristina Fernandez de Kirchner, who had promised to present and pass the Law for IVE. Even though massive mobilisations at each legislative step have provided opportunities for direct engagement through protest tactics, many people also participated in day-to-day activism by carrying the now iconic *pañuelo verde* tied around their neck, wrist or bag.

For many women who are part of La Coordi, #NiUnaMenos was their first engagement with feminist activism. Both Caro and Nadia, who represented San Lorenzo Feminista (an autonomous organisation of fans and members of Club Atlético San Lorenzo de Almagro)[5] within La Coordi, are part of a younger generation of activists who mobilised through the #NiUnaMenos and legal abortion campaigns. During an interview, they described how, as lifelong supporters of San Lorenzo, they had in some ways not fully recognised how their interactions with football had been prefiguring their feminist position. They had developed an understanding that the 'football world [they] loved was *machista*'. Caro explained, 'in the stadium, when I'd give an opinion or would talk [about

---

[5] Professional football teams in Argentina are part of multi-sport membership run by nonprofit clubs that offer a diversity of social, cultural and athletic activities.

the game], other people wouldn't listen or pay attention, and they would belittle me because I'm a woman who couldn't understand'.

Nadia recognised through reflection that she 'always had feminist ideas without knowing it' but also 'a mountain of *machista* ideas because of a society that drags you into them.' The #NiUnaMenos campaign is considered a point of inflection for feminist football activists, and Caro and Nadia described it as an important 'before and after moment' because it provided them with the opportunity 'to put many of the things that happen to [them] as women, particularly in football, into words'. Nadia has been able to affirm her identity as a supporter of San Lorenzo through San Lorenzo Feminista. The group provides an opportunity to 'deconstruct the club' and recognise an institution that is much more than men's football to emphasise the elements that 'coincide with [her] values'.

Participation in #NiUnaMenos exposed many activists to the discourses and practices of feminist politics, generating innovative forms of sociality in football spaces (e.g., organised fan and supporter groups and clubs) that had previously been absent from feminist politics. Supporting the Law for IVE, in turn, provided new opportunities to enact feminist politics and perform feminist football practices during mobilisations, while carrying the *pañuelo verde* became a way to symbolically identify as a feminist.

Football in National Women's Encounters: *What Is Football for You?*

There is a long history of feminist activism in Argentina that prefigured the organising of #NiUnaMenos and the Campaign for Legal Abortion. The Encuentro Nacional de Mujeres (i.e., National Women's Encounter) is an annual event hosted in a different Argentine city each year since 1986. The *Encuentros* (Encounters), which have become the backbone of the movement, consist of workshops on diverse topics organised by activists and are based on principles of horizontality and equality. Even though sports periodically emerged as a topic of discussion during workshops over the years, *football* and *feminism* was only first included in the official agenda at the 2018 *Encuentro in Chubut*. In the years prior, Mónica described how an informal street-football tournament at the 2014 Encuentro in Salta became a space for discussion and reflection.

Similar tournaments became progressively amplified at each subsequent Encuentro. By 2018, the tournament in Trelew included 109 teams of footballers, trainers, sports journalists, academics and supporters from across Argentina with names such as Abriendo La Cancha (Opening the Field) from Cordoba, Las Martas from Santa Fe, and Boca es Pueblo (Boca is the People) and La Nuestra from Buenos Aires (Fernándes Fuks, 2018). Activists organised 'Football and Feminisms' workshops alongside the tournament. For Mónica it was a 'historic achievement' to be officially recognised in the program of the Encuentro.

As a young activist in the Argentine Homosexual Community and as a footballer during the 1980s and 1990s, Mónica felt that feminism was 'very white.[6] [Feminism] belonged to the academics who were very judgemental. They told us if something was feminist or not, and football was not'. Jefferson Lenskyj (1995) conceptualises feminism's distance with sport more broadly as 'sport phobia'. Hang and Garton (in press) argue that this does not mean that there were not feminists concerned with sports, or women who, without perceiving themselves as feminists, fought for female participation in sports. Thus, although it is possible to identify Trelew as a significant moment in feminist football, many in La Coordi are quick to recognise the contributions of women such as activists like Mónica and coach Lorena Berdula who have fought for a feminist football over the years and who have otherwise been made invisible by the patriarchy (Elsey, 2019).

Trelew did, however, mark a coalescing of constituent components in the ongoing and historic struggle for a feminist football. Mónica explained that 'what happened in [Trelew] was marvellous. We made a huge circle and talked about a simple question: "what is football for you? What does it mean to play?" [The discussion] opened a series of wounds that for many hadn't been healed'. Revelations of shared painful experiences—of exclusion, inequality and violence—created a foundation for mutual

---

[6] *Whiteness* in this context refers to the socioeconomic hierarchy and racial-class dynamics in Argentina.

solidarity among participants that since has been centred on feminist football. Emerging from the discussions, participants began working towards creating *La Coordinadora Sin Fronteras de Fútbol Feminista*.

La Coordi is an ongoing project of its participants composed of supporter groups from numerous clubs, sport journalists, athletes, coaches, trainers, researchers and teachers who approach sports from a gender and feminist perspective. Activists emphasised the group's horizontal and polyphonic plurality as emerging through the organising forms of football by blending feminist principles of anti-hierarchies and egalitarian participation with historical practices of making club-based *peñas*, semi-autonomous groups that organise social activities for supporters, whereas players and coaches have organised grassroots community teams that collect resources to make or take over spaces to play. In part, the horizontality emerges from the need to recognise and respond to the diverse realities and challenges faced by women, girls and transgender and nonbinary people in football in the different regions of Argentina.

Within La Coordi, commissions are organised to handle various functions. A social media commission exposes different situations, such as gender-based violence and discrimination in the field of sports. Another commission focuses on activism in the street, occupying space during mobilisations—to set up the *canchas*, for example. Another commission serves as a network for the supporter groups that, as part of La Coordi, turn towards each other for support when navigating the internal politics of their clubs. Nadia from San Lorenzo Feminista argues that as supporters face the distinct realities in each of their clubs, 'we give each other strength. It's like [our participation in La Coordi] also propels our own fight in our clubs, that is, our particular struggles that we have every day. ... So we also constantly learn from the struggles of others'. Practices of solidarity and collaboration between groups from clubs that are otherwise rivals in sports competition, however, can create tension for members of La Coordi, which is explored in the following.

Struggling for a Space to Play: The *cancha* as a Symbol of Appropriating National Identity

The struggle for space for women, girls and transgender and nonbinary people to play is not a novel innovation of *La Coordinadora Sin Fronteras de Fútbol Feminista*. In many respects, the creation of *canchitas* as spaces to play *picaditos* flows from the gendered history of the space-politics of the football field. Embedded within the national myth of *fútbol* in Argentina is the practice of making do and transforming open space into a place to play (Archetti, 2008). The need to create places to play has been a crucial aspect of football's reality in Argentina, particularly in urbanised Buenos Aires, since its arrival and popularisation among working-class players at the end of the nineteenth and beginning of the twentieth centuries. Space in public parks has always been limited in urban centres and maintained grass fields are controlled by private clubs.

Football historian Julio Frydenberg (2011) notes that the economically marginalised men and boys who were 'excluded from the organized spaces, took football to the street as a primordial space [to play]. Novices and enthusiast players appropriated and transformed the streets into social spaces for *men*, youth, and children' (authors' emphasis, p. 93). In other contexts, patches of dirt and livestock grazing fields, called *potreros*, became rough training grounds and spaces to play a free-flowing and now iconic style of play marked by guile and creativity. For Archetti (2008), mythic stories of the *potrero* as an incubator-space for Argentine-style football provided powerful images in the entangled narrative construction of the masculine nation and its territory.

Although these myths and stories revolved around the play of boys and men, including national icons (e.g., Maradona), women's role in the formation of football often went unwritten and silenced, contributing to the hegemonic masculinity over the territory of the football pitch. Given the significance of football to Argentina's national culture (Alabarces, 2014; Archetti, 2016), efforts to silence and exclude the participation of women, transgender, and nonbinary people from the spaces of football translate into a patriarchal effort to exclude their participation in the production of popular culture in general (Elsey & Nadel, 2019; Garton, 2019; Pujol,

2019). The repression, however, has been continually confronted with creative resistance, appropriation and transformation of football, including the long-standing activism of players like Las Pioneras,[7] who represented Argentina at the first Women's World Cup in 1971.

The mythic qualities of the *cancha* encourage a reflection on the entangled significance of feminist football's practice of occupying space through feminist actions and daily life, transforming those spaces into a place to play. British feminist geographer Doreen Massey (1994) recalls passing the football fields along the River Mersey, filled with young players: 'then as a puzzled, slightly thoughtful little girl—that this huge stretch of the Mersey flood plain had been entirely given over to boys. I did not go to those playing fields—they seemed barred, another world' (p.185). Massey points to this formative experience as the beginning of an understanding of space as emergent from the multiplicity of dimensions of social relationships, powerfully including the dimension of gender, that in turn affects the possible social relationships developed across spaces. Mónica vividly describes encountering gendered boundaries while growing up, and how stepping into the boys' spaces of play transformed her relationships with others:

> *Mónica:* I have strong memories of playing in the street. Strong, because I remember watching boys playing football. I was seven or eight. And, watching the boys play in the street from my front door, I wanted to play. A strong, unstoppable desire to play, to make some passes, to throw away the embarrassment and the mountain of things that would happen with all the world watching me. Later, I wanted to be the best I could so that they would accept me.... I was part of the group. The problems began later, how the boys looked at me changed, and so did how my family [looked at me].

Faced with exclusion in the gendered construction of spaces to play, women, girls and transgender and nonbinary people have had to develop practices of appropriating, repurposing and creating their own spaces to

---

[7] The *Pioneras* are a group formed by members of the Argentine national team who played in the 1971 World Cup in Mexico. Former goalkeeper, Lucila Sandoval, more recently reconnected with players from the team to highlight their history, and they have become important symbols for feminism in football (Pujol, 2019).

make it possible to play. Mónica's early life experiences are representative of many others who also encountered exclusionary efforts and little institutional or social encouragement to play. The symbolic placement of the *canchitas* for the *picaditos* on the streets and open park spaces at demonstrations and Encuentros becomes a powerful political act.

Through a feminist positionality, feminist football activists' efforts appropriate and rearticulate the transformative practice of making do with spaces associated with marginalised men and boys, thus asserting an inclusive right to play. Similar practices of appropriating and transforming spaces of football can be seen in other actions by feminist football activists: from taking up space on stadium terraces, entering club administrative positions, to creating teams and clubs explicitly for girls, women and transgender and nonbinary people, feminist football groups have been seeking to reconstruct inclusive spaces in the sports' institutions.

Cancionero feminista. Nutmegging the Patriarchy and Oppression

On Sunday, October 13, 2019, the banner of *La Coordinadora Sin Fronteras de Fútbol Feminista* carried by iconic members of the organisation led the 200,000-person demonstration at the 34th Encuentro through the streets of La Plata. There were hundreds of supporters wearing the colours of their clubs, while players and sports journalists marched behind the banner; it was a massive collective from across Argentina who had participated in sessions organised by La Coordi. They carried drums and flags, the folkloric elements of the Argentine football stadium, and sang songs they had rehearsed the day before while playing *picaditos* on the *canchita* setup on La Plata's central Plaza San Martin. Lyrics in the feminist songbook put to traditional melodies from football stadiums contained verses such as: 'a dissident field is my obsession, where all bodies can celebrate a goal; nutmegging patriarchy and oppression, you will see; football will be for everyone or it won't be; yes, boy, we carry revolution in our [football] boots'.

The reappropriation[8] of popular football songs and chants by members of La Coordi enmeshes practices of feminist politics with football cultures, integrating their passion with the core tenets and values of feminist political organising. Mónica connects the significance of emotions learned through football to La Coordi's presence in the feminist movement:

> *Mónica*: We are called to many political actions because of the force of emotion we transmit when recovering what is ours but from which we've been left out. … We appropriate part of the powerful masculine identity that's in the folklore of football, the part that motivates us to play and motivates us as spectators. It has something to do with how we experience football. Our football songs, for example, are genius; songs that are like anthems are wonderful parts of football in Argentina. If there is a song, you will start to sing it. And you sing and you sing. It's like a repetitive prayer, it doesn't matter if you are winning or losing, what you are celebrating is your identity and belonging. I think that every time La Coordi gets together we are celebrating our identity and belonging to this new little thing we have: feminist football.

Many of the feminist football songs sung by La Coordi appropriate the familiar melodies used in masculine football, as well as melodies common in political mobilisation, in part to generate a shared emotional sense of belonging during marches, demonstrations and events. Within the stadium, the collective singing of the songs creates an effective atmosphere that helps to generate a performative and an embodied sense of collectivity (Hawkins, 2017). According to Javier Bundio (2020), the masculine football songs of Argentine football's culture are statements from their social sphere, of the football stadium and its crowd. Songs are created through a contrafactum process, which involves changing the lyrics of a song or poem while keeping the same melody and/or meter. Melodies are extracted from cultural industries and transformed into part of popular

---

[8] La Coordi intentionally engages in the reappropriation of classic masculine football songs, which historically have stigmatised women, homosexuals and others by modifying their meaning through new lyrics.

mass culture through the lyrics that also influence ideas about football's identities (Bundio, 2020).

An important condition of football identities is their oppositional structure. The peculiarity of the Argentine case is that these identities have been built on the rhetoric of *aguante*, a native category that denotes a system of honour and prestige linked to violence and physical confrontations (Alabarces et al., 2008). The possession of *aguante* by supporters configures a type of hegemonic masculinity, based on tolerance to pain in physical confrontations, having 'balls' and being a man; it is typified by the practices of organised fan groups colloquially called *barra bravas*.

Bundio (2020) demonstrates how cheering and singing at a football match is an antagonistic cultural performance that pits an idealised self-image of the group in opposition to an inferior image of the other. Fans use their performance of songs, relying on masculine ideologies of violent competition, homophobic or xenophobic lyrics, to construct and reaffirm the divide between the two communities of supporters. Representations about 'us' and 'others' are built from a logic of dichotomous, exclusive and oppositional representation using the culturally relevant value system of *aguante* (Bundio, 2020: p.184). Although the *barra brava* is its maximum exponent, *aguante* configures a masculine culture constitutive of Argentine football.[9] For San Lorenzo Feminista, deconstructing masculine stadium songs has been an important site of reimagining the stadium terraces as inclusive spaces:

> We've tried to deconstruct and transform the violence that is implied by the discrimination [in songs against Boca]; it's very uncomfortable to be in the stadium when there is a xenophobic song. Coming from feminism we began to think, 'no more'; you can't tolerate these things in the stadium. It is possible to bring feminism to football and transform what it means to be a fan, the songs, the folklore. … For example, when we started to go watch women's volleyball, it was unbelievable, all the songs were for men. Everyone was singing [for the players to] 'play with balls'. No one was literally thinking 'play with balls', but everything we sang had to do with men, how the *macho* of the terraces experiences football. It didn't translate even

---

[9] *Aguante* transverses into other masculine cultures in Argentina; for example, the rock scene (Garriga Zucal & Salerno, 2008).

though we were supposedly there to support San Lorenzo; as a group we weren't supporting the girls that were playing volleyball. And the violence was there. To sing 'play with balls' to a woman doesn't make sense, and we started to realize it was violent. We needed to deconstruct what we were saying.

Aguante, however, also is related to the folklore in and around the stadiums including drums, flags and songs (Cabrera, 2019; Daskal, 2018). *Aguante* has a dimension linked to the performance of the fans in the stands, which transmits a passion and strength capable of influencing the outcome of the match (Hawkins, 2017). Feminist supporters question the *macho* dimension of this folklore and the violent dimension of football rivalries, without necessarily questioning the rivalry itself or the festive dimension in the stadium. For example, in one of the feminist football songs, the lyrics construct the *other* as hegemonic masculinity in football through the symbolically inferior *barra brava*:

What happened barra brava,
   that the fans are free of machos.
What happened barra brava,
   that in the end they were all *fachos*.[10]
The years go by, the players and leaders,
What happened to the girls? It's the question the people have.
As the girls, we take your place:
Oh oh!
In the streets, in the stadiums, and in the beds.
Oh oh!
While the police look after your football,
Our football is joy,
It's dissident, and it's feminist.

Engaging in the contrafactum of stadium songs is an opportunity for feminist football activists to reflexively engage with football culture more broadly. Naming the *barra bravas* and *machos* calls an idea into existence

---

[10] *Facho* is a local term form denoting fascist sympathies and is used to refer to supporters of Argentina's civic–military dictatorship (1976–1983).

that can be opposed; the opposition also helps to define the idea of what a feminist footballer is. For Caro, it was this:

> The folklore that we experience when we get together with La Coordi's flag, with the flags of all the teams, of all colours, and we are singing all together, it's folklore that we've managed to transform, the ability to think with feminism and our passion … it's the power of what it means to be a fan, the songs and the folklore. The folklore gives us what it means to cheer in the stadium, the passion, the *aguante* for your club. But you can transform it, taking out the violent part that comes from patriarchal football.

In this relationship, feminist football activists appropriate the emotional celebration and popular folklore of the stadium, including aspects of *aguante* that include a rebelliousness and anti-authoritarian disposition, while challenging aspects of the masculine violence of *aguante*. This last dimension is embodied by feminist football activists, who resignify it into feminist folklore. This also is valued by other sectors of feminism: La Coordi is summoned because they convey emotionality. Emotionality is anchored in the body, which is at the centre of feminist football activism: in the songs, the flags, persevering, playing and occupying the field.

The use of stadium songs reflects feminist football's broader engagement with the passion and emotion formed in the rivalries of Argentina's football culture. Rivalries in football are both oppositional and intimately connected through football matches. Feminist football fans continue to reflect on the significance of their clubs' historical rivalries. During fieldwork with the women who are part of the gender area of Club Gimnasia y Esgrima La Plata, Hang (2020) observed that ironic comments about the rival team were common in meetings, and jokes about their rival's stadium or players were told among laughs in private moments. In defining herself as a Gimnasia supporter, Belen described how she must do so in opposition to their arch rival Estudiantes de La Plata. While maintaining their rivalries, Hang (2020) showed that feminist supporters of Gimnasia conduct political work that transforms rivalries through an idea of sisterhood, which implies a shared recognition of common experiences of oppression and inequality.

To construct sisterhood without losing the rivalry, otherwise important to their identity as fans, requires the subtle work of articulating the differences between the supporters, often occurring in the small details of day-to-day actions of enacting a feminist football. Jokes about rivals, for example, function as a way of differentiating fandoms and maintaining the team identity within a wider network of feminist fans. When asked about their relationship to derby rivals Huracán, the first reaction of activists from *San Lorenzo Feminista* was laughter: 'That does not change, we don't like Huracán', Caro and Nadia said. But after thinking for a few seconds, they continued:

> Beyond that, we can even make jokes among ourselves, we shit ourselves with laughter with all the girls from the other teams, but we transform the word *folklore* into really what you see [in La Coordi]. Your head explodes when you see everyone together; it's crazy. … You discover that in other clubs there are many *pibas* like us, we each see each other, learn from others, and we have a lot of the same objectives and shared battles.

Rivalries through sisterhood creates opportunities to develop bonds of solidarity, while maintaining identities of belonging created through the folklore of football.

Conclusion: The Emotionality for 'Recovering What Is Ours'

Throughout this chapter the authors have shown the processes through which activists from *Coordinadora Sin Fronteras de Fútbol Feminista* turn football into a feminist praxis. Vast mobilisations around #NiUnaMenos and the Campaign for Legal Abortion not only enabled a massive arrival of feminism to football but also created openings for football to influence feminism. Within these feminist mobilisations, the long standing but far too often isolated, struggles of women in various spheres of football were able to converge around the project for feminist football. *Picaditos, canchitas* and *cancionero feminista* contribute to La Coordi's folklore, which involves its own identity constructed in opposition to the football they characterise as patriarchal. In turn, feminist football has been engaged in a process of rescuing emotionality and passion from what are seen as the violent dimensions of football. In doing so, feminist football is transforming football folklore into a valuable resource for other sectors of feminism.

Made up of a multiplicity of organisations and activists from various spaces, feminist football manages conflict at a political level, and football rivalries are processed in La Coordi under the idea of sisterhood. They structure their practice on a shared experience of their expulsion and exclusion from football, a sport that in Argentina was almost exclusively owned by men. Mónica recognised that the power of feminist football takes roots in the emotionality transmitted due to 'recovering what is ours, but from which we've been left out'. The praxis of La Coordi is structured under the idea that it is not about completely transforming football, but about the aspects in which macho, homophobic and misogynistic practices are expressed. It is also about recognising the potential of football as political and capable of mobilising unique emotions towards mutual solidarity in diversity. The reappropriation of football folklore reveals how the activism of La Coordi's members entangles practices of feminist politics with football cultures, integrating their passionate engagement with the core tenets and values of feminist political organising.

References

Alabarces, P. (2014). *Héroes, Machos Y Patriotas: El Fútbol Entre la Violencia y los Medios*. Buenos Aires: Aguilar.

Alabarces, P., Garriga Zucal, J., & Moreira, M. V. (2008). El 'aguante' y las hinchadas argentinas: Una relación violenta. *Horizontes antropológicos, 14*, 113–136.

Alvarez Litke, M. (2018). Marcando la cancha: Una aproximación al fútbol femenino desde las ciencias sociales. *Cuestiones de sociología, 18*, e055.

Archetti, E. P. (2008). El potrero y el pibe: Territorio y pertenencia en el imaginario del fútbol argentino. *Horizontes Antropológicos, 14*, 259–282.

Archetti, E. (2016). *Masculinidades. Futbol, tango y polo en Argentina.* Club House

Barrancos, D. (2014). Los caminos del feminismo en la Argentina: Historias y derivas. *Voce en el Fénix, 32.* Retrieved from http://www.vocesenelfenix.com/content/loscaminos-del-feminismo-en-la-argentina-historia-y-derivas

Bundio, J. (2020). *La identidad se forja en el tablón: Masculinidad, etnicidad y discriminación en los cantos de las hinchadas argentinas.* [Doctoral dissertation, UBA/CLACSO]. Retrieved from http://biblioteca.clacso.edu.ar/Argentina/iigg-uba/20201106124857/La-identidad.pdf

Cabrera, N. (2019). *Que la cuenten como quieran: Una etnografía sobre el devenir barra.* [Doctoral dissertation, Universidad Nacional de Córdoba]. Córdoba, Argentina.

Daskal, R. (2018). *Los hinchas militantes del Club Atlético River Plate: Fútbol, pasión y política (1966–2013).* [Doctoral dissertation, Universidad de San Martín]. Buenos Aires, Argentina.

Elsey, B. (2019). Energizadas pelo movimento de mulheres '#NiUnaMenos' as equipes de futebol feminino desafiam os patriarcas do esporte-rei da América Latina. *FuLiA/UFMG, 4*(1), 39–50.

Elsey, B., & Nadel, J. (2019). *Futbolera: A History of Women and Sports in Latin America.* University of Texas Press.

Fernándes Fuks, A. F. (20 Oct 2018). 'Caño, gambeta y gol al patriarcado en Trelew'. *Latfem.* https://latfem.org/cano-gambeta-gol-al-patriarcado-trelew/

Garriga Zucal, J., & Salerno, D. (2008). Estadios, hinchas y rockeros: Variaciones en torno al aguante. In P. Alabarces & M. G. Rodríguez (Eds.), *Resistencias y Mediaciones. Estudios Sobre Cultural Popular.* Paidós.

Garton, G. (2019). *Guerreras: Fútbol, Mujeres Y Poder.* Buenos Aires: Capital Intelectual.

Hang, J. (2020). Feministas y triperas: Mujeres y política en el área de género del club Gimnasia y Esgrima La Plata. *Debates en Sociología, 50*, 67–90.

Hang, J., & Garton, G. (in press) *Maradona and Gender: Rethinking Argentine Feminism through Diego.*

Hawkins, M. (2017). *'This is Boedo': Stories of a lost football stadium, a Buenos Aires barrio, and how the hinchas of San Lorenzo fought to return.* [Doctoral dissertation, Carleton University]. Ottawa, Ontario, Canada.

Hijós, N. (2013). Apuntes bibliográficos para acercarnos a la pregunta por el género en el deporte. *Cuestiones de sociología, 18*, e059.

Jefferson Lenskyj, H. (1995). What's sport got to do with it? *Canadian Woman Studies, 15*(4), 5–10.

Massey, D. (1994). *Space, Place and Gender*. Polity Press.

Natalucci, A., & Rey, J. (2018). ¿Una nueva oleada feminista? Agendas de género, repertorios de acción y colectivos de mujeres (Argentina, 2015–2018). *Revista de Estudios Políticos y Estratégicos, 6*(2), 14–34.

Pujol, A. (2019). *¡Qué jugadora! Un siglo de fútbol femenino en Argentina*. Buenos Aires: Ariel.

Silba, M., & Spataro, C. (2017). Did cumbia villera bother us? Criticisms on the academic representation of the link between women and music. In P. Vila (Ed.), *Music, Dance, Affect, and Emotions in Latin America* (pp. 140–167). Lanham, MD: Lexington Books.

4

Another 'barra' Is Possible: Women, Feminism and 'barras' in Mexico

Claudia Pedraza Bucio

Introduction: Women in the Bleachers

The experience of being a football fan produces identities related to a nation, region, city, neighborhood or specific social sector. In anthropology, sociology and other disciplines, there has been a concern with analysing these identity experiences of football supporter groups (known as *ultras* in international literature) beyond simply enthusiasm (Bairner, 2015; Delgado & Gómez, 2017; Lechner, 2007; Meneses, 2008; Villena, 2002). One such group is the Latin-American *barra de fútbol*. As an object of study, *barras* have generated substantial academic production for more than two decades, focusing on their characterising practices, aesthetics, symbols and structures (Alabarces, 2000, 2004, 2005; Garriga, 2005, 2007, 2015; Garriga Zucal & Moreira, 2006; Moreira, 2005).

C. Pedraza Bucio (✉)
Universidad La Salle, México City, México
e-mail: claudia.pedraza@lasalle.mx

Nevertheless, the analysis of female presence in the *barras* is rare because of the invisibility of women within these organisations, despite the growing number of female fans (GEMBA, 2020; Meier et al., 2015; Pope, 2017). In fact, over the last decade, groups of female football supporters have emerged worldwide (Lenneis & Pfister, 2018; Pitti, 2019). Particularly, adopting the *barra* aesthetic, groups emerged in Latin America seeking to transform sexist male football culture, interconnecting their practices with feminist principles.

The purpose of this chapter is to analyse the experiences of women who created these groups as spaces for feminist action. With this in mind, the first part revisits the approaches of sociology of sport and feminist theory to describe the male culture of *barras*, and subsequently, analyses the ways in which women are embedded in this culture as fans. Next, the third section provides context for the emergence of feminist football supporters' groups in Latin America, including *Barra Feminista* in Mexico, which is the chapter's case study. The fourth section presents the methodology used in the semi-structured interviews that allowed the author to access the experiences of the members of *Barra Feminista*. To conclude, the results of the interviews are discussed that revolve around three notions emerging from the analysis: the gender biases that condition their relationship with football; the mechanisms of otherness that mark their experience as fans; and the need to build other forms, practices and meanings of being part of a football supporter groups like the *barras*.

The Male Culture of *aguante* in Latin American *barras*

Understanding the emergence of feminist football supporter groups would be impossible without characterizing the sport in general and football in particular as gendered spheres 'belonging' to men. The analyses of various authors (Adams, 2011; Archetti, 2002, 2017; Cabello & Manso, 2011; Hughson, 2000; Tajer, 1998) acknowledge this gendering of sport on two levels: (1) as a space built by masculinity, where the values, practices and discourses of the sport are associated with the meanings of 'being a man' and (2) as a space that builds hegemonic masculinity with behaviours, reenactments and interactions for subjects to acquire the traits that define them as 'real men'. Because masculinity is the referent that gives meaning to sport spaces, practices and representations, anything feminine is perceived as the other, the subordinate, the opposite (Meân, 2010; Pedraza, 2017).

In particular, football spaces reinforce this configuration: coaches urge their students not to 'play like a girl', football chants boast that they will 'fuck the rival' and the media talks about 'la hombrada'[1] of winning teams. Football becomes 'a scene of socialisation and education in which the men who participate—footballers, coaches, spectators, fans and media—share a common experience that allows them to consolidate their masculine identity or shape new identities (Cabello & Manso, 2011, p. 87).

The football supporter groups, known as *barras*, are all about this; they are defined as youth spaces 'that produce and reproduce identities or sense of belonging, related yet independent of a football team' (Aponte et al., 2009 p. 12). The set of practices exhibited in this sense of belonging can be summarised in the concept of *aguante* (Alabarces, 2006; Alabarces et al., 2008; Moreira, 2017):

> Etymologically, 'aguante' refers to supporting, to be in solidarity. In football culture, the category is loaded with multiple meanings, all of which lead to ... putting the body into action. You can 'use your body' in many ways: incessantly encouraging the team, going to the home and away matches, enduring the discomfort of stadiums and travel, braving the rain, heat, cold (Alabarces et al., 2008, pp.117–118).

Aguante includes behaviours, interactions and meanings linked to masculinity (Alabarces et al., 2008; Pedraza, 2017), which are shown in the following:

> [A] narrative exaltation of masculinity and a disdain for what is considered feminine, as seen in the explicit sexism and homophobia of chants, cheers and insults against rivals; the desire to show superiority through displays of

---

[1] *Translator's Note:* 'La hombrada' can be roughly translated as 'manning up'. It usually is used by the media to say a team or player(s) behaves bravely, or needs to do so, to defeat a rival.

power, even if this means transgressing the order, space and bodies of others; the use of violence as a legitimate resource to demonstrate this superiority, resolve conflicts and reaffirm the sense of belonging.

This male culture of *aguante* explains the limited female presence in these groups because its practices, discourses and symbols reassert the *otherness* of women. The concept of otherness was originally used by Conde (2008, p. 126) to talk about female fans' emotional relationship with football. This concept is revisited here to define the norm of the relationship between women and the sporting spaces, values and practices that are not deemed *their own*. This otherness is reproduced and maintained in the social imaginary; in media, advertising, journalism and sport streaming the experiences of women as football fans are diminished, mocked or erased (Pope, 2011, 2017).

This marginalisation of female fans permeates academic research, which has typically focused on the importance of sports fandom for men (Pope, 2017), placing great emphasis on the concept of masculinity (Pitti, 2019). Furthermore, the main ways that scholars have approached the question of women's representation in sport tend to analyse female athletes rather than supporters (Toffoletti, 2017). In recent years, however, a growing number of studies have been conducted focusing on women's experiences as football fans. In Latin America, there are a few studies that seek to make women visible in football fandom (Binello et al., 2000; Conde & Rodríguez, 2002; Cruz Sandoval, 2011; De La Vega, 2012; Meier et al., 2015; Ramírez & Restrepo, 2018).

Principally, research on the participation of women in barras (or other ultras groups in diverse regions) indicates that their experiences are marked by a series of negotiations and resignifications of their identity as subjects of gender (Jakubowska et al., 2020; Pitti, 2019). Nevertheless, the ruptures do not entirely transform the gender order because they occur in a space that is symbolically and materially structured by masculinity, even though women also take part in it.

On the one hand, research acknowledges some identity negotiations in the relationship between women and the territory, their bodies, their male peers and their right to enjoyment (Radmann & Hedenborg, 2018; Toffoletti, 2017). Specifically, for women football fans, being in a barra implies: (a) gaining access to places deemed as belonging to men (i.e., the stadium, the streets, a bar) contrary to the closed spaces where female socialisation usually occurs; (b) a reconfiguration of the relationship with their bodies from the appropriation of the physical behaviours of aguante, shown through the intervention, exhibition and risking of their bodies; and (c) self-knowledge of their right to enjoyment through their football fandom (Pedraza, 2017).

On the other hand, some other studies highlight the reproduction of gender roles within barras, where activities (e.g., fundraising, taking care of collective goods and meal preparation) are the responsibility of female supporters (Meier et al., 2018). This gendered assignment of tasks distances them from access to positions of leadership and recognition within the group (Binello et al., 2000). Additionally, some male football supporters 'use their female partners to bring knives and other sharp weapons into the stadium because security screenings are less strict for women' (Clavijo, 2010, p. 56). Thus, not only do women subordinate their actions to the interests of others but also they are exposed to conflicts with the authorities, which could result in a permanent ban from the stadium.

Although the knowledge on the participation of women in barras is limited, it gives one some keys to approach experiences structured through places that are different from those constructed by traditional supporter groups. The author refers to the feminist football supporter groups in Latin America that, in the past few years, have aimed to modify the male culture of aguante.

Kicking Down the Patriarchy: Feminist Appropriation of Latin America's Bleachers

Female presence in the bleachers was inevitable given the way in which football was transformed into a space for the fight for women's rights. The increase in women's participation in several areas (e.g., on the field, in coaching, management and sport journalism) has led to an in-depth questioning of the multiple inequalities, discrimination and violence prevalent in football, along with collective proposals to make these issues visible while preventing and eradicating them.

Notably, the feminist agenda started to gain great momentum in the Latin American bleachers in 2017. Jeréz and Bustos (2020) noted that this was possible thanks to the reconfiguration of *barras* in their struggle to dismantle the stigma of violence that allows for 'the emergence of feminist collectives within supporter groups, putting pressure on internal spaces by questioning aspects of football's patriarchal culture, which is widespread both on and off the field' (p. 40). At the same time, the Latin American feminist movement was growing and becoming more visible while leading campaigns for rights, such as the legalisation of abortion (#MareaVerde), and calling out everyday gender violence (Larrondo & Ponce Lara, 2019; Laudano, 2018; Montenegro, 2018).

Nevertheless, feminist football supporter groups have existed since the early 2000s[2]. The first groups, located in Colombia, are 'Futbola', composed of Club Millonarios' fans; and 'Fortineras', a *parche*[3] affiliated with the group Holocausto Norte Zona 11, a *barra* of Club Once Caldas (Fandiño, 2019; Gutiérrez, 2020). Over the following decade, other women supporter groups of Chilean and Colombian clubs were founded. Between 2017 and 2020, however, more than 30 supporter groups were established in Argentina (16), Chile (10), Colombia (9) and Uruguay (2). In their names, these groups expressed their connection with feminism: *River Feminista* (River Plate), *Sabaleras Feministas* (Colon de Santa Fe), *Feminismo Xeneize* (Boca Juniors), *Sororidad Roja* (Independiente de Avellaneda). Most of the groups were separatists and identified with a professional football club (Arcos, 2019; Burgos & Bazán, 2021). In their social media, they spread slogans reaffirming their feminist identity: *'We kick down the patriarchy'* (Racing Feminista); *'The revolution will include feminism and football'* (Futbola). These slogans go beyond social media; their collective action repertoire included:

---

[2] This data is taken from ongoing research on feminist football supporter groups that analyses their social media to record their repertoires of collective action, the content of their public messages on social networks and their practices.

[3] In Colombia, a 'parche' (patch) is a subgroup of a supporter group or barra.

a) raising awareness and protests on key issues (campaigns against sexist language, murals to make women's participation in football clubs visible, *pañuelazos aborteros*[4] and collective demands against hiring players accused of gender violence);
b) activities for feminist reflection (workshops, discussions and conferences);
c) production of awareness materials and documents for micro and macro events (the *Feminist Anthem Book for the World Cup*, the *Machismo-o-meter* for the bleachers);
d) actions to benefit women fans (free mammography campaigns or grocery donations for unemployed women).

The groups did not act on their own, but rather they came together as a network, founding bigger organizations such as the *Coordinadora Sin Fronteras de Fútbol Feminista* in Argentina, or the *Coordinadora Nacional de Mujeres y Disidencias del Fútbol Chileno* in Chile (Manquepi, 2019; Torres, 2020).

In this context, the emergence of *Barra Feminista* in Mexico is quite interesting. Unlike other collectives, the *Barra Feminista* does not identify with a specific club; it is an organization that supports women's football in general. The group has its origins in social media, not in the bleachers. It first appeared as a group of female fans who shared an interest in exchanging Women's World Cup stickers in 2019 and later arranged to go together to the matches of the *Liga Profesional Femenil* in Mexico. They appeared publicly in March 2020 during a historic match of the Liga[5], drawing the attention of the media and other fans alike (Chavira, 2020; Santiago, 2020).

Barra Feminista has established multiple pillars to achieve their objective of eradicating sexist culture in football, to ensure safe spaces for women (Barra Feminista, 2020):

---

[4] *Translator's note:* A type of protest where women wear green bandanas, a symbol of the pro-choice movement to legalise abortion in Latin American. The name comes from the bandana itself, which is called a 'pañuelo' in Spanish.

[5] It was the first match that the Pumas women's team played in a professional stadium, a place previously reserved only for men's football.

a) In the bleachers and on the field where women's teams play, *Barra Feminista* hack' chant by changing the lyrics (as do some other female *barras* in Latin America) in order to make inequality visible, to transform the sexist narrative in *barras* and to show sorority with female players;

b) through social media, publishing data, dates and statements by female players, as well as other initiatives in favour of women's football;

c) through collaborations with different organizations, in events such as panel discussions, workshops, and conferences, where they reflect on the need to reappraise the feminism of women's football fans, making it visible.

For these reasons, it is relevant to retrieve the experiences of the members of *barras* who desire to turn the bleachers into a space of political action.

Women's Experiences as a Methodology Principle

Patricia Castañeda noted that feminist research identifies the facts of social and personal life that can boost real changes in the generic organisation of the world, for which the recovery of experience constitutes an epistemological and methodological principle (Castañeda, 2008, p. 7). Joan Scott (2001) defined experience as a process, where social subjects are located in the world; she proposed to analyse it not as evidence that gender subjects are different but to explain how these differences are constructed. This implies recovering the narratives through which women have resisted, negotiated and resignified the patriarchal structure in which they live, recognising their independence. Returning to the discussion of football as a masculine space, where the presence of women is marked by *otherness*, the experience of being a female fan entails these processes of resistance, negotiation and resignification.

To recover this experience, semi-structured interviews were used for data collection. With this technique, there is a previously designed guide of questions or issues but that gives space and flexibility to the conversation between the research subjects since its content, order and formulation are entirely in the hands of the person conducting the interview (Blazquez Graf & Bustos Romero, 2008, p. 52). Thus, eight semistructured interviews were conducted with members of the *Barra Feminista* on three issues: (1) identification of gender biases in their experiences as football fans, (2) milestones in their relationship with football and (3) milestones in their relationship with feminism.

The ages of the interviewees ranged between 22 and 32 years old and all hold bachelor's degrees from public universities. They live in Mexico City although three members are originally from other cities. Their employment situation was diverse: there were students, journalists, activists, teachers and so on. All of them were single and without children. Most worked with other feminist groups, not necessarily related to football or sports. None of them had actively participated in a *barra* before although they did identify themselves as fans of a particular club.

To arrange the interviews, the *barra* coordinators were contacted to request volunteers. Each volunteer was informed about the purposes of the interview, asked for informed consent, which was recorded, and provided with a question guide with two options: to conduct a virtual interview (synchronous, which was the choice of four interviewees) or to record the answers to the questions on audio (asynchronous, which was the choice of the remaining four). Both the virtual interviews and the audio recordings lasted approximately one and a half hours.

For the analysis, the responses were organized in meaning matrices, which served to establish links between categories or themes (Hernández Collado & Baptista, 2010). In this research, the author recovered the proposal of Higuita and Restrepo (2017), who suggested analysing the interviews by aggregate matrices (i.e., grouping common testimonies under the same topic), iterative matrices (i.e., grouping divergent testimonies) and finding matrices (i.e., with emerging testimonies not related to the initial categories). From this analysis of matrices, three relevant axes of their experiences were identified: the gender biases that conditioned their relationship with football, the mechanisms of otherness that marked their experience as fans and the need to build other forms, practices and meanings of being part of supporter groups. To present the testimonies of these matrices anonymously, the interviewees have been coded with the letter 'I' and the interview number (e.g., I1, I2, I*n).

Changing the Meaning of Football Fandom

As a starting point for the interpretation of the results, it was necessary to situate the feminist training and praxis of these women (mainly through university professors or activist groups). The initial supposition was that this feminist approach motivated them to form the *Barra Feminista* and denounce the inequalities evident in professional women's football (e.g., unequal salaries, sexist media coverage and lack of institutional support). Yet, the testimonies show the contrary: by reaffirming the feminist watchword of 'the personal is political', it was the identification of the prejudices lived through their experience as fans that generated the need to create a feminist space. First, this space had a personal impact, constructing a safe space for them; then it had a structural impact, modifying the male culture of the barras; and finally, in relation with the political, it became a space of struggle.

Gender Bias in the Introduction to Football

A first finding that stands out is that the initial relationship with football—men's football since it was the only one that was visible in their immediate context—establishes the first marks of *otherness*. Regardless of whether they come from a football family environment (or not) or whether they have developed an identity as fans of a team (or not), the testimonies showed that their initial introduction to football was marked by the sexual division of spaces, gender roles and differentiated practices:

> I3: When we got together as a family to watch a game, the women did not watch it, as though it were not interesting to them, so rather they dedicated themselves to other things. While the men are in the living room watching the game, the women are in the kitchen, cooking or talking about other things and it has always been that way.

Most of the interviewees shared experiences in which it was evident that the role of women is only as guests in football fans' spaces. This result confirmed what authors, such as Pope (2017), observed about how family gender roles shape women's involvement in sports. This shaping occurs: (a) through female roles dedicated to other non-football tasks (i.e., cooking, cleaning, serving food) while matches are being played or (b) through their relationship with male figures who become their reference for fan behaviour: 'brothers, fathers, uncles. They are the ones who teach you, who explain these football things to you' (I2). Even when there are women football fans in their family experiences and family contexts that encourage them to participate in the sport, the sexual division that establishes football as a masculine space remains.

Scholars agree that the male figures play a decisive role in the socialisation of the meanings of fandom, marked by the male ethos, which women accept, reproduce and perform (Binello et al., 2000; Mewett & Toffoletti, 2011; Pfister et al., 2018). Some authors, such as Jakubowska et al. (2020), indicated that although women do not participate in all forms of performance imposed by this male *ethos*, they do not always perceive the gender biases as a problem. Nevertheless, our interviewees did recognise the gendered socialisation, the imposition of male rules and the existence of sexist practices that make it difficult for them to fully appropriate the bleachers, which can even become a factor of rejection:

I3: The stadiums are full of macho dynamics. … Every time I had been to the stadium, with my father, with my brother, I came across with those dynamics that I didn't like. I think that's why it didn't become a habit for me to go to the stadium.

Other studies have shown that women are welcome as football fans if they follow the rules set by men (Binello et al., 2000; Pitti, 2019). Our findings complement this by demonstrating that when female fans do not want to follow the male dynamics, their first option is to move away from fan practices.

Mechanisms of Otherness for Female Fans

In recent years, the literature on women's participation in football supporter groups points out that there are no differences between male and female fans in terms of the ways they show their passion and devotion to a team, but they also underline how women face a more hostile environment, derived from male fan culture (Jones, 2008; Mewett & Toffoletti, 2011; Pitti, 2019). This hostility, in line with our findings, is related to three mechanisms that mark the otherness of women as fans: the stigma of oddness, the dismissal of their passion and the attacks they face in football spaces once they are involved as supporters.

The stigma of oddness is caused by the established belief that women '*are not interested*' in football, produced in part by the effects of the sexual division of space mentioned in the first section. Thus, women who express their love for this sport are identified as strange, rare or out of the norm:

> I1: For example, at a family gathering, it is normal for men to go watch the game and move away from the traditional family gathering, but if a woman does it, they say 'how weird!'. … So, I learned to restrain myself from wasting that passion because it doesn't 'look good' on a woman.

If, as Cabello and Manso (2011) indicated, football gives men a shared experience that allows them to consolidate their masculinity, for women the sport is articulated as a space that puts the desirable model of femininity in stress. Interestingly, although being passionate is something women can demonstrate in other areas, being passionate about football is a male prerogative. Binello et al. (2000) observed that within the groups of supporters, women who are passionate (or passionate 'like men') are rejected because of the belief that they are performing a simulated representation. This is consistent with what other authors have found in more recent research on *ultras* groups in Europe, where women's performances are considered counterfeit or fake (Jones, 2008; Pope, 2011; Meier et al., 2015; Pitti, 2019).

This is directly related to a second mechanism: the dismissal of woman's interests and knowledge of football through trivialisation and constant questioning:

> I5: If my brother comes and says 'I cheer for Pumas', people say, 'Oh, that's great'. But when I say that, they ask endless questions like: 'If you like it so much, tell me the five best players of all time,' or 'Surely, it is because you

like some players'. … It's a bit annoying that you have to keep proving that you only like football for football itself.

On trivialisation, scholars have pointed to the stereotypical assumptions that women's interest in male sports is motivated primarily by attraction to male athletes, which reproduces heteronormativity (Esmonde et al., 2018). Along with this is the constant questioning, which naturalises football as a male field of knowledge. As one of the interviewees points out, 'When a man expresses his interest or opinion on a football topic, he is not questioned' (I5) whereas women are the ones who must demonstrate their knowledge (Hoeber & Kerwin, 2013). In fact, more than half of the research testimonies describe an explicit decision not to talk about football with men in order not to be questioned or mocked.

The third mechanism is manifested in aggressive behaviours that seek to remind women who the symbolic, physical and material owners of the space are:

> I5: Sometimes I go to where *barras* are because of the carnival, but I have to be accompanied by my cousin, my brother, my father, because they come to harass you or say things that are not so cool.

Like other public spaces, stadiums have been experienced as conditioned spaces, where, through different situations, women are told that they cannot occupy any place, they cannot be noticed, they cannot go alone. This differs from the results of other studies showing that women increasingly perceive the stadium as a safe space, mainly because of safety regulations preventing clashes between rival fans (Jakubowska et al., 2020). Still, in the findings here, there is a perception of latent risk because of not only the fights among fans but also the bullying and harassment, the expulsion from certain areas by men as well as the aggressive chants and insults. The fear, insecurity or discomfort when going to the stadium expressed by the interviewees confirms the permanence of the mark the otherness in the bleachers.

Another *barra* Is Possible: Hacking the Culture of *aguante*

From these experiences of otherness emerges the need to create a space where women are not singled out as odd for showing their passion for football, where they are not questioned about their interests and where they feel safe. As mentioned earlier, some studies have focused on the strategies through which women negotiate their presence in these supporter groups, showing that they tend to accept and reproduce the marginal and ancillary position accorded to them by men (Binello et al., 2000; Jakubowska et al., 2020; Pitti, 2019).

In contrast, the recognition of the male culture in *barras* reported by the interviewees makes it difficult for them to accept the rules of belonging to these groups. In fact, none of the interviewees expressed an intention of joining the traditional *barras*, even if they were very fond of a team. Although they recognize the spectacular nature of the *barras'* carnival, the perception of these as violent, masculinised spaces with no female participation was enough to diminish their enthusiasm for joining.

> E5: All *barras* are male spaces, if there are women in *barras*, they don't have a leadership role; for example, you don't see women playing the drums or in the band ... they just let you stand with the *barras* but without taking you seriously.

Thus, for women, another option is to create female supporter groups, a trend that has been described in the literature not only as an alternative but also as a form of resistance to male domination (Lenneis & Pfister, 2018), as well as to openly challenge the sexist and misogynistic cultures of the bleachers (Pitti, 2019). Contrary to the findings of Jakubowska et al. (2020), women in these groups do propose their own forms of support. Particularly, the experience shared with other women at the stadium positions them against the practices of masculinity of *aguante* as the only form of 'being a real fan'. Therefore, with the creation of the *barra*, the purpose is to change this culture in three ways: (1) transforming the explicit sexism and homophobia of chants, cheers and insults against rivals; (2) eliminating the discourse of superiority; and (3) rejecting all kinds of violence, even those that are legitimised as a form of demonstrating *aguante*:

> I1: Instead of chanting misogynistic cheers, we will chant for the respect of the player's work, for them to gain enough money to be full-time football players, for them to have work rights, for them to be treated like professionals by the media.

So, through this change of narratives, practices and meanings, the *barra* becomes a place where personal experiences, through the feminist perspective, articulate a feminist struggle, turning it into a space to make a political statement against inequalities, discrimination and violence against women in football. Still, the need to create a safe space for themselves and others remains at the core where female fans can exist '*without being judged or criticized, because with the barra we can normalize the fact that women like football*' (I1). Contrary to what other studies have observed, where female fans claim to be recognised and accepted as ultras 'despite being women' (Pitti, 2019), these findings highlight the demand of the groups to place women at the centre, arguing that sport is a gendered space and that gender does matter.

This is what makes it possible, in the first instance, to think of these spaces as challenging the masculine culture of the *barras*. A couple of decades ago, Binello et al. (2000) asserted that the absence of symbolic struggle, as well as of other forms of conflict between genders, seems to indicate that the appearance of women in the football universe is not presented as a challenge that implies the possibility of modifying the male culture of *barras*. Nevertheless, what our results showed is that these feminist supporter groups now articulate this symbolic struggle while objecting to being recognised 'just like the men'. They question the gender biases that male culture has impregnated in the meanings of 'being a fan', proposing to resignify *barras*, maintaining their aesthetics and their carnival but without the marks of otherness.

Concluding Thoughts

As Pope (2017) points out, female fans largely have been marginalised in academic research. Nonetheless, the rise of female sports fans forces one to look at the ways in which they are appropriating the bleachers, beyond the acceptance and reproduction of models imposed by male fan culture.

Specifically, it was noticeable that the feminist appropriation of football bleachers is a growing trend among young female fans in Latin America. The presence of these groups makes one think about the possibilities for women to live their love for football without reproducing the male culture previously cited. Particularly, while considering the entry of members of *Barra Feminista* to football, the mechanisms of a relationship with the sport from a position of otherness became evident, conditioning their presence in the stadiums (and other football related spaces) from a place of hostility, discomfort and insecurity. In this regard, personal experiences become political fuel for women to create their own spaces in the bleachers. Therefore, the hegemonic state in which football fanaticism has been built is being hacked, the codes, chants and forms are tapped to understand *aguante*.

The results here show that the feminist perspective among groups of female fans allows them not only to take the bleachers to feel safe but also to transform them into spaces where they can speak out politically against inequalities, discrimination and gender violence. The creation of these spaces goes beyond being recognised as fans, but rather it is about changing the set of practices, values and meanings that condition their experiences of otherness.

With this initial research on feminist football fan groups and *barras*, some edges emerge for further analysis. For example, the author has yet to map the collective actions made in and out the stadiums or to follow the immediate and structural effects that they provoke. Thus, the final challenge is to keep watch over the actions generated by women and the ways in which the feminist praxis can change the meanings, dynamics and structure of football.

References

Adams, A. (2011). Josh wears pink cleats. Inclusive masculinity on the soccer field. *Journal of Homosexuality, 58*(5), 579–596.

Alabarces, P. (2000). *Peligro de gol. Estudios Sobre Deporte y Sociedad en América Latina*. Clacso.

Alabarces, P. (2004). *Crónicas del aguante. Fútbol violencia y política*. Capital Intelectual.

Alabarces, P. (2005). *Hinchadas*. Prometeo.

Alabarces, P. (2006). Fútbol, violencia y política en la Argentina: ética, estética y retórica del aguante. *Esporte & Sociedade, 2*, 1–14.

Alabarces, P., Garriga Zucal, J., & Moreira, V. (2008). El 'aguante' y las hinchas argentinas: una relación violenta. *Horizontes Antropológicos, 14*(30), 113–136.

Aponte, D., Pinzón, D., & Vargas, A. (2009). *Barras de fútbol, juventud y conflictos: mapeo en la localidad de Kenedy, Bogotá*. American Friends Service—CERAC.

Archetti, E. (2002). *Soccer and Masculinity* (pp. 519–524). Duke University Press.

Archetti, E. (2017). Masculinity and football: The formation of national identity in Argentina. In *Game without Frontiers* (pp. 225–243). Routledge.

Arcos, C. (3 de junio de 2019). *La cruzada feminista en el fútbol chileno*. The Clinic.

Bairner, A. (2015). Assessing the sociology of sport: On national identity and nationalism. *International Review for the Sociology of Sport, 50*(4–5), 375–379.

Barra feminista (23 de mayo de 2020) *Principios de la barra feminista (vídeo)*. Retrieved from https://fb.watch/870sBBGhE5/

Binello, G., Conde, M., Martínez, A., & Rodríguez, G. (2000). Mujeres en el futbol: ¿territorio conquistado o a conquistar? In P. Alabarces (Ed.), *Peligro de Gol* (pp. 34–48). Clacso.

Blazquez Graf, N., & Bustos Romero, O. (2008). *Académicas Pioneras. Trayectorias y Contribuciones en la UNAM*. CEIICH UNAM.

Burgos, J., & Bazán, C. (2021). *Las Bulla: La arremetida feminista dentro del espacio masculino de los hinchas de la U*. El mostrador. Retrieved from https://www.elmostrador.cl/braga/2021/01/27/las-bulla-la-arremetida-feminista-dentro-del-espacio-masculino-de-los-hinchas-de-la-u/

Cabello, A. M., & Manso, A. G. (2011). Construyendo la masculinidad: fútbol, violencia. *RIPS. Revista de Investigaciones Políticas y Sociológicas, 10*(2), 73–95.

Castañeda, M. P. (2008). *Metodología de la Investigación Feminista*. CEICH UNAM.

Chavira, P. (20 de marzo de 2020). *Una fiesta feminista en C. U.* Latinus. Retrieved from https://latinus.us/2020/03/15/una-fiesta-feminista-en-c-u/

Clavijo, J. (2010). *Cantar bajo la anaconda, un análisis sociocultural del barrismo en el fútbol.* [Bachelor's Thesis, Pontificia Universidad Javeriana. Bogotá.] Retrieved from https://repository.urosario.edu.co/handle/10336/2087 4?show=full

Conde, M. (2008). El poder de la razón: las mujeres en el fútbol. *Nueva Sociedad, 218*, 122–130.

Conde, M., & Rodríguez, G. (2002). Mujeres en el fútbol argentino. *Alteridades, 1*, 93–106.

Cruz Sandoval, J. (2011). El deporte, los aficionados y las cuestiones de género. In E. Cortés, J. Pedraza, & N. Vázquez (Eds.), *La configuración de nuevos espacios en la cultura. Deporte, comunicación y educación para la paz* (pp. 103–104). UAEM.

De La Vega, M. (2012). *La mujer aficionada al futbol: representaciones de género desde la tribuna.* [Master's Thesis, Iberoamerican University, Mexico City . http://ri.ibero.mx/handle/ibero/422

Delgado, Á. A., & Gómez, G. A. (2017). Mitos, ritos, identidad y alteridad en un estadio de fútbol. *Disparidades. Revista de Antropología, 72*(2), 505–526.

Esmonde, K., Cooky, C., & Andrews, D. L. (2018). 'That's Not the Only Reason I'm Watching the Game': Women's (Hetero)Sexual Desire and Sports Fandom. *Journal of Sport and Social Issues, 42*(6), 498–518.

Fandiño, Daniel (22 de marzo de 2019). *Parches feministas y antifascistas que se la juegan por la igualdad en el fútbol.* Cártel Urbano. Retrieved from https://cartelurbano.com/causas/parches-feministas-y-antifascistas-que-se-la-juegan-por-la-igualdad-en-el-futbol

Garriga, J. A. (2005). Lomo de macho. Cuerpo, masculinidad y violencia de un grupo de simpatizantes del fútbol. *Cuadernos de Antropología Social, 22*, 201–216.

Garriga, J. A. (2007). *Haciendo Amigos a las Piñas. Violencia y Redes Soci(E5)s de Una Hinchada de Futbol.* Prometeo.

Garriga, J.A. (2015). El inadmisible encanto de la violencia: policías y *barras* en una comparación antropológica. In J Garriga Zucal (coord.), *Violencia en el Fútbol: Investigaciones Sociales y Fracasos Políticos.* Buenos Aires: Ediciones Good.

Garriga Zucal, J., & Moreira. (2006). El aguante: hinchadas de fútbol entre la pasión y la violencia. In I. D. Míguez & P. Semán (Eds.), *Entre Santos,*

Cumbias y piquetes. Las Culturas Populares en la Argentina Reciente (pp. 55–73). Biblos.

GEMBA. (2020). *Gemba Insights global sports fan research*. The Gemba Group. Retrieved from http://thegembagroup.com/news/closing-the-sports-fan-gender-gap/

Gutiérrez, E. (4 de abril del 2020). *Mujeres en la tribuna*. Alternativa. Retrieved from https://alternativa.com.co/2020/04/04/mujeres-en-la-tribuna/

Hoeber, L., & Kerwin, S. (2013). Exploring the experiences of female sport fans: A collaborative self-ethnography. *Journal of Sport Management, 16*(3), 326–366. Retrieved from https://www.theclinic.cl/2019/06/03/la-cruzada-feminista-en-el-futbol-chileno/

Hughson, J. (2000). The boys are back in town: Soccer support and the social reproduction of masculinity. *Journal of Sport and Social Issues, 24*(1), 8–23.

Jakubowska, H., Antonowicz, D., & Kossakowski, R. (2020). *Female Fans, Gender Relations and Football Fandom: Challenging the Brotherhood Culture*. Routledge.

Jeréz, M. N., & Bustos, A. C. (2020). Del Estadio a la Calle. Hinchas y *barra*s de fútbol en la revuelta social de Chile. *Espacio Abierto: Cuaderno Venezolano de Sociología, 29*(2), 30–52.

Larrondo, M. L., & Ponce Lara, C. (2019). Activismos feministas jóvenes en América Latina. Dimensiones y perspectivas conceptuales. In M. Larrondo & C. Ponce (Eds.), *Activismos Feministas Jóvenes* (pp. 21–38). CLACSO.

Laudano, C. N. (2018). Acerca de la apropiación feminista de TICs. In S. Chaher (Ed.), *Argentina: Medios de Comunicación y Género:¿ Hemos Cumplido con la Plataforma de Acción de Beijing?* (pp. 138–146). Instituto Nacional de las Mujeres.

Lechner, F. J. (2007). Imagined communities in the global game: Soccer and the development of Dutch national identity. *Global Networks, 7*(2), 215–229.

Lenneis, V., & Pfister, G. (2018). Is There a Life Beyond Football? How Female Fans Integrate Football into Their Everyday Lives. In G. Pfister & S. Pope (Eds.), *Female Football Players and Fans. Football Research in an Enlarged Europe* (pp. 185–210). Palgrave Macmillan.

Manquepi, Belén, (20 de octubre de 2019. *Coordinadora sin fronteras de Fútbol feminista: 'Queremos construir otro fútbol*. La opinión austral. Retrieved from https://laopinionaustral.com.ar/futbol/coordinadora-de-futbol-femenino-queremos-construir-otro-futbol-132966.html

Meân, L. J. (2010). Making masculinity and framing femininity. *Examining Identity in Sports Media, 1*, 65–87.

Meier, H., Strauss, B., & Riedl, D. (2015). Feminization of sport audiences and fans? Evidence from German men's national football team. *International Review for the Sociology of Sport, 52*(6), 712–733.

Meneses, J. A. C. (2008). El futbol nos une: socialización, ritual e identidad en torno al futbol. *Culturales, 4*(8), 101–140.

Mewett, P., & Toffoletti, K. (2011). Finding footy: Female fan socialization and Australian rules football. *Sport in Society, 14*(5), 670–684.

Montenegro, L. F. (2018). El feminismo se ha vuelto una necesidad: movimiento estudiantil y organización feminista (2000–2017). *Anales de la Universidad de Chile, 14*, 251–291.

Moreira, V. (2005). Trofeos de guerra y hombres de honor. In P. Alabarces (Ed.), *Hinchadas* (pp. 75–89). Prometeo.

Pedraza, C. (2017). Señores, ¡yo soy canaria y tengo aguante! Reflexiones sobre la participación femenina en las *barra*s de futbol: la experiencia de las jóvenes en la 'Lokura 81. In G. Cozzi & P. Velázquez (Eds.), *Desigualdad de Género Y Configuraciones Espaciales* (pp. 253–272). CEICH UNAM.

Pfister, G., Mintert, S. M., & Lenneis, V. (2018). 'One is not born, but rather becomes a fan': the socialization of female football fans—A case study in Denmark. In G. Pfister & S. Pope (Eds.), *Female Football Players and Fans. Football Research in an Enlarged Europe* (pp. 211–240). Palgrave Macmillan.

Pitti, I. (2019). Being women in a male preserve: an ethnography of female football ultras. *Journal of Gender Studies, 28*(3), 318–329.

Pope, S. (2011). 'Like pulling down Durham Cathedral and building a brothel': Women as 'new consumer' fans? *International Review for the Sociology of Sport, 46*(4), 1.

Pope, S. (2017). *The Feminization of Sports Fandom: A Sociological Study.* Routledge.

Radmann, A., & Hedenborg, S. (2018). Women's football supporter culture in Sweden. In G. Pfister, & S. Pope (Eds.). *Female Football Players and Fans* (pp. 241–258). : Palgrave Macmillan.

Santiago, Juan. (14 de marzo de 2020) *Pumas y Cruz Azul femenil arman fiesta en el Olímpico Universitario.* Contraréplica. Retrieved from https://www.contrareplica.mx/nota-Cronica-Pumas-y-Cruz-Azul-femenil-arman-fiesta-en-el-Olimpico-Universitario-20201438

Scott, J. W. (2001). Experiencia. *Revista de Estudios de Género: La ventana, 2*(13), 42–74.

Tajer, D. (1998). El fútbol como organizador de la masculinidad. Revista de Estudios de Género. *La Ventana, 8*, 248–268.

Toffoletti, K. (2017). *Women Sport Fans: Identification, Participation, Representation*. Routledge.

Torres, M. (23 de septiembre de 2020). *Nace histórica coordinadora de organizaciones feministas ligadas a las hinchadas del fútbol*, Revista Obdulio. Retrieved from https://revistaobdulio.org/2020/09/23/nace-historica-coordinadora-de-organizaciones-feministas-ligadas-a-las-hinchadas-del-futbol/

Villena, S. (2002). El fútbol y las identidades. Balance preliminar sobre el estado de la investigación en América Latina. *Íconos-Revista de Ciencias Sociales, 14*, 126–136.

5

La Nuestra Fútbol Feminista: A Social Experimentation and Learning Territory

Enriqueta Tato, Jimena Aon, Juliana Roman Lozano, Maria Belén Bramanti, María José Figueroa, Mónica Santino, and Paula Korsakas

For centuries, theoretical, academic and activist feminism dismissed games and sports as practices of the hegemonic and traditional male world. Now, in Argentina and in many South American countries, we are experiencing a popularisation of the women and diversities' movement where feminism is fully understood as a political tool that enables us to fight against all historical oppressions on our bodies, leisure spaces and desires. This is why it is impossible to think of a fairer football without feminism and even more difficult to approach popular education without using a feminist lens.

La Nuestra seeks to expand the field and to continue producing knowledge and transformations, tending towards gender equality within a sport

E. Tato • J. Aon • J. Roman Lozano (✉) • M. B. Bramanti • M. J. Figueroa • M. Santino
La Nuestra Fútbol Feminista, Buenos Aires, Argentina
e-mail: lanuestrafutbolfemenino@gmail.com

P. Korsakas
Universidade Estadual de Campinas (UNICAMP/Brazil), Campinas, Brazil

J. Knijnik, G. Garton (eds.), *Women's Football in Latin America*, New Femininities in Digital, Physical and Sporting Cultures,
https://doi.org/10.1007/978-3-031-09127-8_5

traditionally built from hegemonic masculinity (Goellner, 2005; Knijnik, 2015). Football is the most important sport on our continent and the bearer of multiple meanings and cultural representations (Alabarces, 2003; Guedes, 2002, 2009). Looking at and playing football from a feminist perspective are thus immediate political acts to transform realities and advance the fight against gender-based violence.

In 2020, to reflect pedagogically about this political activity and to revisit coaching practices, the Community of Practice in Popular Education, Feminism and Football (CoP) was suggested by Paula, a Brazilian coach, educator, facilitator of the CoP and coauthor of this chapter. We—La Nuestra and Paula—first met in early 2019, when she visited our football field and led a workshop on Sport Pedagogy and Popular Education organised by Nike and the Laureus Foundation Argentina. The very questions from this meeting awakened the desire to investigate how we coach football, and the CoP was the plan we designed in late 2019 during Paula's second visit.

This chapter shares the journey of the CoP and the individual and collective values created from it as a social learning space (Wenger-Trayner & Wenger-Trayner, 2020) in which we have paved our route to integrating popular education, coaching and feminist practices.

Initial Considerations About Participating in This Book

First, we introduce each of the authors and our positions about writing this manuscript in English.

My name is Enriqueta Tato, and I was born in the city of Azul in the Buenos Aires Province. When I was 17 years old, I moved to Buenos Aires to study physical education. I have played soccer since I was little and, in Buenos Aires, I did so in several teams. For me, La Nuestra is a space where I find happiness, companionship and a lot of learning. In the organisation, I have found a space where I build myself as a person every day, coaching older girls and adult women.

I am Belén Bramanti; born in 1994, I grew up in Junín, Buenos Aires. In 2013, I moved to the capital to study what would become my vocation. I am a physical education teacher and, within this very comprehensive profession, I chose football as a means of activism in educational and political spaces. In 2019, I joined La Nuestra to coach young girls, where I found an inexhaustible source of learning, challenges and the *abrazo de una manada*.[1]

I am Jimena Aon; born in 1979 in Avellaneda, Buenos Aires, I was raised at a shoe manufacturing company, which is my current occupation. In the 1990s, I fought neoliberalism with the Dario Santillan Popular Front. I have studied popular education at the Universidad Madres de Plaza de Mayo (2001), where I researched workshops in territorial social movements. Since 2014, I am a member of La Nuestra, where, through coaching young girls, I can put into practice the knowledge acquired on this journey

I am Juliana Roman Lozano, feminist, football player and immigrant woman from Colombia. I was born in Bogota, and since I was very young, I have been migrating around the world. I am a documentary filmmaker, national football technical director and anthropology student. I have been with La Nuestra for 11 years, and here I have found my place in the world. Here, my social battles are articulated and my passion for militancy, learning and knowing is nurtured while coaching older girls and adult women.

I am María José Figueroa, born in Santa Cruz, Argentina, raised in Cordoba, and have been living in Buenos Aires for the past 11 years. I am studying for a degree in Sports at the Universidad de Avellaneda and want to become a football coach. I am a feminist, football player and have participated in some gatherings in horizontal and collective spaces. I have been a member of La Nuestra for some years, where I coach teenage girls, and it has become a space for co-learning and personal growth.

I am Mónica Santino, born in Buenos Aires in 1965. I am a physical education teacher, sport journalist, football technical director and former football player. I have worked in several women's football community clubs and took an active part in the Argentinian Homosexual Community

---

[1] A 'group hug' in English.

(1989–1996). I played football for the All Boys in the Argentine Football Association's (AFA) Women's League from 1996 until 2000. Since its inception, I am a member of La Nuestra Fútbol Feminista, where I coach teenage girls.

I am Paula Korsakas and was born in São Paulo in 1976. I am a former youth basketball coach, sport scholar, consultant and activist for the right to play sports. I came across La Nuestra in 2019 while working as coach educator in South America.

The invitation to participate in this book coincided with the launching of CoP. We acknowledged the chance to systematise the experience as a valuable opportunity; however, despite our excitement to document the learning journey, we also felt uncomfortable because the text was to be written in English. Most of us do not speak English, and those who do lack fundamental linguistic resources to fully express ourselves. Additionally, as a book aimed to present the historical perspectives and social challenges of football practiced by women in Latin America, we could not help but feel confronted by the fact that precisely those accomplishments and challenges, which are lived, fought and endured in lands where Spanish, Portuguese and more than 420 different indigenous languages are spoken, only had a publishable voice in English.

The history of women and diversities in Latin America and our struggle for spaces of participation and development in sport is permeated by power (Goellner, 2021; Moreira & Garton, 2021). Among the infinite ways in which power oppresses is communication, which frequently results in structural advantages for the dominant language. Language is both an intimate and external phenomenon, a tool to express individual feelings and thoughts, as well as our collective ideas and political constructions (Freire, 2013a). Language is personal, viscera and powerful. It is linked to our lands, struggles, pains and bodies.

Therefore, it seemed relevant to point out the need to create opportunities to express ourselves in a language to fully transmit the depth, texture and matrix of our ideas, our collective knowledge. The marginalisation of nondominant languages, especially in 'international' academic contexts (Phillipson, 2016), is so widespread and normalised in most cultural contexts; it is easy to see it as 'the way things are' rather than as part of the architecture of an experience and, therefore, something open to criticism and revision.

English, like Spanish and Portuguese, are colonising languages in the contexts where they dominate. As Paulo Freire once affirmed, 'it is impossible to think of language without thinking of ideology and power', although he also asserted that grasping the dominant language was a right and a means for the oppressed to make their voices and discourses heard (LiteracyDotOrg, 2009). With Freire's words echoing in our bodies, we wrote this text, originally in Spanish and Portuguese, to then be translated into English by Isabel Lugones, to whom we are grateful.

Nosotras[2]

Villa 31, our territory, is the oldest settlement in the city of Buenos Aires, located between the Recoleta and Retiro neighbourhoods, with its origins as early as 1932. Migrants who worked in the port or were left unemployed began to inhabit the first tin houses in the area. The State also offered housing in empty train cars.

By the end of the 1950s, the Federation of Shantytowns and Emergency Neighbourhoods was created. Villa 31 was soon characterised by its organisational power, and it became a standard-bearer of the informal settlement movement in the city of Buenos Aires. The communist party and the Peronist resistance to the dictatorship of those years are the most important political signs of struggle against injustice and vulnerability. In 1974, Father Carlos Mujica, a fundamental social leader in the history of Villa 31, was murdered by the Argentine Anti-Communist Alliance, also known as Triple A, a far-right death squad founded in Argentina in 1973. Mujica's death left a deep pain and void in the neighbourhood. By the 1978 Men's World Cup in Argentina, the neighbourhood had endured and resisted an eradication attempt by facing off against the bulldozers of military dictator Jorge Rafael Videla. In the 1990s, once again in times of democracy, another attempt to eradicate the settlement occurred.

---

[2] _Nosotras_ is the Spanish word for 'Us', and we chose this term to name this section to represent the work of the first five authors of this text in La Nuestra.

According to the 2010 census, Villa 31 has 40,000 inhabitants originating from various Latin American communities and Argentine provinces, giving the community an immense diversity and cultural richness. Currently, the neighbourhood finds itself in a process of urbanisation, which began in 2009 when the Buenos Aires Legislature passed the Law of Urbanisation. This process has been characterised by a lack of essential services, precarious housing and the inadequate quality of the materials used in improvements as well as by the State's complete lack of a gender and diversity perspective in the allocation and distribution of housing.

As La Nuestra Fútbol Feminista, we have been walking the streets of Villa 31 for 14 years, passing the ball to each other and constantly learning, to build and maintain a safe space for football practice, while reflecting on our actions, lives and identities from an intersectional feminist perspective. We deliver football training sessions two days a week, educational workshops on social and political themes one day a week and different cultural activities for more than 150 women (i.e., young girls, teens, youths and adults) and members of the LGBTIQ+ community throughout the year. All these activities are freely accessible, separated into four age groups[3] and conducted by a coaching staff composed entirely of women and members of the LGBTIQ+ community. Our practice is based on an affective pedagogy of presence and popular education oriented by a community and feminist approach (Davis, 1981; Bidaseca & Laba, 2011), rooted in a particular territory as a permanent space for debate and action. The territories—popular neighbourhoods—are characterised by exclusion, abuse and a permanent feeling of a need to survive at all costs.

When establishing links with the people who inhabit these spaces, we adopt a principle of Liberation Theology practiced by the Priests for the Third World: permanent presence generating solid and indestructible bonds over time is the tool that enables trust. This pedagogy is developed in, with and for the community, in coordination with other organizations and groups, to promote cross-cutting actions. It is a horizontal relationship woven between peers, never from a top-down position of hierarchy.

---

[3] LN activities are divided into four age groups: mini minis (from 5–8 yrs), minis (from 9–11 yrs), cadets (12–14 yrs), youth (16–18 yrs) and seniors (older than 18 yrs).

In this way, we conquered the field. Our presence does not disappear under any circumstances. This footprint for generating ties is also present in our way of playing football.

From this place of safety, sport is a space of support, reflection and expression of those who make up La Nuestra. A point from where we build our own language, our own distinctive identity within feminist football: a platform from which we can experience and forge new meanings and paths, beyond what is strictly known as sport. One of the La Nuestra players once said: 'I stand tall on the field as I stand tall in life'. It synthesises part of the work we do, in which participants are not simply recipients but rather protagonists. Collectively, we are shaping this project we consider to be 'our place in this world', *nuestra manada*[4] (Alvarez Litke, 2020b).

Our motto, *'La cancha es nuestra!'* ('The field is ours!'), asserts that the football field belongs to women and gender dissidents as well. It states that Güemes, the field in Villa 31, is *nuestra cancha*—our field. Holding training sessions on the most in-demand playing field in the neighbourhood, which is also a public space, despite the multiple battles and obstacles faced, represented the first resistance to oppression. When we first came to the field 14 years ago, we were denied our right to play and inhabit the public sphere as football players, but now Güemes is known in the neighbourhood as 'the women's field'. Increasingly, younger women and families began to claim their right to play, acknowledging the safe and caring space offered, as a result of the visibility of our occupation and resistance on the field. The girls who claimed their rights 14 years ago have now become role models for the youngest. In 2007, 12 young women participated. In 2021, more than 150 players and nine coaches make up La Nuestra. We took for ourselves what also rightfully belongs to us after having persistently been denied access by the patriarchal system.

At the same time, we realised that our practice held an enormous reservoir of knowledge, moving us to build ties with other groups and organisations to expand the cartography of football played by women and the LGBTIQ+ community. In recent years, we have made a joint effort to produce theory from practice, systematising our experiences and

---

[4] Our (wolf or dog) pack.

continually reflecting on our collective knowledge, theory 'absorbed from lived practice' (Freire, 1997, p. 22). From this arose the need to generate new networks and, since then, we have carried out football tournaments, health and cultural activities, national and international festivals and workshops that put the spotlight on the transformative and dissident power of feminist sport from a critical and intersectional perspective in society in general, but particularly in hegemonic feminism[5] (Alvarez Litke, 2020a).

As citizens with multiple subordinate identities (Muñoz, 2011)—Latin American women, migrants, lesbians, blacks, youths, girls, nonbinaries—who struggle to play football in particular ways in the face of innumerable and simultaneous structures of oppression and violence, we have turned the field into our battleground, from which other projects led by the members of the organisation have grown.[6] Currently, the leadership of La Nuestra is marked by emerging voices of teens and young adults, in which the assertion of the *villera*[7] identity converges with the appreciation of their identity as footballers and feminists.

Along this journey, tacit knowledge of popular education built from the participation of some of us in social movements was an auxiliary guide to our work, but after a process of systematisation of our praxis through popular education in 2013, it became a foundation for our daily work (La Nuestra Fútbol Femenino, & Co.Co.In, C., 2018). It revealed

---

[5] Since 2013, we have been participating in the National Gathering of Women (ENM) co-organizing the National Gathering of Football Players. In 2017, a workshop on Football and Feminism was included in the ENM grid and the Feminist Football Coordination Without Borders was born, bringing together organisations, gender and diversity commissions, activists, journalists, players, coaches and football leaders from all over the country.

[6] 'Abrir el Juego' (Open the Game) is an example in which we created three booklets with tools to prevent gender-based violence in sport with contents stemming from our territorial background and highlighting the importance of the participation of community-based organisations in the construction of public policies. La Nuestra TV is our television program, which produces counter-hegemonic narratives to transform football. Finally, Cartografiando Nuestro Tejido Villero (Mapping our Villero Fabric) is a project that arose when we asked ourselves about the history of football in Argentina and the history of Villa 31; by locating the protagonists and defenders of human rights in our territory, we were able to break away from the historical invisibility and silencing of girls, women and diversities.

[7] Referred to as the people who inhabit informal settlements. It was originally used as a derogatory term but, currently, to be named as villeres is a vindication of the place where we are born, live and from the place where we think about ourselves and create our narratives.

the chance to construct our own theories anchored in libertarian practices. Democratising speech, bodies and meanings is our path and our political conviction to build a fairer world. Taking popular education to training sessions on the football field to make sure that our pedagogy is embedded with our collective political view has been a constant challenge as coaches, but this is also the driving force of the CoP.

The Community of Practice in Popular Education, Feminism and Football

Belonging to a social group and sharing knowledge is a collective learning process and the essence of a Community of Practice (CoP), 'groups of people who share a concern, a set of problems, a passion about a topic, and who deepen their knowledge and expertise in this area by interacting on an ongoing basis' (Wenger et al., 2002, p. 4). In a CoP, learning is situated in the interaction of people with the social world as an 'act of knowing' that generates meaningful knowledge through reflection on concrete experiences that are collectively shared (Wenger, 1998). It values the exchange of tacit knowledge in informal learning situations that, combined with explicit knowledge, generates new knowledge.

A CoP is a learning partnership with three essential characteristics: *domain, practice and community* (Wenger et al., 2002). Domain defines the identity of a community based on a common interest or shared inquiry; in our case, the search for a praxis as football coaches, guided by popular education and feminism. Community refers to the bonding and relationships nurtured between members that create a sense of belonging, something that is already present and strengthened during the experience. Practice relates to the innovations and practical transformations that arise from the learning we share here.

CoPs have favoured more horizontal learning relationships, breaking with the traditional vertical 'top-down' transmission of knowledge (Wenger, 2010). Likewise, they have been explored in the sport context as a strategy for coach development, valuing practice as an historical and social action that gives meaning to what coaches do and who they are (Culver & Trudel, 2008). It was precisely because of these characteristics that the CoP approach was chosen because it would offer a learning space for us, ethically and politically aligned with La Nuestra's way of (re)existing in the world.

The Meetings

Our CoP was originally planned to take place in 2020, combining virtual meetings and a review of recorded coaching practices. Yet, because of the Coronavirus pandemic, it began when sport activities were already suspended in Argentina. In total, we held 13 virtual meetings (each approximately two hours long) between March and December of 2020, with the intention of producing pedagogical guidelines for La Nuestra.

To prepare for the CoP, as La Nuestra coaches and popular educators, we shared individual questions organised into three thematic axes and generated the guiding question on how to merge popular education and feminism in our coaching practices. Thereafter, the meetings entwined various sources of knowledge, such as academic readings, our practical knowledge as women and sport coaches and the social reality of the pandemic. The meetings also varied in nature; some were more theoretically oriented while others more on applying learnings in practice, both equally important for our praxis (Freire, 2013b). Paula kept a diary of the meetings on a shared online document, and we communicated using a mobile chat app in between meetings.

By the end of the meetings, we reflected individually and collectively on our learnings and the meanings (values) created along the process, based on the Values Creation Framework (Wenger-Trayner & Wenger-Trayner, 2020). In the following, we share reflections and learnings in a nonlinear narrative as a way to make (new) sense of the whole experience.

'La cancha es nuestra!': The Football Field as an Insurgent Feminist Territory

We started exploring popular education through the lens of Argentinean social movements seen as insurgent territories, geographic but also symbolic spaces in permanent resignification and dispute, places to deploy political agency and to reinvent social systems (Aguiló & Wahren, 2014). By reflecting on socio-territoriality, we recognised La Nuestra as an insurgent territory where we act politically and pedagogically for the emancipation of women by living direct democracy and deconstructing patriarchal practices. In this process, we became aware of our diverse experiences with social movements, feminism and popular education and how those learnings culminated in what is now La Nuestra. We also reflected on the idea that popular education, as a way of knowing from political practice, should be the foundation of feminist pedagogy, in content and form, by building new relations between women to co-educate us all as feminist agents for political transformation (Silva & Godinho, 2017).

From the dialogues on popular education and feminism, we reflected on when and how football was oppressive. The challenge was to build more horizontal relationships between coaches and players and to break with traditional authoritarian practices in sport (Korsakas & De Rose Junior, 2002). Questions were centred around decentralisation of power while still generating technical, tactical and physical improvement. In popular education, knowledge emerges from dialogue while in sport, dialogue takes place within the body; we are bodies in dialogue on the field. Football is language. 'The first language is the language of the body' (Freire & Faundez, 2012, p. 73). With that in mind we involved ourselves in coaching football through more dialogic sport pedagogies (Knijnik et al., 2019), reaffirming a feminist and libertarian football for all possible bodies, where repetition and imitation leave the field to make room for creation and emancipation (Korsakas, 2009).

Still, the pandemic raised doubts about our certainties.

La Nuestra's Identity in Movement

Unfamiliar challenges arose with the suspension of training sessions, a drastic break from our daily work as coaches. Not being on the field, somehow, was not recognising ourselves in what was already part of our identity for many who have been there week after week for years. Furthermore, the distancing from the players and Villa 31 families, who were highly vulnerable to COVID-19 because of the precarious living conditions in the territory, was another source of distress.

Suddenly, the power of occupying the football field was weakened by the impossibility to act. Impotence gave rise to doubts about our role with the families and the political meanings we were generating given the emergency. We asked ourselves how to avoid assistentialism. By experiencing this dilemma, we realised that this adversity strengthened the bonds and affection between us because, despite not being on the football field, our actions positively impacted peers and the community.

The actions we carried out were, among others, the organisation of a solidarity campaign in collaboration with feminist networks and friends of La Nuestra. This allowed us to provide, for more than six months, a weekly delivery of bags of food and basic goods for more than 80 families. Furthermore, we were able to make a video of recommendations to prevent COVID infection and another video with formal and informal resources to access test facilities, isolation spaces offered by the government and useful advice to get through isolation. Finally, we made a booklet of games and activities for children, considering that many were enduring the pandemic without Internet access; they were kept away from school and other support spaces, often experiencing overcrowded conditions. Players and families felt cared for and, more importantly, demonstrated a tremendous capacity for autonomy and conflict resolution in this adverse situation as political agents in their own territory.

This moment of fragility and revisiting ourselves as a political–educational collective turned into a new force. When everything was put to the test, we remained faithful to La Nuestra's principles, putting into practice what we have always stood for. Thus, the desire emerged to incorporate that strength when football could return. Pure frustration became an impulse to plan ahead: How could we resume training sessions post-pandemic?

It became necessary to get one more playing field in Villa 31 to guarantee compliance with health protocols, which was also an opportunity to improve the quality of the sport experience by increasing space and playing time. Beyond adding a field, we also located an office, a headquarters to store materials, hold meetings and offer a bathroom for everyone. We resumed training sessions in late October of 2020, having everything planned in advance for the first time.

La Nuestra Theories: What Does Libertarian Feminist Football Coaching Look Like?

We assert that playing football is a right and lay claim the occupation of the field by women and diversities. We refute, however, the discourse of sport as a mere tool for women's empowerment. For us, being able to play libertarian feminist football is an end in itself; it is self-realization, lived citizenship (Korsakas et al., 2021).

Sport is a place in which diverse bodies confront the binary hegemonic ideas of what a female or male body should be (González et al., 2018). We believe sport has the power to bring out the active and transformative character of bodily practices. While providing a safe environment to embrace all bodies and identities, feminist sport practice offers the possibility of living different subjective experiences as bodies and enables bodies to confront, resist and create alternative experiences to what appears to be culturally imposed (La Nuestra Fútbol Femenino & Co.Co.In., 2018).

In this sense, La Nuestra's game model represents our effort to express the football we want to coach and play. If, traditionally, the design of game models represents game concepts and expected player behaviours, placing the tactical dimension at its centre (Casarin et al., 2011), in our case, we articulate sport and political dimensions to communicate our game identity—a strong, organised and solidary football that passes the ball to all possible bodies welcomed onto the field.

After drafting our game identity, we moved on towards the identity of each of the age groups, culminating in the Curriculum of La Nuestra, a long-term development plan that organises sport, politics and history; it has intertwined developmental axes according to which we recognise experienced peers as a reference for the youngest, favouring the sharing of knowledge. The sport axis informs the technical, tactical, physical and psychosocial aspects of training and also embraces learnings related to body self-knowledge and identity as players. The historical axis focuses on the preservation of memories of the struggle for the football field and its protagonists as a means to nurture a sense of belonging and our collective identity. The political axis is devoted to the principles of playing feminist football and living direct democracy.

The very game of feminist football is liberating. The provision of a good sporting experience and its democratization; for us, this is a political act, and sport explored as a metaphorical language of life fuses it with political education (La Nuestra Fútbol Femenino & Co.Co.In., 2018). On the field, libertarian feminist football has been translated into coaching practices (e.g., active listening spaces built for and by players, player leadership in training tasks and learning activities that make room for player creativity), valuing their tacit knowledge and promoting self-management. These are coaching practices that bring theories to life, devoted to promoting individual growth of girls, women and gender diversities as players as much as political agents of social transformation (Korsakas, 2009).

Our Learnings: The Values Created

The Values Creation Framework suggests that values originated in social learning spaces (e.g., CoPs) unfold in different ways, starting from the immediate value the experience generates for participants to the potential value residing in the learnings of each person and the whole group and continuing on to more concrete cycles of transformations (e.g., applied and realized value), related to what participants did in practice, what they learned and the effects this generates in the real world (Wenger-Trayner & Wenger-Trayner, 2020). Participating in the CoP during the pandemic was meaningful per se (i.e., of immediate value). It was an important time and space during an atypical year; everything we gained in communication and joint reflection compensated for the distance from the community that we had never experienced before. Affectively, the CoP meant a moment of care and support to think about peers and ourselves. It was a safe and delightful space to express opinions, to listen and to see how each of us experienced the process.

The CoP was a social space to build on tacit knowledge and gain new insights on popular education (i.e., of potential value) as we 'critically revised and put our collective knowledge(s) in order', we 'put it into words". We theorised our practices. It prompted us to 'de-automatise teaching and think about it critically', 'to break with the linear and think of more participatory dynamics, placing more emphasis on games and circles where everyone can put their voice and body and where we can reflect as a group. … Being able to bring that political stance into the way we design a drill is very enriching.'

Although documentary production could be understood as a potential value 'because it has yet to prove useful in practice' (Wenger-Trayner & Wenger-Trayner, 2020, p. 88), we acknowledge La Nuestra's game model and curriculum by their applied value because planning is part of coaching, not something dissociated or prior to action. The action of planning consequently affected our work on the field. The active participation of girls in suggesting activities, learning football skills from game-like activities, using problem-solving sport tasks inspired by the question's pedagogy (Freire & Faundez, 2012), exploration and dialogue between players as a means of searching for an effective sport skill—these are all examples of how learnings were embodied and lived on the football field.

Despite the limited on-field training time because of the pandemic, we identified qualitative leaps in our practice (i.e., of realised value). Giving more importance to dialogical spaces in training sessions improved communication between us and the players. Players welcomed questioning and are more talkative and comfortable to express what they think and feel. Making sport practice more creative and playful awakened more interest from the players. We believe that the more powerful environment of enjoyment and agency that we have been developing together has contributed to the exponential growth in the number of players who have recently joined La Nuestra.

Another positive effect is that La Nuestra as a whole has been strengthened. We grew collectively and discovered a grand capacity for work and reinvention, for tightening bonds with the community, and greater political clarity about what we do, how we do it and why we do it. We faced situations that arose in a more orderly and robust manner. New paths of inquiry, projects and leadership also have emerged.

In Freirean terms (Freire, 1997), this whole reflective process, lived within the pandemic context, confronted us with a 'limit-situation', extreme conditions that, through praxis, could be overcome. We had recreated ourselves by building a new level of collective consciousness that enabled La Nuestra to generate 'untested feasibility' and create new ways to critically intervene in reality. Among the challenges remaining are the cultivation of this affective learning space by guaranteeing formal moments to continue generating new reflections and ideas while also sharing with new coaches what was built and how we did it because it can become a guide for how to theorise practice. Finally, creating this text together through dialogic writing triggered the latency of the CoP itself, which, although formally finalised in December 2020, was revealed to still be alive, nourished by the feeling of belonging, the desire to meet again and our shared love for what has already been lived. Participating in the CoP, we realised that, in essence, La Nuestra is a potent, living social learning space.

In the same way that we break down walls on the field, tearing down prejudices, we also became stronger by putting our liberating, transformative and collective empowerment processes into words. It is a starting point from which to grow. It by no means ends here. This is what football poses as a game and experience—to risk, make mistakes, recover, learn with others and celebrate passes as essential for goals. The questions we will continue to ask ourselves are the basis for future victories. They will allow us to tie together all possible feminisms so that the right to play sports continues to be guaranteed in the form of a ball accessible to us all.

References

Aguiló, V., & Wahren, J. (2014). Los bachilleratos populares de Argentina como 'campos de experimentación social'. *Argumentos, 27*(74), 97–114.

Alabarces, P. (2003). *Futbologías: Fútbol, identidad y violencia en América Latina.* CLACSO—Consejo Latinoamericano de Ciencias Sociales.

Alvarez Litke, M. (2020a). '¿Fútbol femenino o feminista? Disputas de sentido en torno al género y el deporte en Argentina', en Kula. *Antropología y Ciencias Sociales, 22,* 9–26.

Alvarez Litke, M. (2020b). 'Me paro en la cancha como en la vida': un análisis del fútbol feminista en la Villa 31 desde las teorías de género. *Zona Franca. Revista de Estudios de Género, 28,* 79–104.

Casarin, R. V., Reverdito, R. S., Greboggy, D. L., Afonso, C. A., & Scaglia, A. J. (2011). Modelo de jogo e processo de ensino no futebol: princípios globais e específicos. *Movimento, 17*(3), 133–152.

Culver, D., & Trudel, P. (2008). Clarifying the concept of communities of practice in sport. *International Journal of Sports Science & Coaching, 3*(1), 1–10. https://doi.org/10.1260/174795408784089441

La Nuestra Futbol Femenino & Co.Co.In. (2018). 'La Nuestra' y 'Las Aliadas' sistematización de una experiencia de fútbol femenino en la Villa 31. *Zona Franca. Revista de Estudios de Género, 25*, 256–284. https://doi.org/10.35305/zf.v0i25.64

Freire, P. (1997). *Professora sim tia não. Cartas a quem ousa ensinar.* Olho D'água.

Freire, P. (2013a). *Cartas à Guiné-Bissau: Registros de uma experiência em processo.* Paz e Terra.

Freire, P. (2013b). *Pedagogia do Oprimido.* Paz e Terra.

Freire, P., & Faundez, A. (2012). *Por uma pedagogia da pergunta.* 10ª edição. Paz e Terra.

Goellner, S. V. (2005). Mulheres e futebol no Brasil: entre sombras e visibilidades. *Revista Brasileira de Educação Física e Esporte, 19*(2), 143–151. https://www.revistas.usp.br/rbefe/article/view/16590/18303

Goellner, S. V. (2021). Mulheres e futebol no Brasil: descontinuidades, resistências e resiliências. *Movimento, 27*, 1–12. https://doi.org/10.22456/1982-8918.110157

González, C., Klein, C., Cattáneo, S., Pascual, M., & Cordero, A. (2018). ¿Qué tiene para decir la Educación Física en el campo de la educación popular? Experiencias contrahegemónicas hacia una educación popular del cuerpo. *IV Encuentro Hacia una Pedagogía Emancipatoria en Nuestra América*, Buenos Aires.

Guedes, S. L. (2002). De criollos e capoeiras: notas sobre futebol e identidade nacional na Argentina e no Brasil. In *XXVI Encontro Anual da ANPOCS*, Caxambu (pp. 1–19). https://ludopedio.com.br/wp-content/uploads/043411_Guedes%20-%20Notas%20sobre%20futebol%20e%20identidade%20nacional%20na%20Argentina%20e%20no%20Brasil.pdf

Guedes, S. L. (Traducción Lucia Eilbaum). (2009). Las naciones argentina y brasileña a través del fútbol. *Vibrant, Virtual Brazilian Antropology, 6*(2): 167–185. http://www.vibrant.org.br/downloads/v6n2_guedes.pdf

Knijnik, J. (2015). Femininities and masculinities in Brazilian women's football: Resistance and compliance. *Journal of International Women's Studies, 16*(3), 54–70. http://vc.bridgew.edu/jiws; http://vc.bridgew.edu/jiws/vol16/iss3/5

Knijnik, J., Spaaij, R., & Jeanes, R. (2019). Reading and writing the game: Creative and dialogic pedagogies in sports education. *Thinking Skills and Creativity, 32*, 42–50.

Korsakas, P. (2009). O esporte infantil: possibilidades de uma prática educativa. In *De Rose Junior. Esporte e atividade física na infância e adolescência: uma abordagem multidisciplinar*. Artmed.

Korsakas, P., & De Rose Junior, D. (2002). Os encontros e desencontros entre esporte e educação: uma discussão filosófico-pedagógica. *Revista Mackenzie de Educação Física e Esporte, 1*(1), 83–93.

Korsakas, P., Rizzi, E. G., Tsukamoto, M. H. C., & Galatti, L. R. (2021). Entre meio e fim: um caminho para o direito ao esporte. *Licere. Belo Horizonte, 24*(1) https://doi.org/10.35699/2447-6218.2021.29534664

LiteracyDotOrg. (2009, November 30). *Paulo Freire: an incredible conversation* [Video]. YouTube. https://youtu.be/aFWjnkFypFA

Moreira, V., & Garton, G. (2021). Football, nation and women in Argentina: Redefining the field of power. *Movimento, 27* (e27003). https://doi.org/10.22456/1982-8918.109761

Muñoz, P. (2011). *Violencias interseccionales, debates feministas y marcos teóricos en el tema de pobreza y violencia contra las mujeres en Latinoamérica*. CAWN.

Phillipson, R. (2016). Myths and realities of 'global' English. *Language Policy, 16*, 313–331. https://doi.org/10.1007/s10993-016-9409-z

Silva, M. A., & Godinho, E. (2017). A construção de uma pedagogia feminista latinoamericana na perspectiva da educação popular. In *Seminário Internacional Fazendo Gênero 11 and 13th Women's World Congress* (pp. 1–12). Florianópolis. http://www.en.wwc2017.eventos.dype.com.br/resources/anais/1499344786_ARQUIVO_Trabalhocompleto-MarciaeEliane.pdf

Wenger, É. (1998). *Communities of practice: Learning, meaning, and identity*. Cambridge University Press.

Wenger, É. (2010). Communities of practice and social learning systems: The career of a concept. In C. Blackmore (Ed.), *Social learning systems and communities of practice* (pp. 179–198). Springer.

Wenger, É., McDermott, R. A., & Snyder, W. (2002). *Cultivating communities of practice: A guide to managing knowledge*. Harvard Business School Press.

Wenger-Trayner, É., & Wenger-Trayner, B. (2020). *Learning to make a difference: Value creation in social learning spaces*. Cambridge University Press.

Part II

Mujeres Futbolistas: Experiences and Achievements

6

Power, Policy and Priorities: The Experiences of Colombian Women Playing Football

Sophie Legros, Sarah Oxford, and Ana Margarita Salas de la Hoz

Introduction

Colombia remains one of the most unequal countries in Latin America; citizens are segregated and excluded along class, gender, race and ethnic lines. A history of geographical fragmentation, colonial legacies and uneven development processes has shaped regional differences in socio-economic conditions and cultural practices across Colombia (Safford & Palacios, 2001). Economic and social relations are undergirded by

———————————————

S. Legros (✉)
London School of Economics, London, UK
e-mail: s.c.legros@lse.ac.uk

S. Oxford
School of Public Health and Preventative Medicine, Monash University, Melbourne, VIC, Australia
e-mail: sarah.oxford@monash.edu

A. M. Salas de la Hoz
University of Magdalena, Santa Marta, Colombia

© The Author(s), under exclusive license to Springer Nature Switzerland AG 2022
J. Knijnik, G. Garton (eds.), *Women's Football in Latin America*, New Femininities in Digital, Physical and Sporting Cultures,
https://doi.org/10.1007/978-3-031-09127-8_6

structural racism and economic inequalities, with high concentrations of wealth and land ownership.

In addition to these regional inequalities, the class system also structures social life within regions. Colombia's Public Service Law 142, implemented in 1994, assigns class number through residential property, resulting in neighbourhoods identified by stratum. There is little social interaction and much less integration or movement among the six class groupings, which predominately are visually marked by skin colour. The class system evolved into a method to solidify socioeconomic subcultures. Rodriguez Pizzaro and Ibarra Melo (2013) noted that a Colombian woman's socioeconomic positioning affects her 'living conditions, obstacles, opportunities, knowledge, and choices' (p. 27). The reach of these social markers is profound because they become a complex (re)production of culture, embodied and reenacted through everyday interactions.

Although there is variation, male-centric, heterosexual domination is the pillar of social organisation, and the hegemonic performance of masculinity and femininity is intertwined with individual and family reputation (Sanabria, 2007). Adhering to a strict gender binary based on a hegemonic masculinity that ignores or subordinates women is a critical aspect of Colombian socialisation (Viveros & Guttman, 2005). Gendered socialisation includes sports, where females do not have the opportunities and rewards afforded to males, especially in traditionally masculine sports (Oxford & McLachlan, 2018). Girls and women participating in sports associated with masculinity, however, are nonconforming and thus challenge the gender binary.

Nevertheless, advancements in women's football in Colombia in recent decades include increasing girls' participation in the sport in schools and academies, the creation of a professional league and positive international performances by the women's national team. Furthermore, local governments, community organizations and international nongovernmental organisations (INGOs) have implemented numerous sport for development and peace (SDP) programmes with the objective to foster inclusion, develop life skills of youth or promote peace in conflict-afflicted communities (Parnell et al., 2018). The combination of these visible achievements has resulted in an increase in social acceptability for girls and women to play football.

In what follows, we analyse the various developments of sport policies across Colombia. To understand how this progressive policy space and varied institutional services translate for girls and women on the ground across regions and social classes, we examine women players' experiences in three vignettes (Blodgett et al., 2011). The vignettes were constructed by the authors from their individual research conducted in Colombia about female participation in football between 2015 and 2020. Each author selected an interview participant who demonstrated a mainstream story with women's participation in sport within a respective social class and developed a vignette of the player's trajectory based on the interview transcripts. The vignettes are narratives used to present female athletes' stories, with an emphasis on their own words to bring out women's voices in the analysis.

The first and second authors were raised and studied in the Global North and conducted their PhD fieldwork in Spanish in Colombia; the third author is Colombian and is conducting her honours thesis research in Colombia. All three authors played football competitively at the collegiate level and in various professional capacities, in France and the United States (first author), in the United States (second author) and in Colombia (third author). In the discussion, we draw on the work of Crenshaw (1989) to explore the importance of an intersectional perspective in debates on the effects of women's participation in football and in grassroots sports interventions, calling attention to the varying challenges and achievements for Colombian women from diverse backgrounds.

Policy Analysis

The evolution of sport policymaking in Colombia echoes the country's broader historical, political and socioeconomic developments. Historically, sport has played several roles in Colombia's development trajectory. Early sport policies promoted it as a symbol of progress, using it as a tool to promote 'modern' values and activities, advance the well-being of the nation and cultivate world relations (Ruiz Patiño, 2017).

In the nineteenth and early twentieth centuries, policymakers made efforts to introduce sports in school curricula. Female athletes first made their appearance in the public sphere in the 1920s, in sports (e.g., tennis, horseback riding, golf, or basketball). Their participation was accompanied by concerns about preserving female athletes' femininity, and basketball was the only sport allowed for girls for physical education classes in schools (Cano, 2020).

Until recently, sport was mainly restricted to the wealthy, elite and light-skinned, largely accessible through private clubs or schools. Private sports clubs emerged following economic growth and sociocultural transformations in the first half of the 1900s. With the increase in popular cultural consumption in the 1930s, access to sport activities was extended to some members of the middle and lower classes to promote the idea of a 'cultured' society. Sport policies also were used in campaigns to extend healthy lifestyles and culture to working classes (Muñoz, 2009). Sport acquired a dual significance in Colombian society, reflecting hierarchies of value among the population. Higher class athletes were regarded as successful leaders and entrepreneurs living out their aspirations whereas for the lower classes, sport was to be a tool of intervention used to civilise the population and promote moral and physical values (Ruiz Patiño, 2017). This moralising aspect of sport was part of the broader 'whitening' processes in society (Munera, 1998; Wade, 1995).

In the second half of the twentieth century, mass sporting events became more widespread. In 1948, the first men's football league popularised the sport which became a source of national identity and solidarity for a fragmented society (L'Hoeste, 2015; Watson, 2018). From the 1960s onwards, the State has taken a more active role in sport policies. In 1968, COLDEPORTES, a sport entity separate from the Ministry of Education, was established, and Colombia's participation in several international events (e.g., the 1971 Pan-American games) increased interest for sport policymaking to foster elite performance (Morales Fontanilla, 2020; Sheinin 2016).

Although there are records of women players since the 1950s, competitive women's football emerged in the 1990s in a formal capacity. Women's football grew significantly in the 1970s and 1980s through informal regional leagues and teams owing to the activism of pioneering female athletes. They provided the impetus for *Difútbol*, the organisational body responsible for amateur and youth football development, to officialise national tournaments for women in the 1990s.

In more recent years, further institutionalisation of the sport sector has taken place. The 1991 Constitution led to inclusive laws and policy reforms that promote universality, inclusion and a 'sports-for-all' approach. It recognises the rights, equality and diversity of women and minorities in Colombia, and the State's responsibility in ensuring these principles are respected. The establishment of entities aimed at promoting sports at all levels, together with sport development plans, has led to improvements for female performance athletes and ensuring the rights for all—at least on paper. In 2015, the women's national team qualified for the first time for the FIFA Women's World Cup. A women's football federation (in 2016) and professional football league (since 2017) also have been established but there remains a lack of female representation at the administrative and decision-making levels (Cadavid & Pareja, 2001; Cadena, 2017; Saldarriaga & Sánchez, 2016).

A proliferation of social programmes implemented by a wide variety of actors aims to enact these ideals in practice to increase sport's accessibility in marginalised communities. They include sport interventions addressing peace-building or targeting urban youth as well as local government initiatives to promote physical activity and mobility for all (Cardenas, 2016; Hills et al., 2018; Oxford & McLachlan, 2018; Torres et al., 2013). With high urbanisation rates characteristic of the Latin American region, sport policymaking also became a part of urban planning. Building sport spaces was a key part of Medellín's 'social urbanism' approach (Drummond et al., 2012; Echeverri & Orsini, 2015), where top-notch infrastructure—from libraries, outdoor gyms to synthetic sport fields—was built in underserved urban areas, increasing access to sporting facilities (Parnell et al., 2018). This model has since been replicated in other cities in Colombia.

Some democratisation of sports has thus taken place. Women's football has become more visible, and, despite negative stereotypes about women players, there has been a shift in attitudes with a greater demand for women's football teams and an expansion in public and recreational spaces available to women. Nevertheless, female football players lack stable and secure financial support, and the women's football league is lacking in resources. Despite discourses of nondiscrimination and inclusion in policy documents, female athletes face persisting constraints to full participation.

Policies are designed by policymakers who understand social problems based on their visions of the world and biased understanding of social groups' experiences. Feminist theorising about the policy process underscores the assumptions that define the policy process (Cornwall et al., 2008). Examining the policy process through a feminist lens encourages one to reflect on how the problem is represented, how that representation has come about, who is unheard and who has a say in this representation (Baachi, 2009).

The next section links macro-level policies and structural factors with women's lives and experiences. Starting from women's personal descriptions of their achievements and challenges can increase understanding of their actual experiences, attempting to increase the 'interpretive power' (Cornwall et al., 2008) of female football players regarding their own trajectories. This can lead to distinct policy insights and priorities.

Vignettes

We selected three women born into differing classes and from several geographical regions: one from the upper (five or six), the middle (three or four) and the lower (one or two) classes to analyse their experiences playing football in Colombia. The data comes from interviews collected for various projects. These vignettes illustrate the array of women's experiences in Colombia's unequal and class-based society.

> Case Study 1—Maria. Upper class, mid-thirties: María's initiation into football was inevitable: football has been played, watched, analysed and discussed at her family reunions throughout generations. As is custom in traditional wealthy families in Antioquia, weekends are spent at the family's *finca* (farm)—a secondary home in the outskirts of Medellín. On Fridays after school, she would go to the finca along with her cousins. As the second granddaughter among many grandsons, she had to play what the older boys wanted to, and football was the preferred sport.

María's parents educated her about the importance of sport; she tried many sports, including playing football with friends in the gated apartment building where she lived. There were few opportunities for girls to play competitively. She attended an all-girls religious school, and the nuns did not consider football appropriate for girls.

Negative comments, name-calling and stereotypes discouraged many of her eager female friends from playing. Her parents clarified the negative comments to her and explained that football was acceptable for her like barbies were acceptable for her brother.

She learned the rules of football by watching games and casually playing in the streets. Her role models were male football players like Faustino Asprilla, Alexis García or Andrea Pirlo. Without cable television, she did not know women's football existed at the global level. Her first reference in women's football was Mia Hamm; she admired her attitude in interviews in addition to her football skills, how she navigated questions that were uncomfortable or biased.

When she arrived at a private university to study civil engineering, the opportunity arose to live out her passion for football to the fullest. She advocated in the university's sports department with a small group of attracted students to create a female league within the university. They selected the best players and started practicing with the men's team's coach during a trial period to assess the women's commitment and discipline.

After three months, the university hired the first female coach, and the team started competing in a university tournament and in the region's football league. The university provided them with new equipment and balls. They also supported players with transportation costs, food and authorisations when travelling for tournaments. The university regarded them as a legitimate team representing the institution. Maria played on the team for nine years while she completed her university degree, her master's and one more as a visiting member. In 2009, they won the national university tournament in Armenia.

Through football, Maria learned values, such as discipline, compassion and dedication, that helped her develop. She considers her university team as family. She cherishes her opportunity to compete at the university level, particularly the experiences of setting goals and pursuing ambitions collectively. Nowadays, she plays twice a week recreationally with friends, renting her university's synthetic turf fields for an hour in the evenings after work.

Maria believes that the stigma around women's football that she experienced as a child does not exist anymore. She asserts that now if a girl wants to play football, her dad will buy her shoes, a ball and sign her up to a team. She considers that things started changing about ten years ago when Colombians became more aware of women's football at the global level and when football academies and schools began incorporating women's football in their projects. Today, even the nuns at her primary school have come to terms with the sport—the school has an intercollegiate girls' team. Girls no longer have to wait until university to be able to compete in an official tournament

Case Study 2—Camila. Middle class, early twenties: Camilla liked football ever since she was little; she always saw her brothers play and claimed that she could too. Early on, she began to play with her cousins and brothers on her neighbourhood's streets in Santa Marta. She didn't know of other female players; she didn't even know that women's football existed. Her family always supported her. At first, when there were no female teams, her mother did not want her to play with boys. When women's football initiatives started in her city, her mother gave her unconditional support.

Camila's football journey was not always easy. She faced social barriers because football was considered a 'man's sport'. People commented that football 'attracts lesbians' and she often heard people refer to female players in derogatory ways. This never stopped her, and because of her family's support, she did not care about what other people said or thought.

When she started playing football, economic and material resources were very scarce. The players had to pay for uniforms, travel costs and the coaches' salaries, even when they played in tournaments to represent their region. Camila's perspective about football began to change following the emergence of the first women's teams in Santa Marta and the integration of new regional teams in national championships. When she started, she had considered it a temporary hobby, but with these new opportunities and the excitement she felt playing football, she started considering it her life project.

When she was 13, Camila started taking football seriously and training regularly, which led her to be selected for youth teams at the regional and national level. Following the creation of the women's league in 2017, she had the opportunity to play for the Magdalena Union club and afterwards with another professional team when Magdalena Union dropped out of the league. These experiences played a part in her selection for the Colombian U17 national team, which she considers her biggest achievement so far. This event established football as a genuine life project for her, making her realise that she could pursue everything she wanted in her own country—playing football and studying at the same time. Previously, she thought she would have to leave Colombia, moving to Spain, for example, to continue playing football.

Football has had a positive impact in Camila's life. It contributes to her emotional and personal growth; it makes her happy and motivates her to improve every day. Through football, she has met people who inspire her to set new goals and achieve them. Although not substantial, football became a source of economic support that allows her to pay for her university studies and contribute to her brother's studies, alleviating her mother's financial responsibilities as the family's principal earner while her dad works in the informal economy as a motorcycle taxi driver.

Camila believes that there is still much progress to be made for women football players in her city. From conversations with some of her teammates from other parts of the country, most notably those from the 'interior' (central cities like Bogotá or Medellín), she realised that many had received some form of financial support to cover expenses to participate in selections and had access to more resources than were available in her region.

That being said, she highlights that there are now noticeably more girls who dare to play football. The female player that she most admires today is Daniela Montoya, who has been advocating for better labour conditions in women's football. Camila believes that getting involved in football will still be a difficult path for future female players, but that it is worth fighting for what they love.

Case Study 3—Yuliza. Lower class, early twenties: Yuliza loves football. She started playing at eight years old with her brothers and male neighbours in the dirt streets near her concrete uninsulated tin-roof house. Her house is in a neighbourhood defined by the Colombian government as an informal settlement, represented on the news as violent, and called home by thousands of Colombians internally displaced because of conflict.

She began to take football seriously at 12 years old when she joined GOALS, an SDP organisation. GOALS closed, but before it did, an employee suggested she join another SDP organisation called VIDA. Around the same time, a VIDA employee gave a presentation to her church congregation about it's methods. At church, Yuliza's father learned about VIDA's methodology to teach kids football, lessons about values and social support offerings. Her father thought it sounded like a great idea; he signed her and her little sister up. Her mother was less committed to her daughters' playing football but could not stop them.

The fields where VIDA operated included government-funded projects, such as a paved court with metal fencing taller than the houses and a grass field where cows roamed. When the government reallocated the grass field for an infrastructure project, VIDA changed locations to a fenced-in grass field provided by the catholic church. Field options and playing spaces near Yuliza's home were minimal.

As a child, Yuliza saw girls watch her play with interest and heard the girls' mothers refuse their requests to join. As a teenager, she listened to her female friends explain they wanted to play too. Their parents denied their participation because either an SDP organisation did not exist near their homes or their parents' rules limited their movements to walking to school and back.

When Yuliza played on the street with her brothers, people called her derogatory names, such as tomboy and lesbian, which made her feel bad. She did her best to ignore them. Her love for football was more important than bad feelings. At VIDA, girls and boys played football together. After she joined VIDA and improved her skills, she did not hear those bad words. Furthermore, instead of putting her down, her community discussed her impressive football abilities, which made her proud.

As a teenager, Yuliza began mentoring younger kids at VIDA after school. Also, she played in girls' football and futsal tournaments in her neighbourhood on the weekends. Sometimes she would travel by a combination of walking and riding on a public bus to play for an elite team that practised in a slightly wealthier area across a mega-highway located on the edge of a big city. A donor, organised through VIDA, paid for her to participate on that team.

Yuliza believed that football and VIDA changed her life. Before she joined, she angered easily and was physically aggressive with other kids. Her formal position with VIDA as a mentor led her to feel respected. She then wanted to be a positive role model. Football became her passion; it occupied her time. Yuliza experienced much stress in her life, but she noted that all of her stress disappeared when playing football.

Only 10–20 percent of VIDAs participants are girls depending on the field and day. Yuliza believed that change to girls' inclusion in football was happening in her neighbourhood. She highlighted that she does not hear the derogatory names anymore and that at VIDA girls playing football is normal. A normality, she argued, that is being extended to her broader community and throughout her neighbourhood.

Discussion

The trajectory of women's football and sport policies should be understood in the context of broader societal change influencing women's rights and autonomy. These include the advancement of women's education, the role of the feminist movement's mobilisation and progress in women's labour-force participation and political representation, and how these are partially offset by continued constraints to women's empowerment in a context of gender discrimination, economic and social exclusion and sustained levels of violence and internal conflict (Bradshaw et al., 2019; Domingo et al., 2015; Iregui-Bohórquez et al., 2020; UN Women, 2018).

In recent years, female players and activists have taken a stand to condemn the unfair treatment that women players experience and the existing gender inequalities in football. In 2019, members of the women's national team denounced experiences of sexual harassment and inadequate economic compensation. As a response, the football authorities suspended the women's football season. The 2020 coronavirus outbreak further laid bare the precarious conditions with which women players are confronted.

The vignettes illustrate differences and similarities between the women's experiences, revealing intersecting inequalities. Despite the emergence of relatively progressive sport policies and institutions noted in our policy analysis, inequalities in football persist, suggesting a difference between formal equality and equality in practice. In this discussion, we apply a gender and intersectional lens to sport policy analysis. This involves considering the multiple and intersecting power relationships that shape women's experiences because multiple social identities can lead to experiences of inequality that combine, overlap and amplify each other (Crenshaw, 1989).

Despite differences in contexts, all three women demonstrated a resilient mentality a deep and committed passion for the sport and benefitted from some form of family support. These shared characteristics were essential as they made room for themselves in a traditionally masculine space to navigate stigma and negative social sanctions. All three pursue acts of activism and resistance according to their resources and social position—from mentoring other children in their neighbourhoods to advocating for the creation of the first female team at their university.

Their stories demonstrate the importance of role models and seeing a critical mass of women playing the sport at the local and national level, which has been facilitated by an increased policy space and community interventions for women's football in Colombia. Although from a higher class, Maria did not have the same opportunities as younger players today because she grew up in a time when formal female teams and leagues did not exist for young girls. Generational differences also interact with social class to shape female players' football trajectories.

Nevertheless, contrasts between the three experiences can be drawn as sport policies interact with underlying inequalities. Opportunities and constraints are not just distributed differently along what might be considered the 'metropole' and the 'interior'. Geographical location and social positioning within a particular area can compound in a variety of ways and one might experience greater disadvantages in a marginalised community in a major metropolitan city because of urban segregation; this could include long and costly commuting distances and limited opportunities because of structural conditions (e.g., unemployment, job precarity and a lack of access to higher education).

Furthermore, Afro-Colombians and indigenous communities tend to be concentrated in peripherical regions with fewer resources or government support—as is the case for the Coastal or Amazonian regions—and in marginalised communities within urban centres, especially those with a high number of internally displaced populations. This has profound implications for how policies are applied. Regions, such as the Caribbean coast, have historically been abandoned by central authorities or their social context and local needs neglected in government interventions (McGraw, 2007). This is evidenced in Camila's story, when she expressed the lack of institutional support and that the development of the sport initially had to be sponsored by players themselves, uncovering how sport policies are implemented differentially. Dark-skinned female athletes thus can be exposed to multiple forms of discrimination because of racial divisions and institutional neglect in addition to their status as women and their social class.

Also revealed in the women's stories are various opportunities to be competitive in the sport, to develop not just life skills but to be fulfilled by aspiring to and working towards ambitious goals. Social class shaped their aspirations: all three worked to improve and reach new echelons, but what echelons are achievable depends on their context and the local authorities' decisions and policymaking. Among them are the repurposing of sport spaces for other political interests (e.g., education, infrastructure, housing and so on). As their stories show, aspirations are dynamic and respond to structures of opportunities and constraints.

Finally, we note differing perspectives of change. Yuliza's point of reference was her own neighbourhood, Camila focused on comparisons with other regions of Colombia, and Maria framed her trajectory with relation to women's football at the global level. Their perspectives on the evolution of women's football are indicative of their distinct realities, the various spheres in society in which they operate, and how they position themselves within Colombian society.

The potential impact of football policies on women and girls' lives is thus mediated by their social position. The vignettes and the discussion illustrate how underlying inequalities condition women's ability to take advantage of progressive sport policies. Intersecting inequalities limit opportunities, but they also mediate the extent and ways players can benefit from participation in sport or the meaning football might have in their lives. Both the positive consequences of playing football (e.g., economic compensation or the friendships built) and the negative sanctions (e.g., the stigma connected to homosexuality, gender stereotypes and material costs) will matter more or less to various women and girls. For example, economic aspects might heighten the difficulties for players with fewer economic resources, or they might expand the perceived benefits of the sport compared to other players. Attention to women's life stories provides insights into how sport policies actually are lived out by female athletes 'on the ground', and how policies can have distinct consequences depending on the institutional context and women's social position within that same context.

Conclusion

In this chapter, we argued for an intersectional perspective in sport policy analysis. First, we demonstrated that an understanding of the class and gender system is pivotal in understanding the historical development of sport policies and their implementation in Colombia. Second, through a focus on women's experiences in the three vignettes, we examined how the impacts of sport policies can vary for women in various contexts and social positions. Feminist scholars have categorised programmes and policies into those that are discriminatory, gender-neutral, gender-aware or gender-transformative, according to the degree to which the policy or programme reinforces, neglects or purposes to tackle upfront gender inequalities and remove barriers towards greater equality (Cole et al., 2020; Fernandez, 2016).

Although a programme may not be outright discriminatory, it might even be inclusive of diverse social identities, it could still disadvantage women and girls depending on the local context (Oxford & McLachlan, 2018). Underlying conditions (e.g., safety, gender norms or risks of sexual harassment) can discourage girls from using outdoor sport places. What might appear to grant free and universal access also depends on local power dynamics and control of spaces.

From our review of sport policies in Colombia, many appear universal or gender-neutral; others are targeted towards specific populations such as at-risk youth or indigenous populations, aiming to be inclusive. The problem to be addressed through sport is often represented as one of life skills and moral values or as one of access—a lack of infrastructure or organised sport activities. Sport policies rarely aim to tackle the broader structural conditions that influence gender inequality and youths' aspirations (e.g., unequal gender norms, poverty, insecurity, lack of decent jobs or uneven development).

Furthermore, we consider what is missing in sport policymaking. The literature is often concentrated on interventions in Bogotá and Medellín, the country's two largest cities. Certain regions do not have local sports' offices or strategies, much less infrastructure, especially where State presence is lacking. As mentioned earlier, these often correspond to regions with higher concentrations of Afro-Colombian and indigenous communities, which have historically been marginalised, discriminated against and racialised. The lack of case studies coming from these regions is informative and calls for more diverse settings in future research on Colombia's sport for development programming. As the vignettes illustrate, sport policymaking could benefit from a richer analysis and an intersectional lens, paying attention to the broader areas of female players' lives and how they interact to shape their participation in sports.

References

Baachi, C. (2009). Introducing a 'what's the problem represented to be?' approach to policy analysis. In C. Baachi (Ed.), *Analysing policy: What's the problem represented to be?* (pp. 1–24). Pearson.

Blodgett, A. T., Schinke, R. J., Smith, B., Peltier, D., & Pheasant, C. (2011). In indigenous words: Exploring vignettes as a narrative strategy for presenting the research voices of aboriginal community members. *Qualitative Inquiry, 17*(6), 522–533. https://doi.org/10.1177/1077800411409885

Bradshaw, S., Chant, S., & Linneker, B. (2019). Challenges and changes in gendered poverty: The feminization, de-feminization, and re-feminization of poverty in Latin America. *Feminist Economics, 25*(1), 119–144. https://doi.org/10.1080/13545701.2018.1529417

Cadavid, L. E. G., & Pareja, L. A. (2001). A propósito de la salud en el fútbol femenino: Inequidad de género y subjetivación. *Educación Física y Deporte, 21*, 15–25.

Cadena, J. D. (2017). *Percepción de la equidad de género en el deporte élite colombiano.* Master's thesis, Universidad Autónoma de Nuevo León. San Nicolás de los Garza, Mexico. http://eprints.uanl.mx/19478/

Cano, D. (2020). *El futbol profesional femenino en Colombia: una mirada politologica.* Honours monography, Pontificia Universidad Javeriana. Institutional Repository, Pontificia Universidad Javeriana. https://repository.javeriana.edu.co/handle/10554/52132.

Cardenas, A. (2016). Sport and peace-building in divided societies: A case study on Colombia and Northern Ireland. *Peace and Conflict Studies, 23*(2).

Cole, S. M., Kaminski, A. M., McDougall, C., Kefi, A. S., Marinda, P. A., Maliko, M., & Mtonga, J. (2020). Gender accommodative versus transformative approaches: A comparative assessment within a post-harvest fish loss reduction intervention. *Gender, Technology and Development, 24*(1), 48–65. https://doi.org/10.1080/09718524.2020.1729480

Cornwall, A., Harrison, E., & Whitehead, A. (2008). *Gender myths and feminist fables the struggle for interpretive power in gender and development*. Blackwell.

Crenshaw, K. (1989). *Demarginalizing the intersection of race and sex: A black feminist critique of antidiscrimination doctrine, feminist theory and antiracist policies*. University of Chicago Legal Forum.

Domingo, P., Menocal, A. R., & Hinestroza, V. (2015). Progress despite adversity: Women's empowerment and conflict in Colombia. https://odi.org/en/publications/progress-despite-adversity-womens-empowerment-and-conflict-in-colombia/

Drummond, H., Dizgun, J., & Keeling, D. J. (2012). Medellin: A city reborn? *Focus on Geography, 55*(4), 146–154.

Echeverri, A., & Orsini, F. M. (2015). Informality and social urbanism in Medellin. In *Medellin: Environment, Urbanism and Society* (pp. 132–156). Universidad EAFIT.

Fernandez, B. (2016). *Transformative policy for poor women: A new feminist framework*. Routledge.

Hills, S., Gómez-Velásquez, A., & Walker, M. (2018). Sport as analogy to teach life skills and redefine moral values: A case study of the 'Seedbeds of Peace' sport-for-development programme in Medellin, Colombia. *Journal of Sport for Development, 6*(10), 25–37.

Iregui-Bohórquez, A. M., Melo-Becerra, L. A., Ramírez-Giraldo, M. T., & Tribín-Uribe A. M. (2020). The path to gender equality in Colombia: Are we there yet? https://repositorio.banrep.gov.co/bitstream/handle/20.500.12134/9903/be_1131.pdf?sequence=6&isAllowed=y

L'Hoeste, H. F. (2015). Race, sports, and regionalism in the construction of Colombian nationalism. In R. Irwin, J. Poblete, H. F. L'Hoeste, & R. Anker (Eds.), *Sport and Nationalism in Latin/o America* (pp. 85–105). Palgrave Macmillan US.

McGraw, J. (2007). *Purificar la nación: Eugenesia, higiene y renovación moral-racial de la periferia del caribe colombiano, 1900–1930*. Universidad De Los Andes.

Morales Fontanilla, M. (2020). Sport policy in Colombia. *International Journal Of Sport Policy and Politics, 12*(4), 717–729. https://doi.org/10.108 0/19406940.2020.1839531

Munera, A. (1998). *El fracaso de la nacion: region, clase y raza en el caribe Colombiano (1717–1821)*. Banco de la República / El Áncora Editores.

Muñoz, C. (2009). To colombianize Colombia: Cultural politics, modernization and nationalism in Colombia, 1930–1946. University of Pennsylvania, Dissertations available from ProQuest. AAI3363572. https://repository. upenn.edu/dissertations/AAI3363572

Oxford, S., & McLachlan, F. (2018). 'You have to play like a man, but still be a woman': Young female Colombians negotiating gender through participation in a Sport for Development and Peace (SDP) organization. *Sociology of Sport Journal, 35*(3), 258–267. https://doi.org/10.1123/ssj.2017-0088

Parnell, D., Cárdenas, A., Widdop, P., Cardoso-Castro, P.-P., & Lang, S. (2018). Sport for development and peace in Latin America and the Caribbean. *Journal of Sport for Development, 6*(10), 1–5.

Rodriguez Pizarro, A. N., & Ibarra Melo, M. E. (2013). Los estudios de género en Colombia. Una discusión preliminar. *Sociedad y Economía, 24*, 15–46.

Ruiz Patiño, J. H. (2017). Juventud y deporte en Colombia en la primera mitad del siglo xx. *Boletín Cultural y Bibliográfico, 51*, 57–71.

Safford, F., & Palacios, M. (2001). *Colombia: Fragmented land, divided society*. Oxford University Press.

Saldarriaga, J. D., & Sánchez, J. A. (2016). *Del estereotipo al reconocimiento, avances en equidad de género de las deportistas antioqueñas entre 2012–2014*. Corporación Universitaria Minuto de Dios, Bello, Antioquia. https://hdl. handle.net/10656/5267

Sanabria, H. (2007). *The anthropology of Latin America and the Caribbean* (1st ed.). Pearson.

Sheinin, D. M. K. (2016). The 1971 Pan-American games and the search for Colombian modernities. *International Journal of the History of Sport, 33*(1–2), 147–163. https://doi.org/10.1080/09523367.2015.1121869

Torres, A., Sarmiento, O. L., Stauber, C., & Zarama, R. (2013). The Ciclovia and Cicloruta programs: Promising interventions to promote physical activity and social capital in Bogotá, Colombia. *American Journal of Public Health, 103*(2), 23–30. https://doi.org/10.2105/AJPH.2012.301142

UN Women. (2018). *El Progreso de las Mujeres en Colombia 2018: Transformar la Economía Para Realizar los Derechos*. https://colombia.unwomen.org/es/ biblioteca/publicaciones/2018/10/progreso-de-las-mujeres-2018

Viveros, M., & Guttman, M. (2005). Masculinities in Latin America. In S. Kimmel, J. Hearn, & R. Connell (Eds.), *Handbook of studies in men and masculinities*. Sage Publications.

Wade, P. (1995). *Blackness and race mixture: The dynamics of racial identity in Colombia*. Johns Hopkins University Press.

Watson, P. J. (2018). Colombia's political football: President Santos' National Unity Project and the 2014 Football World Cup. *Bulletin of Latin American Research, 37*(5), 598–612. https://doi.org/10.1111/blar.12634

7

Bolivian Women as Professional Footballers: The Voices and the Feminism of the *karimachus*

Eliana Aguilar Aguilar and Ana Alcazár-Campos

First Half—Introduction

As in many other Latin American countries, football is part of Bolivian society. Rinke (2006) argues that football is practically part of the Latino identity. Even though football did not originate in South America, it became popular quickly. As Galeano (1995) mentions and Rinke (2006) confirms, Latin American footballers have allowed the world to rediscover Latin America, see it beyond the conquest, with distinct eyes. In Bolivia, people enjoy the sport and support the nation's footballers even though it is last in FIFA's South American ranking. Taking this into account, when Bolivians talk about football, there is an automatic

E. Aguilar Aguilar
La Salle University, Bolivia, La Paz, Bolivia
e-mail: consulta@superateconpsicologia.com

A. Alcazár-Campos (✉)
University of Granada, Granada, Spain
e-mail: alcazarcampos@ugr.es

association with men's football, by the force of the order that dispenses with justification (Bourdieu, 1998). Men's practice in most sports became the 'neutral' and normalised version, so it became necessary to add the feminine adjective to refer to women's sport practice.

Unfortunately, football also reflects a *macho* society in which women do not have the same opportunities as men (Hernández, 2014; Ruiz, 2011). The presence of women on the field challenges the masculine hegemony within the football context, where women have been prohibited from entering, breaking heteronormative expectations (Aguilar, 2014). Football does not discriminate, but those who manage it do. In Bolivia, the football federation has always been led by men who have prioritised men's football, until 2018 when FIFA regulations called for the promotion of women's football with the risk of sanctions against associations that did not comply (FIFA, 2018). Thus, in 2019, departmental leagues were quickly set up to avoid FIFA sanctions, but several factors (e.g., spaces to play or players' ages) were not considered. Currently in Bolivia, there is only one all-ages category in the women's league. In 2019, in a match in La Paz, a 13-year-old footballer played against women who were twice her age, some even older (Aguilar, 2020).

The obvious differences between women's and men's football (e.g., the lack of competitions and opportunities to engage in competitive matches, absence from media coverage and economic gaps) prompted the authors to look at the country's social history of women's football. We started to ask if any Bolivian football lovers and supporters knew about female footballers, such as Maitté Zamorano, who was the top goal scorer in the 2013 and 2017 Women's Copa Libertadores, or Zdenscka Bacarreza, former head coach of the Bolivian women's football team. As a child, Bacarreza had to pretend to be a boy with the name Marco Antonio to be able to play football and hide herself from being judged by La Paz society (Calatayud, 2020).

When we started researching Bolivian women footballers, their story appears to begin very recently, but in fact, Bolivian women have been playing football for many years. Reviewing newspapers, we found photographic evidence from as early as 1983 (Gutierrez, 1983); however, there were no studies or official data available. The Bolivian Football Federation's (FBF) website includes limited information about women's football and only from the last three to five years. Nevertheless, the Bolivian women footballers of the 1990s changed the course of their sport in the country while opening doors for future generations of female players, breaking gender taboos and supporting younger girls and women to find their way within the sport. This chapter attempts to understand how these women built and negotiated their femininity while they achieved professionalism in Bolivian football. The experiences of these footballers from various cities offer one the opportunity to know which barriers and impediments they encountered along the way while giving voice to those historically relegated to the margins of football.

Bolivian society has various myths associated with women's football because the traditional roles of women, especially as housewives, carers for their elderly parents or family members and caregivers of children, are still important for society, particularly in rural areas (Yapu, 2010). Bolivian women who did not follow these traditional roles were called *karimachus*[1]—the Quechuan word for tomboy (Castro, 2008).

To analyse the current orthodox gender order in Bolivia and its implications on the football field, we employed the theories of Simone de Beauvoir and especially Betty Friedan. Friedan (1963) describes how the role of a good wife, mother, and housewife created the notion of the 'feminine mystique'. At the same time, she demonstrated that boys do things to prove that they are boys, while girls learn they are girls by avoiding acting like boys, thus denying their masculinity (Friedan, 1963). In the early 1990s in Bolivia, being a woman within the public sphere of football, either as a spectator or player, was considered unfeminine in social narratives, so one could be called a *karimachu*. Ana Huanca, a player who participated in this study, confirmed that people constantly used to yell at her: 'Playing football is for men. The *karimacho* is playing!'

In this study, the authors intend to start building Bolivian women's football history and try to uncover the voices of players who for several decades were left in obscurity. Thus, we employ feminist research methodologies to uncover their stories and, while doing so, shape new meanings for Bolivian

---

[1] The word *karimachu* underwent changes, like many other words in Quechua, because of internal migration in the country and the imposition of the Spanish language. For this reason, nowadays the term can also be written as *karimacho* or *carimacho* (Zuna, 2017). It is important to consider that *karimacho* refers to an effeminate man and *warmimacho* to a manly woman, but the word *karimacho* later became popular to refer to homosexuality or to those who do not follow traditional gendered social roles (Opinión, 2009).

football history, showing how women have contributed across the country to build a powerful popular football culture. Next, after presenting the methodological background and procedures used in the research, we tell the *karimachu's* stories. By listening and analysing their voices, it is possible to demonstrate how their resistance can be considered a feminist struggle that gives new meaning to being a Bolivian, a woman and a footballer.

Halftime—Methods

Qualitative research was the method that best allowed us to collect the voices of women footballers, but it was not enough to complete this research. For this reason, we use feminist epistemology because it allowed us to overcome the positivist and patriarchal objectivity that underpins science, putting participants, the players, at the centre of the study; this helped us to challenge our initial understandings and access a more in-depth version of the participants' world (Haraway, 1991). As Marta Luxán and Jokin Azpiazú (2016) argue, subaltern experiences allow one to have a more complex perspective than those of a position of social privilege. At the same time, as Sandra Harding (1996) observes, feminist epistemology goes beyond simply adding women to research; as Donna Haraway (1991) states, feminist epistemology is a responsibility of which one must be aware from the beginning of an investigation while recognising that the production of knowledge is always a political act.

Our research included interviews with 11 current players from various cities across Bolivia (i.e., La Paz, Santa Cruz, Cochabamba and Tarija). They were chosen according to their accessibility and experience. Subordinate knowledge and subaltern voices are a way of confronting the androcentric ideal of science and hegemony in football. Four of them, Janeth Morrón, Ana Huanca, Maitte Zamorano and Luzdana Rivera, have been part of the Bolivian national football team in several call-ups, all currently work as physical education teachers or head coaches and are still playing in championships and tournaments in their cities. On other hand, we interviewed Zdenscka Bacarreza, the head coach of the Bolivian women's national team at the time of the interview, although she still plays football in seniors' championships.

Bacarreza is the first woman to coach the women's national team (Calatayud, 2020). Three players interviewed (I,e., Marta Poma, Nieves Condori and Irene Tolin) are *cholitas*; *Chola paceña* or *cholita* are terms that refer to *mestizo* women from the Bolivian highlands characterised by their use of the traditional costume of the city—a long skirt that they do not take off even to play. They play in various amateur tournaments, almost always crowning themselves as winners. Finally, the other three women (i.e., Viviana Rojas, Amancaya Barreda and Katherine Gallardo) used to play football as amateurs. Although they wanted to reach the professional level, they had to stop playing for several reasons and currently continue to play football as a recreational activity.

We conducted semi-structured interviews in Spanish with all 11 players. These interviews were later translated from Spanish to English by the authors. Most of the interviews were face to face, but four were online because of restrictions in place in response to the COVID-19 pandemic. We always respected the idea that the interviewees are the ones who have the knowledge as well as the practical and embodied experiences of playing football. Van Dijk's (1999) theory of discourse analysis was employed to understand their conversations as emotional narratives that formed memories within each individual participant about events that occurred at the social and collective levels. Their responses were then analysed and thematically organised into three broad categories: (1) how they became footballers, (2) how they entered the public sphere of football and (3) how they have continued in the sport.

Van Dijk (1999) maintains that everything learned—body movements, even the way we express ourselves—is in social memory. Likewise, we believe it is important to value this while giving space and voice to subordinate knowledge to better understand the lives and social realities of the trailblazers of Bolivian women's football.

Second Half—Results and Discussion

This section initially discusses how the research participants became footballers for which they were labelled as masculine *karimachus*, but they brought new meanings to the word *karimachu*. Then, we explore how the footballers occupied a space from which they were systematically excluded. Finally, we intend to show how they resisted and persisted in the field and which strategies they used to continue playing football.

Karimachus

'Playing football was like an illness and a shame for the family', says Luzdana Rivera. This footballer's words reflect the stories of many Bolivian women who wanted to play football during the 1990s and found themselves trapped in a hegemonic and macho structure. Sylvia Burrow (2016) discusses the notion of a double bind in sport that constrains women; there is a possibility of marginalisation if a woman decides to play a sport deemed onlly for men. This was the case for Bolivian women who were categorized as *karimachus* when entering the public sphere of football during the 1990s.

Irene Tolin told us: 'When I enter the field, I forget everything, the stress of home and work. ... I don't even think about people because people always call us "*karimachu*" or other vulgar things'. It is interesting how the word *karimachu* has been used to pigeonhole and discredit women who are passionate about football; thus, instead of simply being called 'footballers', they were labelled *karimachus*. Although there are 36 other native languages in Bolivia, the word *karimachu* has been used throughout the country, regardless of a player's cultural background, to discriminate against women footballers.

At the same time, labelling women footballers as *karimachus* has been a way to protect men's place in football spaces as the only ones who can play and enjoy the game. Moreno (cited in Hernández, 2014) argues that the various insults used against women in football are for being both feminine and masculine at the same time. Marta Poma, another footballer interviewed said 'people used to say about us, these women aren't going to be able to play'.

In the Bolivian case, our participants mention how their footballing bodies have been labelled as 'masculine'. Thus, a concept arises about a straightforward link between 'masculine' postures and gestures and sexual preferences outside the heterosexual norm (Moreira & Garton, 2021). Yet, the idea of stigmatising women who play football as homosexuals is not only an issue in Bolivia but also internationally (Moreira & Garton, 2021). Footballer Viviana Rojas recalled: 'My friends used to ask me: are you a lesbian?' Amankaya also explained: 'A lot of people thought that I had a lot of lesbian friends just because I played football'. We can see that society continues expecting women to be, as Friedan (1963) described: a porcelain doll, sensual and feminine enough to fulfill men's heterosexual desires.

Katherine remembers: 'Nobody said anything to me face to face, but it was in people's discourse that the girl who played football, I mean, I was the *karimacho*'. Nevertheless, the footballers followed their dreams, they put all the insults behind them and continued playing because they understood that football has no gender. 'Football is for everyone, men, women, children and us *cholitas*', affirmed Nieves Condori. It would have been easy for them to stop playing football to avoid comments, but through their examples and perseverance playing football, they managed to resignify and adopt a new meaning of being a *karimachu*. As Viviana Rojas explained: 'People knew me because I was the girl who played football; they always told me that it was not for girls and because of that I was a *karimachu*, and that made me feel better, thinking that I was special'.

This is how they continued to play football, some of them alone or supported by their families, but against society's expectations. 'I was lucky that my family loves sports... my father motivated me to play; he was with me all the time, at all my matches, and always took me to the field', Maitté Zamorano said. Luzdana also remembered: 'There was no women's football tournament for me to train. In a street tournament, my brother and dad spoke because in the invitation there was no prohibition for girls to play. They [the tournament organisers] made my dad sign a document to take responsibility for me. This is how I started playing'. For these women, playing football in their childhood gave them more opportunities than those girls subjected to the traditional roles associated with the feminine mystique (Friedan, 1963).

The beginning of this path was very hard and lonely for the players interviewed, but nowadays, the word *karimachu* is not heard as frequently. Nevertheless, the tendency to associate the term with women who do not do something typical of 'a woman' still persists. According to Ana, 'Sometimes *karimacho* is still heard, but less now than before'.

Voices of the *karimachus*: Occupying a Masculine Space

One of the main problems faced by Bolivian women footballers is that the only body allowed to play football is the idealised image of a virile man's body (Knijnik, 2014). Rojas (2002) mentions that in a globalised society, football is a performance of the male gender and the attributes of the masculine condition. Thus, a hegemonic masculinity is (re)produced that excludes women from football. At the same time, women continue to be challenged by expectations of traditional femininity (Friedan, 1963), considered 'complementary' to hegemonic masculinity, according to which any other body that does not comply with the established parameters is considered a 'transgressor'.

For many years, these players had to live and get used to hearing people call them *karimachu*, but that didn't stop them from doing what they wanted—playing football. Luzdana Rivera recalled: '

> When I started playing, I was the only girl around boys. I thought I was the only female footballer in the world. There was no internet, no social networks to connect with other women like now. I was happy when I saw more women a few years later'.

It is interesting how finding another woman who plays football generates joy for the player. She does not see other players as her rivals, but rather uses sorority as a fundamental value or as a strategy to continue playing football in such a hostile environment. One of the most important values in football, fraternity, was adopted from the motto of the French revolution because, for many authors such as Galeano (1995), football was associated with war. Beauvoir (1949) states that fraternity, as understood by the French revolutionaries, has a clear masculine character. Men are free and equal and establish fraternal relationships; they are friends who collaborate with each other, but women are not their 'brothers' (Beauvoir, 1949). Fraternity did not exist for women in Bolivian football during the 1990s, so meeting other women who played football was an opportunity to create a new and different bond.

It is important to highlight that the practice of football adds another meaning to the female body, adopting new ways of feeling and being on the field (Hernández, 2014). This new social representation of women's bodies on the field helps change the collective imagination, subverting the macho structures of football while leaving behind the myth that Friedan (1963) calls the 'eternal feminine'—the idealised woman as mysterious, magical, virgin, martyr, lover, mother. It even challenges society's idea that women's bodies appear helpless and as the negative, while men represent the positive and neutral (Beauvoir, 1949).

Even the uniform in football is an important issue to discuss. All Bolivian women must wear men's shirts and uniforms. One of the footballers, Katherine, asserted that: 'The uniforms were never made for our bodies, we used men's ones; there was only one size adapted to a male body. In that sense, the lack of women's uniforms serves to maintain male hegemony within football and keep the association of football with the male body in the social collective.' As Connell and Messerschmidt (2005) argue, hegemonic masculinity promotes the dominant social position of some men and the subordinate social position of women and other 'inferior' men. Likewise, this is an issue that came to light years ago in various feminist discussions because of the declarations of Joseph Blatter in 2004, the ex-president of FIFA, who insisted that women footballers' shirts and shorts should be different from men's but should accentuate their figure to attract more male attention (Hidalgo, 2017).

The belief that women's bodies belong to someone else is part of the sexualisation of them in football and has always been present. Moreira and Garton (2021) argue that since the beginning of the practice of football, women have experienced the stigmatisation, silencing and disciplining of their bodies. During the 1990s, the hyper-sexualisation of women's bodies had been the most accepted way for women to enter this public space as amateurs, as an adornment of the game, as in the Olympic Games of ancient Greece, to satisfy and please the male gaze (Macías, 1999).

It is worth clarifying that the masculine image as the only idealised and permitted body in football leans on the discourse of biological disadvantage and enters the collective imagination of society in childhood (Díaz & Martinez, 2017). Biological difference is constructed from the moment in which, during children's games, girls' physical development is limited in the 'feminine' games because of the expectation of delicacy connected to 'being a woman', while boys have the opportunity to use their bodies to play and develop greater physical ability to help them play sports (Hernández, 2014). In this way, if women try to follow the feminine mystique, they will not have freedom of choice (Friedan, 1963).

Resistance and Persistence on the Field

Friedan (1963) states that society wants women to adapt into a culture and believe that if they adapt, they will be happy and achieve full realisation of themselves; but Friedan found that this does not necessarily allow for a full realisation of a person's being. For this reason, every person should find how to be in the world and not just follow society's expectations. Femininity has been a construct supported by numerous experts (most of them men describing a reality other than their own) that largely went unchallenged until feminism appeared and questioned the nature of 'being a woman' (Scott, 1986; Butler, 1990; Lamas, 1996). Friedan (1963) mentions that she started enjoying being a woman when she stopped chasing the idea of being feminine. Bolivian footballers resisted and persisted on the football fields, even though society considered them unfeminine because they found personal fulfilment in football, far beyond cultural expectations.

The players' statements seem to reaffirm a feminine ideal related to tradition. Janeth Morrón explained: 'Regarding my femininity, I don't feel anything out of the ordinary, the fact that I play and love football doesn't change anything, only the clothing changes'. Yet, in practice, by occupying spaces and participating in activities considered masculine (e.g., playing football), these women are revolutionising what it means to be a woman in the Bolivian context.

Thus, the strength of the *karimachus* on the football field has helped break with the notions of femininity and the fragility of women in a context where they did not stop facing obstacles. Zdenscka declared: 'My generation was stopped by nefarious leaders! We could not compete for 10 years and we could not be part of a Bolivian team because the requirement was to be in a club that plays in the association, and we didn't have an association in the city'.

Friedan (1963) argues that when women go outside of the feminine mystique searching for a new and more liberating life, they will usually pay for it with various types of violence and resistance from macho social structures. De Beauvoir (1949) adds that many women continue to be trapped by conventional values because change implies discomfort, fear or loss of a privileged situation, requiring a painful pathway.

Likewise, the players interviewed considered that they have managed to consolidate and strengthen their femininity through the practice of sport, taking into account and respecting the way each one conceives of the concept of femininity while not abiding by what social norms stipulate about 'being a woman'. Although people have been led to believe that there is a femininity conceived within the parameters of the feminine mystique, the reality is that when a woman steps outside of this heteronormative idea, she can understand that the structure of femininity is personal, cultural and political. This depends on the diverse narratives and bodily experiences that each woman encounters daily. Femininity is not unique. According to Judith Butler (1990), women perform it every day, and playing football introduces one more possibility of 'being a woman'.

As Janeth Morron asserted, 'I do not feel more masculine by playing football, as I do not feel less feminine…I just feel myself, a normal person'. Amankaya built on this idea, 'On the field, you can see me be aggressive, effusive, all you want, and off the field too'. The interviewed players live their femininity as they feel fit, sport does not take away their femininity. De Beauvoir (1949) mentioned that leaving traditional roles could deprive a woman of her attractiveness, losing her power, if she ever had it, because traditional beauty has a submissive component; this is where the idea of the complementarity of hegemonic masculinity and femininity comes into play.

Similarly, the disadvantages that women could face when playing football were compensated by their discipline and work ethic. They all admit they worked very hard to achieve their football objectives. Ana Huanca described her typical routine: '

> I work every morning in a school as a physical education teacher; three afternoons a week, I work as a football trainer and the other two afternoons I practice by myself. If I have a call up for the national team, I train at night, but it is very tiring'.

Now, there are more women on the field, but equality within football is far from being achieved. Some authors maintain that one way to achieve equality in football would be through equal wages while other authors defend the idea of coed football to break paradigms (Pereira, 2019; Hernández, 2014). Aguilar (in Hernández, 2014) states that equality in football between women and men will not be easy to achieve. The reality is that there are many obstacles and barriers that make it impossible for women to become professionals. One of the main barriers is the macho mindset of football institutions; however, the constant presence of Bolivian female footballers on the field since 1990 allows new footballers to be more visible today.

Another major barrier is that women footballers do not earn money from their sport like men, which is why they must have other jobs to both achieve their football objectives and sustain themselves. As seen in Ana Huanca's statement earlier, it can be seen that footballers strive to achieve their goals, giving up various activities that do not allow them to concentrate entirely on their game, which is mentally and physically exhausting and can affect their on-field performance.

In 2018, FIFA presented a strategy to increase women's participation in football, but the agenda does not cover the basic needs of women nor does it mention gender pay gaps and maternity, a main concern for women (FIFA, 2018). As Zdesncka Bacarreza points out, 'I told myself: You cannot play anymore! You have a daughter! Although I did want to, I thought I didn't have time'.

As a result of FIFA (2018) regulations, most Bolivian cities today have an association and organise women's tournaments. Women can play football without facing as much discrimination as in the past, and they also have more options to demonstrate their ability and play in various tournaments or on the national team. Ana observed, 'Now there are many opportunities; I did not have them, but if I had, I would have left the country to play … sometimes I think it's unfair'. Similarly, Amankaya stated, 'If this league thing had come up earlier, when I was in school or university, I would have given it my all And I have several teammates who say the same thing'.

Today, almost all the players who were interviewed are still connected to football in some way. From wherever they are, they work towards equality on the field. For example, in 2014 Zdenscka and a friend,

Carmen Pozo, opened the first football academy for women, 'Las Super Poderosas' (Calatayud, 2020), which allows for the consolidation of the idea that Bolivian women can play football in the country's collective imagination. Now, most of the football academies in Bolivia train both women and men.

Extra Time—Conclusions

The patience and strength of Bolivian footballers during the 1990s helped challenge the stereotypes of the feminine mystique that were part of Bolivia's narratives. Friedan (1963) mentions that when women can use their full strength, their full ability will be able to destroy the mystique. Although they have had to endure being called *karimachus*, and in some cases, other kinds of insults (e.g., lesbians, little men and tomboys) as an attempt to keep them off the field, silencing their voices and making them invisible, Bolivian women footballers have built a new way of being on the field.

These women are the ones who can best describe the reality of Bolivian football because they have experienced it. They are the reason why it is now possible for girls to play football and why it is even possible to find football academies for them; this has helped normalise female football in the country. At the same time, new concepts have been resignified in the collective imagination, which was built according to male hegemony. Women can leave a position of subordination to change the relational logic with which they have lived until today, expanding the possibilities for the construction of alternative femininities. These women, with their presence in the public sphere of football, are not committed to the feminine mystique, but rather through football they have found the liberating and emancipatory path that Friedan describes—a new way to personal fulfilment, well-being and happiness. They are breaking with the norm, creating a new way of living femininity through football.

Today, the daily work and silent effort of these 11 footballers, and many other Bolivian women who play or have played football, must be recognised and made visible. They broke down the barriers; they redefined the word *karimachu*. It is no longer a woman who does men's things, but rather a *karimachu* is a powerful and brave woman who goes after her dreams, who builds her life day by day, no matter what people think or say to stop her, because she believes in herself. Women could develop many other meanings for the term *karimachu*. This is why we dare to say that *karimachus* could become feminist icons.

At the same time, footballers' experiences help one analyse the football agenda presented by FIFA in 2018 and understand how far we are from equality in the sport. The governing body's agenda should focus on taking into account women's real needs (e.g., gender pay gaps, equal opportunities in training, equal rights), as well as issues of violence and sexual harassment while taking motherhood into consideration instead of firing players or prohibiting maternity in their contracts. For these reasons, women's football needs to go against the system of extractivism, creating a space where women and men can work together to reach equality, for it will be necessary to have a feminist perspective to fight for equal rights in football.

Taking Simone de Beauvoir's words to the football field: 'One is not born a football player, but rather becomes one'. Although not all interviewees had played for the national team, each one had faced the same macho structure, no matter where they were from. Each footballer contributed from their place to make Bolivian women's football visible around the country. Even though they were labelled *karimachus*, these women's experiences, resistance and perseverance might ensure that future generations of Bolivian women who are interested in football do not have to suffer what these women have experienced. These players, by their example, have changed life for many Bolivian women.

References

Aguilar, E. (2020). Equipo de fútbol de mujeres: Marcando historia en el clásico femenino. In K. Gallardo (Ed.), *Las Más Fuertes* (pp. 176–183). La Paz, Bolivia: Editorial 3600.

Aguilar, F. (2014). Desde la barra femenina. In E. Hernández (Ed.), *Las que aman el futbol y otras que no tanto* (pp. 122–129). Elementum SA.

Beauvoir, S. (1949). *El segundo sexo*. Siglo Veinte.

Bourdieu, P. (1998). *Dominación masculina*. Anagrama.

Burrow, S. (2016). Trampled autonomy: Women, athleticism, and health. *International Journal of Feminist Approaches to Bioethics, 9.* https://doi.org/10.3138/ijfab.9.2.67

Butler, J. (1990). Muñoz, M. Traductora (2007). *El género en disputa, el feminismo y la subversión de la identidad.* Paidós Ibérica S.A.

Calatayud, O. (2020). Zdenscka y Piña: Dos nombres para una causa, el fútbol femenino. In K. Gallardo (Ed.), *Las Más Fuertes* (pp. 98–110). Editorial 3600.

Castro, M. (2008). *Los determinantes socioculturales en la salud sexual y reproductiva de mujeres indígenas.* Retrieved April 10, 2021, from: http://www.revistasbolivianas.org.bo/pdf/umbr/v1n18/v1n18a10.pdf

Connell, R., & Messerschmidt, J. (2005). Hegemonic Masculinity: Rethinking the Concept. *Gender and Society, 19*(6), 829–859. Retrieved June 15, 2021, from http://www.jstor.org/stable/27640853

Díaz, J., & Martinez, A. (2017). '¡Mundialistas! Pero Son Mujeres'. Ideología, discurso radial, fútbol y sexismo. *DeSignis: Publicación de La Federación Latinoamericana de Semiótica (FELS), 26*, 187–195.

FIFA. (2018). *Estrategia de futbol femenino.* Retrieved April 2, 2020, from https://resources.fifa.com/image/upload/women-s-football-strategy.pdf?cloudid=jor8jikrnmjulndmyoip

Friedan, B. (1963). Martínez, M.Traductor (2016). *La mística de la feminidad.* Cátedra.

Galeano, E. (1995). *El futbol a sol y sombra.* Siglo Veintiuno Editores.

Gutierrez, O. (1983, November 7). Strongest campeón. *Hoy.* El deportivo, p. 16.

Haraway, D. (1991). *Ciencia, Cyborgs y Mujeres: La Reinvención de la Naturaleza.* Cátedra.

Harding, S. (1996). *Ciencia y Feminismo.* Ediciones Morata.

Hernández, E. (2014). *Las que Aman el Futbol y Otras Que no Tanto.* Elementum SA.

Hidalgo, M. (2017). Las 5 muestras de que a Joseph Blatter sólo le interesó el físico de las futbolistas. Retrieved April 20, 2020, from https://www.elespanol.com/deportes/futbol/20171111/261224318_0.html

Knijnik, J. (2014). Gendered barriers to Brazilian female football: Twentieth-century legacies. In J. Hargreaves & E. Anderson (Eds.), *Routledge Handbook of Sport, Gender and Sexuality* (pp. 121–128). Routledge.

Lamas, L. (1996). *El Género. La Construcción Cultural de la Diferencia Sexual.* UNAM.

Luxán, M., & Azpiazú, J. (2016). *Metodologías de Investigación Feminista. Material didáctico del Máster en Igualdad de mujeres y Hombres: Agentes de Igualdad.* Universidad del País Vasco/Euskal Herriko Unibertsitatea.

Macías, V. (1999). *Estereotipo y deporte femenino, la influencia del estereotipo en la práctica deportiva de niñas y adolescentes.* Retrieved April 30, 2020, from: https://hera.ugr.es/tesisugr/15755368.pdf

Moreira, V., & Garton, G. (2021). *Fútbol, nación y mujeres en Argentina, redefiniendo el campo del poder.* Movimiento Revista de Educação Física da UFRGS. https://doi.org/10.22456/1982-8918.109761.

Opinión. (2009, November 12). Aún se practican ritos de iniciación sexual. *Opinión.* https://www.opinion.com.bo/articulo/sin-categoria/aun-practican-ritos-iniciacion-sexual/20091112012527328509.html

Pereira, H. (2019). *Estudio sobre la existencia de una brecha salarial entre la selección femenina y masculina de fútbol en EE.UU.* https://www.researchgate.net/publication/337294091

Rinke, S. (2006). ¿La Ultima Pasion Verdadera? Historia del Futbol en America Latina en el Contexto Global, 100. Retrieved May 20, 2020, from http://www.iai.spk-berlin.de/fileadmin/dokumentenbibliothek/Iberoamericana/2007/Nr_27/27_Rinke.pdf

Rojas, F. (2002). *La deportivización del cuerpo masculino* (Vol. 18(113), pp. 47–57). El Cotidiano. Retrieved June 26 2021, from https://www.redalyc.org/articulo.oa?id=32511306

Ruiz, J. H. (2012). Futbol femenino: ¿Rupturas o resistencias? *Lúdica Pedagógica, 2*(16). https://doi.org/10.17227/ludica.num16-1355

Scott, J. W. (1986). Gender: A useful category of historical analysis. *The American Historical Review, 91*(5), 1053–1075. https://doi.org/10.2307/1864376

Van Dijk, T. (1999). *El Análisis del Discurso en Anthropos. 186, September–October 1999* (pp. 23–36). Retrieved May 18, 2020, from 'http://www.discursos.org/oldarticles/El%20an%E1lisis%20cr%EDtico%20del%20discurso.pdf

Yapu, M. (2010). *Primera infancia: experiencias y políticas públicas en Bolivia.* Fundación PIEB.

Zuna, G. (2017). El idioma quechua. In *Americanía. Revista de Estudios Latino Americanos* (pp. 145–156). Nueva Época.

8

Socio-Political Dynamic of Women's Participation in Football in Venezuela

Rosa López de D'Amico and Lesbia Verenzuela

Introduction

In Venezuela, more women are participating in women's football, breaking barriers, limitations, prohibitions and stereotypes in a quest to achieve gender equality. Yet, there is a dearth of research or critical review on women and football in Venezuela. Women have always actively participated in the construction of society; female participation in the economic, social and political arenas has been acknowledged throughout the past decades. The same cannot be said, however, about sports. The greatest obstacle that women's football has is the sport's continued management by men with a patriarchal generative perspective (Hinojosa, 2016). A cultural change in football institutions and the educational sector is

R. López de D'Amico (✉)
Universidad Pedagógica Experimental Libertador, Maracay, Venezuela

L. Verenzuela
Universidad Nacional Experimental Politécnica de las Fuerzas Armadas, Cagua, Venezuela

© The Author(s), under exclusive license to Springer Nature Switzerland AG 2022
J. Knijnik, G. Garton (eds.), *Women's Football in Latin America*, New Femininities in Digital, Physical and Sporting Cultures,
https://doi.org/10.1007/978-3-031-09127-8_8

131

necessary to make the presence of women visible in a sport in which males have historically maintained hegemonic control.

Despite the disadvantages surrounding women's claims in Venezuelan football in its various roles, there is a history of women and football, a history of challenges and triumphs, needs and absences, exclusions and continued defiance. Perhaps, these realities guide its most significant development phase. In addition to the sport itself and the physical benefits of participation, women's football empowers women; their participation is a form of activism that breaks barriers and challenges obstacles. The idea is not to go against the system, but for society to understand the value of women. Clearly, it is not enough only to allow women to play football, rather they should be empowered through this sport. More female voices and viewpoints that refute the patriarchal discourse and show other forms of gender identity in football should be presented.

Venezuelan Football

Football in general is a space that has great social and cultural relevance, but there are aspects that need to be addressed to consolidate a scenario that promotes equal opportunities and development for all, particularly for women in the sport. This chapter seeks to answer the following question: What are the socio-political elements present in women's football in Venezuela?

In Venezuela, by the mid-1970s some women's competitions were organised by the Minor Football League (LFM) but were not recognised by the Venezuelan Football Federation (FVF). In 1991, Venezuela participated in the first South American Women's Championship, which the FVF considers the starting point for women's football in the country. The first Women's Football World Championship, organised by FIFA in 1991 in Canton, China, represented the global promotion of this discipline. This event pushed the South American Football Federation (CONMEBOL) to organise a women's South American championship for its teams to compete for qualification for the world championship. Venezuela was absent from the 1995 edition of the South American Championship but participated again in 1999. Some of the pioneeering women in those years were Teodora González, Josefina 'Pita' Rodríguez and Milagros Infante, among others. These women were the first in Venezuela to struggle for women's recognition in this sport, which had been socially considered a male domain (Dunning, 1992). Women's football became a way to challenge for gender equality.

Since then, Venezuelan women's football has advanced. The creation of the Female Super League (i.e., professional women's football championship) in 2017 initiated the professionalisation of the discipline in the country (Requena, 2017). According to the FVF, through the Department of Women's Technical Development, the following are the statistics on women in football as of 2019: 24,247 total players of which 11,473 are older than 18, 12,684 are under 18 and 338 are registered with professional contracts; there are 269 female football clubs, 240 female coaches, 120 female referees, 92 teams in youth leagues for girls under 14 and 157 teams in youth leagues for girls under 16. Of the 109 employees of the FVF, 48 were women. Beyond this data, there is limited information about women, football and gender in Venezuela.

Literature Review

'Gender' refers to the socially structed roles, behaviours, activities and attributes that a given society considers appropriate for women and men (Council of Europe, 2014); gender equality can be defined as the result of the absence of discrimination on the basis of a person's sex in opportunities, allocation of resources, benefits or access to services and equally valuing the responsibilities and roles of women and men (UN Women Turkey, 2021). Concepts of gender mainstreaming, gender equality, gender equity and women's empowerment have been identified as key drivers for promoting women's quality of life and sustainable social change. Prioritising gender as an element of social change involves implementation, monitoring and evaluation of policies and programs central to achievement of gender equality (Kluka et al., 2013; United Nations, 2020). Thus, it is important to have data or studies to carry out the respective analysis.

Other concepts used in Latin American literature that are important to define are the terms 'patriarchy' and 'chauvinism'. In this study, a patriarchal society or system is one in which men have all or most of the power and importance (Valdivieso, 2007). Male chauvinism is the belief that men are superior to women; in this text, the authors use it to refer to the belief or attitude that women are naturally less important, intelligent or able than men (Hernández, 2014). It is essential to keep in mind that sport and gender are both social constructs (Connell, 2009).

Valdivieso (2007) indicates that feminism is a social theory, a socio-critical theory, a political proposal built on the questioning of the patriarchal structure of human existence; it is a concept created from the resistance and conflict with the domination imposed by the hegemonic establishment. Castells (1996) explains feminism as all persons and/or groups, reflections and attitudes oriented to eliminate subordination, inequalities and women's oppression and to achieve, therefore, emancipation and the construction of a society in which there is no place for discrimination by sex or race. Feminism promotes social transformation in favour of human rights and women in all sectors of society. Feminist theories are related to the knowledge, respect and interpretation of the new relationships that women develop with sport and in particular with football.

Feminism and Sport

Feminists in sport are the men and women who seek to eradicate gender discrimination (Ordoñez, 2011). Feminism in sport represents the struggle of men and women for women's access to traditionally male activities, and football is one of these (Ordoñez, 2011). This chapter examines the socio-dynamics of women's participation in various roles in football and considers the issue of equal access. Football in the global context has started to provide a platform for women's participation and has the chance to change from being part of the problem to being the solution.

Gallo and Pareja (2009) indicated that families were the institutions that most questioned girls' inclusion in boys' games and conditioned them to other roles and occupations they considered appropriate for girls.

Later, however, girls no longer just wanted to accompany their brothers to play a small-sided football match, suddenly they were also on the field running alongside them (Pimentel, 2018).

'Football' has been defined in the male discourse as a sport that demands virile strength and is a representation of machismo or patriarchal inspiration (Hernández, 2014). According to De Certeau (1986), football is a space that allows for an understanding of society because it provides a space to observe popular culture and understand how people use this stage. Football is more than a game; it is a phenomenon that allows for the study of modern culture and new societies from multiple perspectives. This sport has become a global mass phenomenon and a source of cultural identity with distinctive cultural, economic and political effects that have been legitimised with its own tradition and history.

Nevertheless, football is the team sport most practiced by women around the world, and many countries have professional leagues (Chavisnan, 2018). Female football represents a social space, a path to empowerment that opens the door to gender equality (Verenzuela & López de D'Amico, 2018). Women's football has evolved significantly in the last 40 years; however, until 1970, it was only played by a minority and was even forbidden in some countries, such as Germany and England (Weeks, 2015). Currently, more than 30 million girls and women play football all over the world in 209 FIFA-member associations (Williams, 2011).

In Latin America, Hinojosa (2016)—based on her research with women players from Argentina, Costa Rica and México—concluded that gender inequality will not be solved by including more women in football. Rather, inequality is related to the cultural marginalisation and unequal economy that contributes to the notion that football is a sport made by and for men, which creates difficulties for women to develop professionally.

In Ecuador, McCann (2016) observed that women's football has faced certain challenges in competitive sport, but if women can continue playing, football can provide lifelong mental benefits and abilities that could help women succeed in the world and challenge a system with patriarchal and chauvinist values. At the 2014 Women's Copa America in Ecuador, a study about social representation found that women players' femininity and sexuality are put into doubt through a biological perspective that questions their capability and abilities to perform this practice traditionally considered just for men (Martínez & Goellner, 2015).

Methodology

The socio-political view of women in football from a gender perspective in Venezuela was approached with a blended quantitative and qualitative methodology. Hermeneutics was used to interpret socio-political reality, with various opinions organised by categories. 'Hermeneutics' is the action of interpreting a text; it is a method applicable to interpretation science (González, 2007), so it reveals meanings that are part of what is evident and explicit.

A sample of 10 women was selected for interviews. The following criteria were used for the selection of the participants: participation in football as a player coach, referee and/or administrator; at least two years of experience in each one of the roles; and availability to participate in the interview. The interviews were conducted in several contexts and on average lasted 45 minutes each. Four of the interviewees were abroad at the time of data collection while the others were in four different states. The main focus of the study was on the in-depth interviews regarding women's experiences in football. The interviewees' responses were analysed in the light of hermeneutic theory and the literature reviewed.

A survey also was carried out with the purpose of gathering the opinions of the audience, those that attends women's football training sessions and matches, about women's participation in the sport in Venezuela. This social technique of data collection helped to get to know the voices of the audience and their position regarding Venezuelan women's football. The survey was made up of 13 questions and was distributed during training sessions, football camps, matches and a workshop session. It was a nonintentional sample with no other requirement than to be present as part of the audience. Answers from a sample of 100 people were collected. The respondents were 75% female and 25% male; participants were separated into two age groups—the first between 36 to 50 years old and the other 51 and older. Participants (i.e., mothers, fathers, grandmothers, grandfather and others) attended women's football training sessions, tournaments, camps, and/or workshops.

Results

Through the analysis of the in-depth interviews and the survey results, seven categories emerged. The first category is the 'Introduction to and interaction with women's football through the game with males'. When most of the interviewees started to play football in the 1980s, they played with males and on male teams. Some indicated that they started refereeing because of a friend's influence. There was a positive and motivational interaction, in which passion and love for the discipline made it part of their daily lives as players, coaches, referees and leaders; however, women's presence in football was not easily accepted.

In the beginning, many faced resistance from a parent because it was not considered a sport appropriate for girls or women. They often attended training sessions secretly; nevertheless, in general, their families supported the interviewees' participation in football. In most cases, support was influenced by an inclination towards the sport in the family group. Despite the progress of women's football around the world, this has not been mirrored in Venezuela because more women players, coaches, referees, manages and leaders still need to be incorporated into the sport.

The interviewees credit the development of women's football in the country to the recent export of Venezuelan players to professional teams around the world. At the same time, some women referees have emerged with opportunities to officiate in international competitions. Still, they acknowledge that a chauvinist culture persists in society that has conditioned the practice and mass expansion of the sport. Consequently, this culture impacts the political agenda, which shows little to no interest in the development of women's football, leading to a lack of credibility, sponsorship, institutional support and promotion of it. The interviewees indicated that women saw sport, and particularly football, as a powerful means to carry out their struggle for equal rights and opportunities.

The number of female referees is increasing, and women are beginning to have opportunities to earn a living in the sport and thus defend women's position in football even though they have been subjected to insults and abuse from fans. Nevertheless, they hope that the position of women in Venezuelan football will improve as FIFA promotes initiatives specific to women. Similarly, the rise of new talented players and their contribution to the national team's success will raise the sport's profile in society.

The second category is the 'Influence of family support on women's football'. According to the interviewees' testimonies, many initially were prohibited from playing because football was considered a waste of time or inappropriate for women. In other cases, their families embraced football because other family members played the sport, so they allowed the girl(s) to play. The literature reinforces that parents should support their children's choice of sport and guide them but never use their bias to influence what the child wants to do during their time of leisure (Comellas, 2007). Family plays a key role in the creation of habits and autonomy (Comellas, 2007) and can influence the shaping of sport practices, particularly during the early stages of life (Ruiz & García, 2003).

The third category is 'Women's presence in female football'. Women's football in Venezuela has grown significantly in recent years, but even though society has been evolving and the stereotypes associated with male and female spaces should be a thing of the past, the latter has not yet been accomplished. It is true that female participation has increased, but levels are still low. In the office, in positions of management, on the field and in the stands, football has not achieved gender equality. According to Alfaro (2012) in the sport sector, statistics are often used as a smokescreen to hide the real problems faced by women; these include male-dominant sport structures, minimal budget allocation, lower quality resources, less media coverage of female success and activities and restricted access to decision-making roles. Nevertheless, there is hope as FIFA president Gianni Infantino in 2016 indicated that female football is a priority for the organisation and that there is much more potential for growth in women's football than in the men's game (Galán, 2020). Also, the memorandum between FIFA and UN Women established the importance of gender equality (ONU Mujeres, 2019).

Category four is the 'Socio-cultural prevalence of women in football'. Women are active in the sport and to become involved they have had to overcome discrimination, rejection, social exclusion, continuous questioning about their physical capacity and doubts about their gender identity and sexual orientation. Nevertheless, women's presence in the sport has contributed to eliminating myths and socio-cultural barriers that have kept women at a disadvantage in relation to their male counterparts. Peña and Jaramillo (2001) highlight other kinds of discrimination faced by women who play football: social strata, poor access to training spaces, lack of sponsorship and chauvinist attitudes of their family and fans in the stands.

'Unequal opportunities for women in football' is category five. The football world is still unequal, not just in economic terms but also historically, symbolically and culturally (Elsey & Nadel, 2016). The number of female athletes has grown, but they still receive unequal treatment, particularly because of the belief that some sporting behaviours are not feminine. Although women's competitions are emerging, there is no comparison with salaries earned by male athletes. These differences are because of a devaluation of cultural roles attributed to women. If female players are provided with better working conditions, it is very likely that the number of players in teams and leagues will increase and the quality of the game also will improve. Most of the reasons for the oppression and subordination of women in sport are related to the use of power and privileges (Janson, 2008).

Category six is 'Discrimination against women in football'. Interviewees described situations of discrimination or exclusion, indicating that they experienced bitter situations, mistreatment, a lack of adequate spaces to practice and develop along with poor salaries and working conditions in professional football compared to male players. A major obstacle for women's football is that it is still administered by men who do not value women in sport and maintain a patriarchal generative perspective. In the world, there are few female coaches, so women's football is often not perceived through the needs and specificities of female players, coaches, referees and leaders. Women are in a male space and are constantly faced with discrimination, exclusion and prejudice in their daily routine, particularly in their practice. As Tamburrini (in Marugan, 2019) said, sport is the last bastion of machismo. It is not enough to have more female football players; more voices and perspectives are needed to refute the patriarchal discourse and begin to display other gender identities in football.

The last category is 'Football and women'. To a certain extent, women have been included and participate in this sport. There is, however, still a long way to go and many obstacles to overcome. There is great hope because the success of the national women's team has brought pleasure in spite of the difficulties they have faced. In addition, there are now official competitions under the guidance and management of the FVF as well as tournaments organised by CONMEBOL and FIFA. The interviewees suggested that women's football could be a helpful tool to promote equality in society and contribute to improving women's experiences in sport. They see it as a step towards achieving real equality between men and women, eliminating gender stereotypes, promoting inclusion and diversity, integrating a gender perspective in business and politics and contributing to the improvement of public health.

The interviewees' careers in football have been difficult and full of obstacles, and although the sport will not change immediately, recent data is optimistic. Nevertheless, more financial support and opportunities for development are needed for all girls, teenagers and women who want to pursue a career in any role in this sport. Peña and Jaramillo (2001) have indicated that football represents a kind of social empowerment for women, in which there is an emancipative act that frees them from social ties. Historically, football has been monopolised by men, and all forms of monopolisation create inequalities and subordination. Thus, women's struggle in football is one of gender equity and an attempt to overcome the resistance of male power in football.

Regarding the survey results, the majority surveyed (86%) expressed that they had a relative in the session. When asked about their relationship to the player, they indicated: daughter (79%), sister (15%), niece (4%) and friend (2%). The number of daughters is significant because it suggests that their parents have decided to support their right to play despite negative stereotypes. Of them, 63% indicated that women have managed to be empowered through Venezuelan women's football whereas 37% believe that empowerment has not yet been accomplished.

Those who believe that football has empowered women relate this empowerment to the international success of the national team and its players. Nonetheless, women's football at the grassroots level is also growing. The under-17 national team has achieved significant levels of recognition after having qualified twice for the world championship (2010, 2014), achieving fourth place in 2014; they also won the South American title in 2013 and achieved third place in 2010. In general, the presence of women in Venezuelan football has grown, and despite ups and downs, their presence has been made known and they continue to fight for more space in the sport. Nevertheless, 73% of those surveyed strongly believe that there is still discrimination against women in the sport, 13% believe there is some form of discrimination and just 12% believe that maybe there is no discrimination; however, no one denied that there is discrimination.

Regarding the perception of women's participation in Venezuelan football today, the respondents believed that 61% are players whereas only 10% are believed to be referees. Women's inclusion in refereeing has not been easy, and it has been tough to break the old structures of society and sport. Respondents perceived that just 15% are present as coaches, which is still a low number. Women only coach female teams, and the number is ironically contemptible. In leadership positions, only 20% are perceived to be active in women's football. In terms of the women's presence in the stands for women's football, the response was 100%. Their agreement with the statements is shown in Table 8.1.

Table 8.1 Social Views about Venezuela Women's Football

What is your opinion about women's football in Venezuela?	Percent (%)
It is a discipline that has advanced in the last years.	78
It is perfect for women's development in society.	83
It brings health benefits.	62
It allows women's qualities in sport to stand out.	30
It is a male space, but women have gained respect with lots of dedication and effort.	100
It is a sport that has provided a future for women in the world in their sport through quality exportation.	92
It is a challenge for women in the fight for gender equality.	71

The survey results demonstrate poor promotion of women's football in Venezuela. Just 12% indicated that there is a push, but 88% indicated that there is no promotion of women's football. Therefore, more investment and dissemination are needed to encourage women to build an identity of female football, creating its own image and language, which could allow women in various roles in football to see themselves as being part of this sport.

Final Remarks

The socio-political dynamic of women's football in Venezuela indicates that its practice has grown because of important factors such as family support, particularly motivation or interest that parents provide to the girls and women who play football regularly. Still, parents' concern regarding their daughters' practice of a male sport is conditioned by the cultural belief that football is a boys' game that does not encourage feminine behaviour. In this study, the nuclear family and their sporting habits influenced the decisions of the interviewees; the barriers, limits and prohibitions implemented by parents were circumstantial and based on the typical belief that 'football is not for girls'. Even so, parents thought that playing football gave their daughters confidence and optimism.

Women's representation in football has increased, but it is yet to equal that of men, which was evident in the survey results. The interviewees pointed out that there are some female figures who have reached significant managerial positions even though this is perceived as a male space. There are also women in administrative positions at the FVF, such as Milagros Infante, former head coach of the women's national team and current CONMEBOL instructor. Although there are initiatives (e.g., the offering of courses through FIFA, CONMEBOL and the FVF) to increase the number of women referees and coaches, these actions are still not enough.

The findings of this study in the Venezuelan context agree with the literature on women's football around the world, especially in terms of women's struggle to enter this space. It is necessary for more women to be involved in all areas of the football system. For example, football needs more female journalists in the media who could bring a critical view of female amateur and professional players; more female referees to lead the development of the sport; more commentators who could impose their style when narrating a game; and more female leaders in the institutions that organise and propose changes in football. In general, we need more female voices and insights to challenge the patriarchal voices and provide new possibilities not only for women but also for the sport itself.

References

Alfaro, E. (2012). El liderazgo de las mujeres en la dirección y gestión del deporte. In *Actas del I e II Ciclo de Conferencias: Xénero, Actividade Física e Deporte* (pp. 31–49). Universidad da Coruña.

Castells, C. (1996). *Perspectivas Feministas en Teoría Política*. Paidos, Estado y Sociedad.

Chavisnan, S. (2018). Futbol femenino. https://prezi.com/p/6kkredhmpgks/futbol-femenino/

Comellas, M. J. (2007). *Escuela Para Padres. Las Claves Para Educar a Nuestros Hijos*. Ariel.

Connell, R. (2009). *Gender* (2nd ed.). Polity.

Council of Europe. (2014). Council of europe convention on preventing and combating violence against women and domestic violence. https://www.coe.int/en/web/conventions/full-list/-/conventions/rms/090000168008482e.

De Certeau, M. (1986). *La Invención de lo Cotidiano*. I. UIA.

Elsey, B. & Nadel, J. (2016). South American soccer is ignoring its women. *Vice Sports*. Retrieved January 20, 2018, from https://sports.vice.com/en_ca/article/pgnazz/south-american-soccer-is-ignoring-its-women

Dunning, E. (1992). O deporto como uma área masculina reservada: notas sobre os fundamentos sociais na identidade masculina e as suas transformações. In E. Norbert & E. Dunning (Eds.), *A busca da excitação* (pp. 389–412). Lisboa: Difusão Editorial.

Galán, P. (2020, October 18th). Fútbol femenino y la mujer en el fútbol: presente y futuro. https://www.sennferrero.com/2020/10/18/futbol-femenino-y-la-mujer-en-el-futbol-presente-y-futuro/

Gallo, L., & Pareja, L. (2009). A propósito de la salud en el fútbol femenino: inequidad de género y subjetivación. *Educación Física Y Deporte, 21*(2), 15–25.

González, F. (2007). *Investigación Cualitativa y Subjetividad. Los Procesos de Construcción de la Información.* Mc Graw-Hill.

Hernández, E (2014). *Las que aman el fútbol y otras que no tanto.* Elementum SA de CV.

Hinojosa, D (2016). *El fútbol femenino profesional. Una perspectiva de género desde Argentina, Costa Rica y México.* Tesis Doctoral. Universidad Autónoma del estado de México.

Janson, A. (2008). *Se Acabó ese Juego que te Hacía Feliz.* Aurelia Rivera.

Kluka, A., Goslin, A., López de D'Amico, R. & Doll-Tepper, G. (2013). Women: Are they changing the face of global sport management. *ICSSPE Bulletin, 65*, 430–439 Retrieved from https://www.icsspe.org/content/no-65-cd-rom

Martínez, M., & Goellner, S. (2015). Representaciones sociales de la selección femenina de fútbol de Colombia en la Copa América 2014. *Educación Física y Deporte, 34*(1). https://doi.org/10.17533/udea.efyd.v34n1a03

Marugan, B. (2019). *El deporte femenino, ese gran desconocido.* España: Universidad Carlos III de Madrid.

McCann, M. (2016). *El fútbol femenino: Los implicaciones de ser una futbolista femenina en una cultura machista.* Independent Study Project (ISP) Collection. Paper 2322. http://digitalcollections.sit.edu/isp_collection/2322.

ONU Mujeres. (2019). Comunicado de prensa: FIFA y ONU Mujeres firman su primer memorando de acuerdo. https://www.unwomen.org/es/news/stories/2019/6/press-release-fifa-and-un-women-sign-mou.

Ordoñez, A. (2011). Género y deporte en la sociedad actual. http://perio.unlp.edu.ar/catedras/system/files/ordonez_genero_y_deporte_en_la_sociedad_actual.pdf

Peña, N. & Jaramillo, E. (2001). Fútbol femenino: estigma de discriminación cultural de las mujeres que practican fútbol en la ciudad de Manizales. *Lecturas en Educación Física y Deportes,* 6(32). https://www.efdeportes.com/efd32/futbolf.htm

Pimentel, L. (2018). *Volando sobre tierra: investigando sobre el fútbol practicado por mujeres en Uruguay.* Tesis de Licenciatura. Universidad de la República. https://www.colibri.udelar.edu.uy/jspui/bitstream/20.500.12008/20409/1/TS_PimentelLucia.pdf

Requena, F. (2017, May 5). *FVF presentó oficialmente la superliga femenina.* https://www.eldiariodeguayana.com.ve/fvf-presento-oficialmente-la-superliga-femenina/

Ruiz, F., & García, M. (2003). Tiempo libre, ocio y actividad física en los adolescentes. La influencia de los padres. *Retos. Nuevas Tendencias en Educación Física, Deporte y Recreación, 6*, 13–20.

UN Women. (2020). *Gender Equality: Women's Right in Review 25 Years after Beijing*. EE.UU: Autor.

UN Women Turkey Office. (2021). *Guidelines for gender-responsive sports organizations*. Author.

Valdivieso, M. (2007). Una mirada desde el feminismo en Venezuela. De la colonialidad y a la descolonialidad. Ponencia en el *Seminario Colonialidad del poder y giros descoloniales. Las insurgencias político-epistémicas de nuestro tiempo*. Caracas, del 15–18/5.

Verenzuela, L. & López de D'Amico, R. (2018). La mujer venezolana en el fútbol femenino. *Revista Actividad Física y Ciencias*, Edición Especial 'Mujer y Deporte' (pp. 127–138).

Weeks, J. (2015). De cómo la Federación inglesa prohibió el fútbol femenino. https://sports.vice.com/es/article/jpwee3/como-federacion-inglesa-prohibio-futbol-femenino-dick-kerrs-ladies-inglaterra-preston

Williams, J. (2011). *Women's Football, Europe and Professionalization 1971–2011*. A Project Funded by the UEFA Research Grant Programme.

9

Invisible Champions: An Ethnography of Peruvian Women's Football

Mark Biram

Introduction

JC Sport Girls is an amateur women's football club formed in Lima, Peru, in 2003 by women keen to promote the sport in the metropolitan Lima and Callao region of Peru. Driven by enthusiastic volunteers, the club began recruiting players at open trials, solidifying a reputation as a place where women, systematically excluded from the country's national sport, could participate and thrive. The JC denotes *juventud comprometida* (i.e., committed youth) and comes from feminising the name of long-standing Callao neighbour Sport Boys—that was formed in 1927.[1]

From humble beginnings holding trials for local amateur players, the club quickly gained momentum, attracting promising young players

---

[1] Sport Boys Women joined the women's league in 2019.

M. Biram (✉)
University of Bristol, Bristol, UK
e-mail: mb17689@bristol.ac.uk

© The Author(s), under exclusive license to Springer Nature Switzerland AG 2022
J. Knijnik, G. Garton (eds.), *Women's Football in Latin America*, New Femininities in Digital, Physical and Sporting Cultures,
https://doi.org/10.1007/978-3-031-09127-8_9

from across the country. In the absence of sustained efforts from many of the country's professional clubs (excluding perhaps Club Universitario), the stated ambition of becoming a leading club in Peruvian women's football was quickly attained—they have four national championships as of 2021. For this reason, they have represented Peru four times at the Women's Copa Libertadores, the same number as the aforementioned professional club Universitario.[2] These achievements have not gone unnoticed, and the club has an excellent reputation in their local *barrio* (neighbourhood) Miraflores. Despite changes across the continent hinting towards an increased agency through football for women (Wood, 2018), findings from this chapter indicate a significant lag in the case of Peru in even starting to dislodge the meanings of hegemonic masculinity that football continues to signify (Panfichi, 1999, 2014; Ruiz Bravo, 2000).

This lies in stark contrast to incursions that have been made in other areas. For example, Afro-Peruvian women came to embody the nation as successful volleyball players in the 1980s (Wood, 2012, p. 15) while women surfers have also enjoyed considerable success (Wood, 2009). Comparatively the profile of women's football in Peru remains extremely low. Indeed, many of the JC Sport Girls' players commented to the author that it saddened them that no one back home even knew that they were competing in the 2018 Women's Copa Libertadores in Brazil.

I met the team on several occasions in the Amazonian city of Manaus at the aforementioned tournament held in November and December 2018. Here, I got a feel for the situation of Peruvian women's football with a clear comparison with teams from other countries at the tournament. It is far from coincidental that after this tournament they have not represented Peru again at the continental showdown. It owes much to the paradigm shift that women's football in South America is currently undergoing. In particular, it can be traced to a flagship CONMEBOL policy colloquially referred to as *obligatoriedad,* which (quasi-)obligates professional clubs into having a women's programme by denying them entry to any CONMEBOL-sanctioned international men's competition; this would include the Copa Libertadores as well as the Copa

---

[2] Sport Girls won the Peruvian Women's Championship in 2010, 2011, 2012 and 2017.

Sudamericana—a less prestigious continental competition like the Europa League—should they resist.

For the purposes of this chapter, the focus is on how a paradigm of top-down changes is blind to effects on smaller independent clubs like JC Sport Girls. This case study notes how the accumulated cultural capital of such clubs has been in some sense disparaged with the onset of *obligatoriedad*, posited by institutions as a year-zero, marking the start of professional women's football. Moreover, for the players, *obligatoriedad* is bittersweet. Peruvian players felt that *obligatoriedad* would probably trigger more opportunities to earn an income from playing, but this alone does not afford the women's game the dignity, social standing and support that it needs. In an increasingly marketised polity, by focussing solely on well-known (men's) clubs, the longer and more substantive contribution of smaller, independent clubs has been decisively marginalised.

In a cold economic sense, the larger brand-name clubs are best placed to offer the physical infrastructure necessary to advance the women's game. Clearly, the pull of brand-name clubs is not purely economic—it is also derived from the accumulated cultural capital of clubs like *los tres grandes* (the big three): Alianza Lima, Universitario and Sporting Cristal. Men and women players alike have grown up supporting these clubs and thus want not only to earn salaries and benefit from the conditions and infrastructure of brand-name clubs but also to become part of those traditions. It is important to consider all the factors involved rather than simply to understand the situation within the framework of a familiar economic reductionism.

First, this chapter argues that in the absence of any concrete support from the Peruvian Football Federation (FPF), clubs like JC Sport Girls have been influential over the last 18 years in challenging the deep-rooted societal prejudice that has sidelined women from the game. Indeed, such has been the institutional neglect that the first Peruvian Women's Championship organised by the FPF only happened in 2019, after this fieldwork had taken place. Nonetheless, the inherently limited role of amateur independent clubs is acknowledged. Without significant financial support, the profile of JC Sport remains relatively low outside and even within Lima. For this reason, it is important to acknowledge that the challenge the club extends to a highly gendered sporting identity is largely symbolic.

Nonetheless, women's football finds itself at an important juncture where affirmative action is required from football policymakers to ensure the contribution of pioneering clubs like JC is recognized; JC is far from being an isolated case. Prior to the incursion of the brand-name clubs in each country, there are several clubs that have made a largely unacknowledged but significant contribution to women's football in their respective nations. Just a few representative examples, without the intention of excluding many others' outstanding work, include Formas Íntimas in Colombia; Kindermann, São Jose and Ferroviária in Brazil; and Estudiantes de Guárico in Venezuela.

This author argues that, with sufficient institutional support, these clubs could provide an important counterweight to the large male clubs, where dislodging hegemonic masculinity (Connell, 2005) to any meaningful extent is challenging. With the accrued cultural capital of these clubs in their local regions, it is reasonable to assume each could be capable of attracting significant home-match support, as has been proven by a number of cases of popular women's teams in Brazil.

Methodology

This chapter brings into dialogue the results of four semi-structured interviews with club directors with the results of an anonymised survey and follow-up semi-structured interviews carried out with all 22 players of the JC Sport Girls squad at the 2018 Copa Libertadores in Manaus. Taking advantage of my stay in Manaus, I also was able to meet the other teams present in the city for the three-week tournament. Using this opportunity, I could attend teams' training sessions and matches, including those of JC Sport Girls, talk to players more informally and carry out a standardised survey and follow-up interviews with them.

This method, known as 'convenience sampling', involves drawing sample data from a target group who is close at hand at a given time (De Vaus, 2013; Fowler Jr, 2013). This allowed me to collect a wide range of comparative data that shed light on the various positions of women's football across the continent. The tournament was comprised of 12 teams in total: There were 10 national league champions (one from each member association of CONMEBOL), an extra team from the host country (Iranduba of Manaus) and the defending continental champions, Audax (formerly Corinthians-Audax from São Paulo). JC Sport Girls was present at the tournament as Peruvian national champions.

The survey was self-administered through group administration; the rest of the club delegation left me for half an hour to first explain the survey to players and then allow them time to carry it out. Group administration normally results in a higher rate of response (Fowler Jr, 2013, p. 65) although it was clearly explained to players that participation was entirely voluntary. In this case, all players were keen to participate, safe in the knowledge that their participation would be anonymous. Similarly, information from follow-up interviews has been anonymised.

The survey was explained using simple short words to ensure a consistent meaning to all respondents and to minimise any possibilities for ambiguity (Fowler Jr, 2013). Moreover, piloting was carried out in Bristol prior to fieldwork and questions both for the survey and semi-structured lines of inquiry were adapted according to feedback and suggestions kindly offered by native speakers. Once again, it is fair to note that those piloting were academics who were unaware of the lived realities of women footballers. This turned out to be particularly apparent during fieldwork when it became clear that answers to certain questions were skewed by the wording in subtle ways. For example, there is a significant difference in asking if the gender of a team manager is important or asking whether players would prefer a female manager. In response to the first question, players, as might be expected, said that competence was the more important factor whereas, in the second instance, players often responded that they did prefer a female manager.

The possibility of carrying out follow-up interviews allowed me to clarify any such ambiguities and probe further in more nuanced ways to represent players' opinions as well as I could. Moreover, the diverse realities of women footballers in Brazil, where the majority of the research was carried out and where the sport is on a comparatively stronger footing; and Peru, where at the time of doing the research, women's football remained heavily marginalized. This was also abundantly clear when meeting with the JC Sport Girls.

The survey largely respects the conventions of survey research insofar as the majority of questions were of a closed nature to guarantee the comparability of data from which to draw meaningful conclusions (Fowler Jr, 2013, p. 93). Considering the dearth of information available on the subject matter, at my own discretion I added five more open questions to produce qualitative data. The survey also touches on the role of the media and on allowing players an opportunity to suggest how future improvements ought to be made.

These results were brought into dialogue with material from semi-structured interviews with directors of JC Sport Girls, which were carried out in the early months of 2021 to supplement the earlier material collected in Maraus in late 2018. Owing to the ongoing COVID-19 pandemic and to practicality, the more recent interviews were carried out using Skype. These interviews explored the same broad themes contained within the survey, albeit with the inevitably looser structure afforded by one-to-one interviews. For both the follow-up interviews with players in 2018 and the more recent interviews carried out with institutional figures, the length of the interviews varied between 20 and 40 minutes. This depended entirely on the level of detail offered by interviewees as well as on the direction of the questioning. The data this chapter draws on underwent full ethical review at the University of Bristol in September 2018 prior to commencing fieldwork.

Context

When carrying out the initial survey with the Peruvian players, a number of them pointed out immediately that much of the phrasing of my questions pertained more to countries like Brazil where, in many cases, players could already earn a full-time living from the game and where national league games appeared, at least sporadically, on cable or public television channels. Similarly, they pointed out that there was an enormous disparity in terms of the length of the women's football season and that even speaking of a season for women's football in Peru was often not appropriate or—at best, a stretch.

The case of Peru was clearly stages behind the current struggle in Brazil, where women's football was trying to incorporate itself into a masculinised invented tradition (Biram, 2021). The breach between the official rhetoric and the lived reality of women footballers at the time of the fieldwork was much greater in the case of Peru. Indeed, it made a particularly compelling case study because it took place in the final days of amateur clubs representing Peru at the continental competition.

The first mentions of gender equality (watered down to inclusion) appear in the FIFA Statutes in April 2016 (FIFA, 2016; Soares, 2019). It can be speculated that this shift towards official recognition at a global level has triggered the domino effect that caused CONMEBOL, the South American football governing body, to initiate the aforementioned policy of *obligatoriedad*. In this way, the potentially progressive and transformative moment of women's football in the country (and on the continent more generally) mirrors the wider deliberative moment in Latin American politics and society; that is, insofar as there is an ever-present danger of widespread street protests and social pressure neutralised by nominal concessions that are not matched by lived reality. This disjuncture is one familiar to Peruvians and thus colours many of the interactions I had with players and directors from Sport Girls.

In other areas of civil life, Peruvians are accustomed to lofty rhetoric falling short in practice. For example, the influence of the great Brazilian educator Paulo Freire is present in Peruvian Ministry of Education policy documents (Ramírez, 2018). The discourse promising critical emancipatory pedagogy is not matched by the threadbare and traditional positivistic ethos of state education (Espinal, 2021, p. 370). This gulf between rhetoric and reality is present in the players' views. As one player succinctly summarized: '*para nosotras, lo que dicen es puro cuento, no se siente acá en Perú todo eso de inclusión y la política de obligatoriedad*' (for us, everything they say is just hot air, all the talk of inclusion and *obligatoriedad* is not felt here). Their view of the present and future is framed by a scepticism rooted in lived experiences of hollow rhetoric. The following section considers some of the recurring themes during my interactions with the club hierarchy of JC Sport Girls and subsequently the viewpoints of players themselves.

Discussion

The Club Hierarchy

JC Sport Girls runs four categories, an under-12, under-14 and under-17 team in addition to the senior side which is generally dominated by players in their late teens or early twenties looking for a springboard towards playing for larger clubs. Each year the club brings in large numbers of new players at all levels with the goal of developing them. Prior to *obligatoriedad*, the club provided several players to the Peruvian women's national team, although the club hierarchy emphasised a shift towards the selection of players from brand-name clubs.

Without entering into great detail about the policy of *obligatoriedad*, from the perspective of a club like JC Sport Girls, tying the growth of women's football to an economic sanction against brand-name clubs, the sole focus of which generally has been men's football until the onset of the policy, is problematic. The economic clout of larger men's clubs means they are likely to dominate women's competitions despite having done none of the foundational work to get the women's game off the ground. Moreover, the number of teams realistically likely to reach the men's Copa Libertadores, a tournament for the highest positioned teams in each country, reflects the ever-decreasing circles of a stale development model. The financial rewards for participation in the men's Copa Libertadores have increased greatly in recent years—meaning those who qualify frequently have pulled away from the rest, mirroring the global trend of subdivisions within national leagues. Peru is a prime example of this, with clubs (e.g., Alianza Lima, Sporting Cristal and Universidad San Martin) now embracing women's football to maintain their position at the continental table in the men's game.

The incursion of these teams to the women's game has brought long overdue financial recognition for players. Nonetheless, well-informed sources told this author that at present monthly payments fell between 200 and 1000 soles (between US$52 and 260 as of May 2021). At present in Peru, the legal monthly minimum wage is 930 soles a month. These stipends, concentrated largely at the lower end of the scale, are insufficient for players to dedicate themselves solely to football and are also clearly ridiculous relative to monthly earnings reported to fall between 16,000 and 32,000 soles ($4000–8000 as of May 2021) for first-team male players at the same clubs (AS Peru, 2019). Furthermore, these salaries are only available to the better-known players—those who have represented the women's national team; have competed at international events, like the women's Copa Libertadores; or perhaps even those with the most active social media profiles.

Broadly speaking, directors at Sport Girls feel that they have been usurped by clubs who have not invested in women's football and still lack much-needed long-term programmes for player development. Even though CONMEBOL policy stipulates the need for at least one youth category, there is a danger that clubs only pay lip-service to this aspect rather than carry it out wholeheartedly across a range of age categories in the way that Sport Girls has done for the preceding 18 years.

Players' Views and Experiences

A difference that distinguished the JC Sport Girls from other clubs was the marked lack of insecurity and instability that characterises women footballers' lives. Generated by a reluctance to fully formalise the position of women footballers within a changing scenario, ambiguity and precarity (often two- or three-month contracts) are the norm in many semi-professionalised settings like Argentina and Colombia (ACOLFUTPRO, 2020; Garton, 2019). A consequence of this is constantly having to relocate to another city, country or even continent to continue their activities. The developing transnational market and migration of players already has been covered in the literature (Agergaard & Tiesler, 2014); however, the focus of this work is on the push–pull factors that tend to lead players to look largely to Europe or North America for a career. Clearly, the great majority of players do not have these opportunities available and have to relocate regionally or even internationally on numerous occasions within a given calendar year.

For precisely that reason, I was initially surprised by the level of attachment players felt for JC, an aspect that contrasted sharply with the more transitory contexts. Seven or eight players highlighted that '*JC Sport Girls es como una familia para nosotras, una familia más unida que ninguna*' (JC Sport Girls is like a family for us, a family that is more united than any other). This resonates with the experiences of UAI Urquiza players in Argentina, who offer a similar expression—'*nunca te olvides de dónde viniste*' (never forget where you came from)—in acknowledging the club's ethos and formative influence (Garton, 2019, p. 75). For this reason, it is important to acknowledge the diversity of experiences of women's players not only across countries but also within national contexts.

From this discovery, I continued questioning to discover that many of the players had spent more than 10 years with the club. They spoke warmly about how it had helped their emotional development and given them opportunities to socialise in wider circles. Players spoke of how key figures at the club reached out to girls from a variety of social backgrounds and dedicated time to each of them individually. The club's base in the affluent suburb of Miraflores is deceptive. Players told me that the club's hierarchy is driven by bringing together a group from diverse backgrounds, and they were keen to point out the various areas they each come from. This aspect of the club has not gone unnoticed with the passing of time. For example, JC Sport Girls has benefitted from significant funding from the local Miraflores Municipality, which recognises the social role of the club in the community.

The players are extremely positive about the opportunities that Sport Girls has given them—for example, travelling to Manaus to play in the Copa Libertadores. Still, when approached individually for their opinions on the wider state of women's football in the country, the players were initially much more reticent to comment on topics they obviously consider far from satisfactory. After a short period of breaking the ice, they became much more forthright. Once again, unlike players I met from elsewhere on the continent, the Peruvian players were yet to feel any differential or trickle effect from *obligatoriedad*. They were, however, aware of it, and curious to converse with players from other teams as to what this may mean for them in the short, medium and long term.

Players felt that the development of women's football on the continent could broadly be divided into three or sometimes four tiers, with Brazil as the most developed and countries, which they also felt to be semi-professionalised, in the middle (Garton et al., 2021). In all cases, they grouped Peru together with Bolivia and to a lesser extent Ecuador in the final tier. The three-week Libertadores tournament for them represented a unique opportunity to be in contact with their counterparts from other teams.

Informatively, in the hotel where JC Sport Girls were staying, organised by CONMEBOL, there were only two other teams (the tournament had 12 teams in total)—Deportivo Ita of Bolivia and Union Española, an amateur Ecuadorian women's club, not to be confused with the Chilean professional outfit of the same name. At the time I met them in December 2018 in Manaus, they remained unpaid amateurs, thrust fleetingly into the limelight to play in a lopsided group including two past winners of the women's Copa Libertadores—Santos of Brazil and Colo Colo of Chile. The players were keen to underline the fact that the game that most resembled their domestic calendar would be the dead rubber for third place in the group with Deportivo Ita of Bolivia.

The gulf in development at the group phase spoke to the deep-rooted challenges of uneven development in women's football across the continent. The Peruvian case warns against the temptation to extrapolate broad conclusions for an entire continent based on one or two emblematic cases, as happened in the early Anglo literature on South American football (Mason, 1995). Fortunately, in the case of women's football, a burgeoning literature is bringing the necessary nuance, calling into question institutional claims of professionalisation in Brazil (Goellner, 2021), Argentina (Garton et al., 2021) and also in Colombia (Biram & Mina, 2021; Mina et al., 2019). In each case, claims of professionalisation were placed under scrutiny with the idea of a state of semi-professionalisation proposed.

For the duration of the Copa Libertadores tournament, the team was accommodated in the industrial area of Manaus and was able to access high-quality training facilities made available by the local women's club,

3B da Amazônia. Perhaps for this reason, foremost in the players' minds at the time of carrying out the fieldwork was the comparatively appalling standard of the pitches in their native Peru. They spoke of pitches that would more accurately be described as a beach, others that were uneven and could easily cause injuries. At times they even spoke of pitches where the grass was so long that they struggled to see the ball. This is not limited to smaller clubs or even to Peru—similar findings have been found in Santos in Brazil (Biram, 2021). All of this is a by-product of the way Peruvian women's football has been structured for a number of years. The league is also Lima-centric, a quasi-desert terrain where maintaining grass is difficult and prohibitively expensive.

The tournament essentially runs first at district level, after which district winners compete at a provincial level and only then does the final tournament at a national level take place. In this way, responsibility for running a women's tournament is passed down to the provinces and even to local districts. It is at least theoretically possible that the involvement of Peru's larger clubs will slowly start to remedy the lamentable conditions in which tournament games are played. Nonetheless, it is worth noting that several professional clubs from across the continent have already chosen to base the women's operation at entirely separate facilities to the men's team, using training grounds for official matches. Thus, nothing can be taken for granted in this regard.

The players had no trouble joining the dots in terms of the interconnected nature of their marginalisation. One, for example, proffered the following: '¿*Cómo podemos esperar que los medios de comunicación se interesen por nosotros cuando se juega siempre en tan malas condiciones?*' (How can we expect the media to be interested in covering us when we always play in such poor conditions?). This remark is representative of the players' awareness of the complexities of the problem.

An agenda for change would require the full incorporation of women's football into national federation calendars—this includes a full friendly schedule for national teams and a season of reasonable length for women's teams held at appropriate facilities. The players were acutely aware of what needs to be done and were able to spell out a coherent agenda of changes in less than five minutes. The players realise that only when these steps are completed will it be possible to get a reasonable audience from national and international media.

Academically, there has been a tendency to focus on the shifting nature of pejorative media coverage (Mina & Goellner, 2015; Mourão & Morel, 2008), or on the lack of visibility of women's football (Goellner, 2005; Rial, 2013). This certainly rings true in the Peruvian case, but players felt that much of the problem stems from institutional neglect of the women's game. Along similar lines, there has been a disproportionate focus on national teams, rather than on the everyday experiences of women's football and the gradual transition towards professionalisation. This has been addressed in part by the insightful participant ethnography of Gabriela Garton (2019), *Guerreras: fútbol, mujeres y poder,* in which she reflects on her experiences with Club UAI Urquiza. There is a clear need for further in-depth research on countries like Peru, which lags significantly behind other countries on the continent, as the players were keen to impress on this author.

When asked about their aspirations for the coming year, with the onset of *obligatoriedad,* one player offered optimistically: '*El próximo año todo se vuelve profesional, nos gustaría ganar un poco de dinero para que nos sirva de algo. Siempre lo hemos visto como un hobby. Lamentablemente en el fútbol femenino no hay apoyo económico acá*' (Next year, it will all become professional; we would like to earn a bit of money so all the effort is worth it. We've always seen it as a hobby. Sadly, women's football has no financial support here). These comments underline how Peru was a couple of development stages behind many of its neighbours at the time of carrying out fieldwork, but they also hint at the gradual drift towards change. Understandably, players were eager for their efforts to be rewarded by being paid and recognised as professionals, but from some of their remarks about belonging to a family, there are many positive aspects of an endeavour, like Sport Girls, that many would also like to retain.

As alluded to earlier, certain players have greater reach than others because of substantial followings on social media. For example, Xioczana Canales and Xiomara Canales, two sisters who have both starred for the Peruvian national team, have 10,000 and 22,000 followers on Instagram, respectively.[3] This was, perhaps, a contributory factor in attracting a brand-name club wishing to make a marquee signing to signal their seriousness when they opened female divisions in 2019. Understandably, given their status as international footballers, they were keen to gain experience, but many questions remain about the level of commitment of professional clubs in Peru set against the highly committed amateurism of Sport Girls. This is to say, despite the prestige attached to the brand-name clubs, there are still no guarantees in Peru of a serious operation being run for the women's teams.

With the thrust of current policy, which focuses almost solely on brand-name clubs, there is a danger of an abrupt transition from players participating at clubs like Sport Girls, which see their role in terms of social responsibility and community value, to transitory roles playing for indifferent brand-name clubs, which have often done little or nothing to support women's football, and now are involved in satisfying CONMEBOL legislation. Of course, this is not always necessarily the case. Of the big three, Universitario had a women's team long before *obligatoriedad*, about which JC players spoke positively. For this reason, recognising the agency of each club to run their operation as they see fit, further research into specific cases would strengthen the current literature. Moreover, strategic support for smaller independent clubs may smooth this, until now, abrupt transitional period that brings opportunities but also challenges.

Conclusion

The case of JC Sport Girls is a representative one for several smaller independent clubs that have made considerable efforts to promote women's football and tackled deep-rooted societal stereotypes with motives that go beyond economic gain. For that reason, a progressive polity would look to harness and grow the cultural capital of such clubs to create a sense of tradition in the women's game.

---

[3] Their Instagram handles are @xiomara_canales_oficial and @xioczana-canales.oficial, respectively.

Women's football on a continental level has reached an important intersection whereby progress needs to be underscored not only by legislation but also by affirmative action to address structural inequalities and to offer much-needed accountability. The perspectives and experiences of players, discussed in this chapter, speak to this breach. Players are reluctant to believe in the rhetoric of football authorities because they are too accustomed to their lived reality. They are acutely aware of the lack of media coverage in Peru. They are conscious of the egregious playing conditions they have had to tolerate for a long time, and they know that in many cases, until the onset of *obligatoriedad*, many of the brand-name clubs had done little or nothing to address the highly gendered nature of football in the country. Conversely, they recognise the genuine intentions behind smaller independent clubs.

Much of this can be addressed only with a coordinated plan juxtaposing policy with accountability. Moreover, it is crucial that the route women's football takes in Peru is not governed by prevailing economic reductionism. Brand-name clubs may have better resources financially than clubs like Sport Girls, but they are not necessarily better equipped. To operate at their best, players need stability and much of the development work JC Sport Girls offers players. For this reason, capital alone does not mean that large clubs will 'do women's football' better. Indeed, brand-name clubs could learn a lot about the needs of women's football by learning from the experiences of clubs like JC.

Only by involving the actors who have sustained women's football for the past decades will Peruvian women's football be able to guarantee that the necessary level of commitment and vitality meets the coming challenges. In turn, this would require, if not wholesale institutional changes, at least representation in the Peruvian Football Federation for actors who have given so much to the women's game.

References

ACOLFUTPRO. (2020). *Situación de las futbolistas de la liga femenina 2020*. https://acolfutpro.org/informe-acolfutpro-situacion-de-las-futbolistas-de-la-liga-femenina-2020/

Agergaard, S., & Tiesler, N. C. (2014). *Women, soccer and transnational migration*. Routledge.

AS Peru. (2019, March 29). *Así está la brecha salarial en el deporte profesional peruano*. AS Perú. https://peru.as.com/peru/2019/03/29/masdeporte/1553869600_184347.html

Biram, M. D. (2021). Mermaids in the land of the king: An ethnography of Santos FC women. *Movimento, 27*, 275.

Biram, M. D., & Mina, C. Y. (2021). Football in the time of COVID-19: Reflections on the implications for the women's professional league in Colombia. *Soccer & Society, 22*(1–2), 35–42.

Connell, R. W. (2005). *Masculinities*. Polity.

De Vaus, D. (2013). *Surveys in social research*. Routledge.

Espinal, S. (2021). Impacto del COVID-19 sobre las capacidades en educación: Discusión para el caso peruano. In *COVID-19 & Crisis de Desarrollo Humano en América Latina* (pp. 367–379). Pontificia Universidad Católica del Perú.

FIFA. (2016). *FIFA Statutes April 2016*. https://resources.fifa.com/image/upload/the-fifa-statutes-in-force-as-of-27-april-2016

Fowler, F. J., Jr. (2013). *Survey research methods*. Sage.

Garton, G. (2019). *Guerreras: Fútbol, Mujeres y Poder*. Capital Intelectual.

Garton, G., Hijós, N., & Alabarces, P. (2021). Playing for change: (Semi-)professionalization, social policy, and power struggles in Argentine women's football. *Soccer & Society, 22*(6), 1–15. https://doi.org/10.1080/1466097 0.2021.1952692

Goellner, S. V. (2005). Mulheres e futebol no Brasil: Entre sombras e visibilidades. *Revista Brasileira de Educação Física e Esporte, 19*(2), 143–151.

Goellner, S. V. (2021). Mulheres e futebol no Brasil: Descontinuidades, resistências e resiliências. *Movimento (ESEFID/UFRGS), 27*, 21001.

Mason, T. (1995). *Passion of the people?: Football in South America*. Verso.

Mina, C. Y. M. Goellner, S., & Rodríguez, A. M. O. (2019). Fútbol y mujeres: El panorama de la liga profesional femenina de fútbol de Colombia. *Educación Física y Deporte, 38*(1).

Mina, C. Y. M. & Goellner, S. V. (2015). Representaciones sociales de la selección femenina de fútbol de Colombia en la copa américa 2014. *Educación Física y Deporte, 34*(1), 39–72.

Mourão, L., & Morel, M. (2008). As narrativas sobre o futebol feminino o discurso da mídia impressa em campo. *Revista Brasileira de Ciências Do Esporte, 26*(2), 73–86.

Panfichi, A. (1999). Representación y violencia en el fútbol peruano: Barras bravas. *Contratexto, 012*, 151–161.

Panfichi, A. (2014). *Ese gol Existe: Una Mirada al Perú a Través del Fútbol.* Fondo Editorial de la PUCP.

Ramírez, R. F. M. (2018). La pedagogía crítica y la educación actual. *Revista Ciencias y Humanidades, 7*(7), 175–190.

Rial, C. (2013). El invisible (y victorioso) fútbol practicado por mujeres en Brasil. *Nueva Sociedad, 248*, 114.

Ruiz Bravo, P. (2000). Desde el margen. Representaciones de la masculinidad en la narrativa joven en el Perú. *Revista de Estudios de Género. La Ventana, 12*, 244–271.

Soares, C. (2019). O Estatuto da FIFA e a igualdade de gênero no futebol: Histórias e contextos do futebol feminino no Brasil. *FuLiA/UFMG, 4*(1), 72–87.

Wood, D. (2009). On the crest of a wave: Surfing and literature in Peru. *Sport in History, 29*(2), 226–242. https://doi.org/10.1080/17460260902872669

Wood, D. (2012). Representing Peru: Seeing the female sporting body. *Journal of Latin American Cultural Studies, 21*(3), 417–436. https://doi.org/10.108 0/13569325.2012.711748

Wood, D. (2018). The beautiful game? Hegemonic masculinity, women and football in Brazil and Argentina. *Bulletin of Latin American Research, 37*(5), 567–581. https://doi.org/10.1111/blar.12633

10

Mexican Women and Academics Playing Football

Ciria Margarita Salazar,
Isela Guadalupe Ramos Carranza,
and Emilio Gerzaín Manzo Lozano

Introduction

Risk, strategy, skill, strength and movement have always been considered man's domain. Sport is a field that seems to exemplify this view. Mexican women live at a crossroads between historical tradition and the change of roles demanded by current times and equality policies. The economic, social and scientific development of Mexico, a country centred on male power (Kuper, 2015), constitutes a panorama of various social ranges, idiosyncrasies and identities. There is an advance towards progress in areas originally intended for men, and at the same time, a challenge to leave behind the roles and labels that have defined women's participation in public life (Galeana, 2013).

Sports, football in particular, used to have an exclusively male presence, hegemonic in sporting development and television audiences

C. M. Salazar (✉) • I. G. Ramos Carranza • E. G. Manzo Lozano
University of Colima School of Education, Colima, Mexico
e-mail: ciria6@ucol.mx; iramos5@ucol.mx; manzolozano@ucol.mx

© The Author(s), under exclusive license to Springer Nature Switzerland AG 2022   **165**
J. Knijnik, G. Garton (eds.), *Women's Football in Latin America*, New Femininities in Digital, Physical and Sporting Cultures,
https://doi.org/10.1007/978-3-031-09127-8_10

(Ramirez, 2013). Now women are making progress on the football field with the creation of the Professional League five years ago and, beyond the sporting model of the maximum circuit's affiliates, Mexican women have also found a niche of opportunity to continue promoting football with a gender perspective from and within academia.

Such is the case of the present chapter on women academics and professors at Mexican public universities, former and current players who combine study and human resource training with their participation in semi-professional and local leagues. The academics, from their respective fields, have promoted feminist actions, encouraged participation in amateur contexts and reached national teams, drawing attention to the need for growth during the years prior to the emergence of Liga MX Femenil (i.e., Women's MX League). Therefore, it is relevant to understand the positions and perspectives on the advancement of women in football and the sport of women's football players who study and/or teach at Mexican public universities.

The chapter was prepared in two sections, the first with an anthropological and narrative approach that includes the following four topics: (1) the evolution of Mexican women's public participation, (2) the Mexican women's body in movement—from illegitimate to legitimate, (3) the football culture in Mexico and the arrival of women and (4) university football as the platform for the Liga MX Femenil. The second section discusses the results and is based on the empirical method used to describe the initiations and motivations for playing football, as well as gender stereotypes, social transformations and the perception of change or the development of women in the sport field.

Evolution of Mexican Women's Public Participation

The figure of the Mexican woman with a languid, dreamy look rests in a window frame and listens to a young man serenade her on a horse accompanied by a mariachi or a guitar. She waits, barely smiles, and at the end of the song the man approaches her and takes her in his arms. There is no resistance, only a surrender and placidity that reflects the scene of many nationalist films of the 1930s and 1940s—the so-called Mexican Golden Age (Blanco, 1993).

Overtaken by social reality, the imagery of cinema provokes effects that are not favourable for the development of women; it seems that meeting one's beloved and marrying him will result in the resolution of any female's conflict. Femininities are even limited because it is a matter of imposing a model without accepting variations (Loaeza, 1995a). The male–female polarisation and the weighing/hierarchisation of the former over the latter has historically led to the invisibility of the female's actions.

Let us think of a form of a Mexican ecosystem built on a masculine axis, while everything feminine is kept on the periphery, a cognitive centre-periphery metaphor (Lakoff & Johnson, 1983), where power is concentrated at the axis (i.e., in men). At the same time, a silent construction of movement provokes the feminine lethargy, the simulation of doing nothing—translated into the denial of the fact—into becoming an alternate movement that remains parallel so as not to narrow and thus destroy the metaphor from which it was posed.

During the Spanish conquest, the role of Malitzin (Glanz, 2013) was decisive for the Spaniards to dominate the Aztec people because the princess became a slave and was given as an offering to those of the peninsula. She stands out for her gift of languages and her knowledge of customs and idiosyncrasies, attributes that brought her closer to Captain Hernan Cortes and enabled her to subjugate the imperial city of Tenochtitlan.

The reviled interpreter—from then until today—had a dark end, and her role in the history of Mexico remains a matter of debate. Sor Juana Ines de la Cruz (Soriano, 2020) was noted for her great literary ability, captivating several viceroys while in defiance of the almost angelic status of a woman at the time. Although her work is now recognised, she remains a unique case in all of colonial Mexico. She lived cloistered to pay the price of knowledge.

On the path to independent Mexico, among the many women who took part in the rebellion against the Spanish crown, the name of Leona Vicario appears. She, along with her husband Andres Quintana Roo, took up the fight and entered the battlefield. Later, she refused to join the court of the Austrian Empress Carlota, wife of Maximilian, who founded the Mexican Empire without much success and with a tragic end

(National Institute of Historical Studies of the Revolutions of Mexico, 2020).

The vicissitudes of Mexican women can be enumerated one by one; names are gradually uncovered and ennobled, breaking through the wall of silence that once restrained them. The transgressions are not long in coming: Amelio Robles (Rocha, 2019) participated in the armed movement of 1910 and was recognised for his military capacity, for his brave character in confronting the enemy. He retired with honours, but his real identity appears in the records as Amelia de Jesus Robles Avila. A transman—a woman who joins the war hiding her gender.

The panorama of outstanding women in Mexico during the twentieth century moves the mechanisms of the present, and in another millennium, it will be necessary to build a clean, wide and luminous path for equitable treatment where diversity is the great difference that unites humanity.

Movement of Mexican Women's Bodies: From Illegitimate to Legitimate

Without the advances generated by the women of the twentieth century, it would have been difficult to make inroads into unimaginable fields (Galeana, 2013). The actions of these women allowed progress to make its way ever more firmly into the public sphere and into originally masculinised fields, including the body and movement (Salazar & Manzo, 2020).

The public figure of Mexican women, as elsewhere, is framed by stereotypes. From childhood, being a woman implies differentiation in treatment, a subordination to the presence of men in the home, whether fathers, brothers or close relatives. Their physical development presupposes less resistance and competitive power to respond to patterns where creativity and intellect are less important than their sensitivity (Blanco, 1993).

The management of the female body is at a crossroads between objectification, where the physical body is overvalued and directly related to the satisfaction of exclusively sexual and reproductive male pleasure, and the transformative proposal to break with the stereotypes and imposed schemes to achieve liberation and control of its structure (Coral-Diaz, 2010). Beauty (entirely relative and abstract), fragility, enduring youth, the immobile state of their corporal image (Loaeza, 1995b), only provoke a permanent state of dissatisfaction in the face of the changes that the present time offers.

The body, male or female, is surrounded by the group, class, geographical region and culture (Bourdieu, 2000) and provokes a rapprochement by affinity, the identification by resemblance of the one who holds the strength and power with the one who is endangered. As occurs between nations, as seen throughout history, with similarities to colonisation, one gender dominates another; memory makes masculinity seem more important (Jimenez, 2012). The male body suggests strength, achievement, triumph. The feminine is assumed, on the contrary, to polarise the coexistence of both, a situation that takes on distinct tones in today's societies but that, for reasons of permanent memory (Gonzalez & Melero, 2012), is anchored in the tradition—that is, where everything that refers to confrontation, achievement, strength and movement evokes the man.

In recent generations, the feminine, in a process of structuring–destructuring–restructuring, opens the possibility of establishing new forms of male–female relationships. This paradigm shift is proactive and likely to increase, on the one hand, the visibility of feminine work in all social fields; and on the other, the recognition of its potential in the change of tasks dedicated or defined as masculine (Venegas et al., 2015).

The practice of football has allowed the social figure of Mexican women to make inroads into a patriarchal field. Subsequently, with the support of gender policies during the 1960s and 1970s, together with the expansion of opportunities through the International Olympic Committee (IOC), female participation in the sport grew with a higher competitive level and professional character (Ulloa et al., 2017).

The various ways of experiencing football within Mexican society must be observed from several spheres; contextual and historical considerations provoke permanent discussions from and within the feminine vision. Football mobilises women in a social and sporting sense, and the horizons of this process are analysed in the following. In Mexico, the public practice of football dates back to the 1960s, preceded by the English feminist movements (Santillan & Gantus, 2010).

Mexico's Football Culture and the Arrival of Women

The historical roots of football in Mexico date back to the nineteenth century with the arrival of British immigrants, who initiated the practice of football as a form of recreation and entertainment. In a short time, this new sport spread to the children and young people of the country, especially Mexico's upper classes, who played it in their schools, where football had been incorporated into the curriculum with the intention of motivating students through collective entertainment (Angelotti, 2008). Football, as a pedagogical tool, constituted the ideal means to train the new generations in the benefits of associative activities, promoting actions organised around common objectives, even though it would ultimately become a professional, massive, normalised and institutionalised sport through the form of club companies (Angelotti, 2005).

Traditionally, football has become part of Mexican culture, with various meanings as a manifestation of nationality or masculinity, within the considerations for coexistence in a communal party. Likewise, it involves artistic, political, social and economic manifestations that produce approaches beyond the sporting field (Alabarces, 2003). In this sense, Ferreiro (2003) mentions that football is an ideal laboratory to understand the complex antagonistic ritual between fans.

Rivalries do not recognise borders, race, religion nor social position, but they do identify gender in terms of a label placed on a person. At the same time, there has been an assumption that only men play football; that is to say, for spectators, men are a reference for practice. There is a certain masculinisation of football; male footballers take into account the criteria of winning or participating, even as female footballers highlight other values such as helping or encouraging (Acuna-Gomez & Acuna, 2016)

In 1970, the press played a fundamental role in the dissemination, promotion and development of women's football when the first Women's Football World Championship was held in Italy and a year later when it was organised in Mexico. These competitions led the International Federation of Association Football (FIFA) to consider the option of a women's version of the World Cup. An invitation was made and only 12 nations agreed to participate, including Mexico; however, the first FIFA Women's World Cup would not be held until 1991 in China (Santillan & Gantus, 2010).

In Mexico, since the 1960s, women have openly played football; however, it would take dozens of years for there to be a professional Women's Football League there. On December 5, 2016, Enrique Bonilla,[1] president of the Liga MX Varonil (Men's MX League) at that time, announced the birth of the Liga MX Femenil to be launched in 2017. The women's teams correspond directly to the men's teams of each MX league-registered one, ushering in a new era of women's participation in football (Lopez & Robles, 2019).

University Football as the MX Professional League's Platform

Women, as the story goes (Angelotti, 2008), began to play in the streets or on the courts of the Mexican plains in the company of friends, neighbours and/or relatives; later came the organisation of neighbourhood clubs or teams, followed by the integration of federated sport and the creation of municipal and state leagues (Angelotti, 2005). This expansion allowed schools to participate in national events for children and youngsters, as well as first-division tournaments sponsored by phone or soft drink companies.

Then, hand in hand with the promotion of the University Games, women's sport was opened in the universities, and the growing push led

---

[1] *Source:* Lopez, C. & Robles K. (2019). Mexican women's football: almost half a century of history and barely three years of being a reality. https://cnnespanol.cnn.com/2019/04/10/el-futbol-femenino-mexicano-casi-medio-siglo-de-historia-y-apenas-tres-anos-de-ser-una-realidad/

these institutions to find the best football players in the country and give them scholarships to build competitive teams. Some of the Liga MX Femenil teams are now university franchises made up mostly of female players who have been recruited with the primary idea of studying and playing at the same time, as Coronado (2020) mentions; and their performance in the classroom and on the field synergise to consolidate Liga MX Femenil during each season.

The proposal to use university players to reinforce the Liga MX Femenil is based on the university sports model in the United States. The university competitions are separated into State-level, then national and then the teams are inducted into professional football. Its main characteristic is its diversity and decentralisation without the intervention of the Ministry of Education (Terol, 2006).

The sense of identity that a football team can generate is closely linked to the university or team to which a person belongs. University football teams are a link to professional identity; prior to 2017, it was the closest thing to being professional. Yet, players were limited to competing for four or five years depending on their degree. Nonetheless, university sport became a platform for young people to select academic continuity through sports scholarships that consisted of financial support to pay for their studies.

University sport creates situations of professional belonging where wearing the team's shirt is also assuming the identity of professional practice. The university as an institution that generates knowledge is a place where the sport of football is an object of scientific study and a generator of the knowledge that society seeks to produce (Rivera, 2005). In the same way, being part of a group, collective or team breaks with daily university life. According to Connor Bracken (2020), in the case of women football players who compete at a high level and study, they remain highly motivated in both academic and sporting spheres. Also, research has indicated that women who exercise get greater brain stimulation and increased energy levels, which leads to the improvement of their perception of well-being, self-esteem and regulation of cognitive processes, leading to better academic performance (Yoshiharu, 1996; Gruber, 1986; Ceballos et al., 2000).

Women academics and university students playing football are a new category of study; nowadays, the conditions of sporting opportunities, advances in terms of public gender policies and the social perception of women playing football have changed. Today, these women are academics, but they are also top-level and/or professional players in a national league.

The Methodological Process for Broadening Women Footballers' Perspective

To approach this group of women located in the country's public universities, a qualitative methodological process was designed with an anthropological and constructivist approach. In the absence of references to previous similar studies, it is useful to confront the object of knowledge and order the data available for analysis (Arnold, 1998). Constructivist research makes it possible to analyse the human experience and provide the structure for data analysis. '

> Human-observer and social systems are suspended in networks of meanings, co-participatively produced and externalised through language, which constitute their horizons of reality' (Arnold, 1998, p. 32).

The data-collection technique used was the interview, which Roberto Hernandez-Sampieri and Paulina Torres (2018) define as a meeting in which a person (the interviewer) and another person or persons, converse and exchange information about a topic through questions and answers, and communication and co-construction of meanings regarding the topic addressed is carried out. The instrument used was a semi-structured interview guide consisting of 34 questions divided into three main sections: (1) gender tasks and their current discussion (14 items), (2) gender stereotypes and social transformations (7 items), and (3) the changing female paradigm in sport versus academic life (13 items). The interviews offered access to the interviewees everyday life and experiences, perspectives and opinions on the topic addressed.

Female academics who play football were selected using the snowball technique—'a technique for finding research subjects. In it, one subject gives the researcher another name, and the researcher provides the name of a third, and so on' (Atkinson & Flint, as cited in Baltar & Gorjup, 2012, p. 132). At the end of the process, there were 14 subjects, all Mexican women who study at a postgraduate level or work in public universities as professors and play at a university, semi-professional and/or professional level.

The application of the instrument was carried out between the months of February and April 2021 through videoconferencing on the Google Meet platform. This facilitated access to these women, as their sporting and academic commitments kept them busy while the distances between cities in the context of the COVID-19 pandemic made face-to-face meetings difficult.

University Women Playing Football: Reality and Challenges

The analysis of the construction made by university women who play football, referring to the tasks of gender and its current discussion was developed under the scheme of semantic association (Arellano, 2015) and interpretation of discourse (Leon, 2015) and applied to each response to the questions asked. The participants in the study were composed of 10 women who live and play football in the State of Nuevo Leon, an industrial locality—one of the three most populated in Mexico—bordering the United States, whereas the rest of the participants were from the central and western regions of Mexico.

The average age of the interviewees was 31.9 years of age; 4 have a master's degree, 2 have a doctorate and 2 have a bachelor's degree. Seven of the women have a job associated with exercise science and three were in administration. Half were teachers or members of the academic community, 30% collaborate with university centres and 20% were postgraduate scholarship students and have sporting functions at the institution.

Eight informants had a late start in their sporting careers; they were not able to begin until secondary school or even had to wait until they came of age before deciding to play at the university. In their experiences, we found a lack of sport initiation opportunities or programmes, sport promotion campaigns, sport role models, social and sport support from family and peers and a gender-sensitive sport culture. It is the student sport system that allows these women academics who play football to access the sport in an autonomous, independent and socially protected way through school representation and the comprehensive training provided by the sporting discipline (see Table 10.1).

Social labelling of women footballers is associated with discrimination or aggression because of prejudice and lack of social recognition. In other words, labelling women with words that associate incomplete masculinity (i.e., homosexuality) or anomaly (Butler, 2007), as Didier Eribon (2004) points out, perpetuates mental and cultural structures that sustain inferiority, condemnation and rejection. Strauss (in Butler, 2007), from the theory of sexual oppression and the limitations of the body, explains how these representations of women footballers condition the equality of men and women in relation to a political, social and cultural systems that explains their capacities within the framework of a hostile sexism in which patriarchal culture oppresses women in various areas of life. It is understandable that many women drop out at an early age or wait until an advanced age to take up football again (Montoya, 2012).

The words related to masculinity are: *machorra, marimacha and guacha,*[2] whereas those associated with homosexuality are lesbian and *Ranma 1/2*[3] (see Diagram 10.1). Luisa Orozco and Dignora Usuga (2018) define 'butch' women or tomboys as masculine women who develop longings for other women and have short hair and masculine clothing, posture and movement. These adjectives express a fear of the masculinisation of women (Eribon, 2004) as well as significant discrimination against women who participate in disciplines that break with the feminine—the delicate.

---

[2] Translated to English, these terms mean butch, tomboy and slut.

[3] *Ranma 1/2* is a character from a Japanese Anime, which tells the story of a young martial artist who was cursed by falling into a lake. When he encounters cold water, he turns into a woman and returns to his male version in warm water.

Table 10.1 Beginnings in the Practice of Football and the Motivational Elements for Deciding to Enter Competitive and Professional Football

Informant	Beginnings in football	Motivation for starting football
1	In secondary school is when I started to know about *sporting events*, and that's when I became more interested in being or belonging to a team.	I saw a live match of the Mexican national team versus Barcelona.
2	I had certain skills that distinguished me from the *rest of the girls and boys*, but I couldn't play.	I struggled to find a place to start playing on a team and it wasn't until high school that I was able to.
3	I started playing football when I was five years old, and I have played football all my life. *I played in a team of adults.*	The team belonged to the family, so social support was an important motivation.
4	Very interested in participating in the *different activities that were carried out in the schools.*	Motivated always by the coach that I was included in the teams.
5	Until I was 11 years old, I was playing *in the street and in physical education classes in primary school*	I was encouraged to go to university to play football; they had a team there.
6	I started at the age of five *in a children's football team.*	I was attracted by the matches and the press reports, the coverage of the Mexican national team.
7	I started in the sport very young, when I was five or six years old *when I entered primary school*, so I was always aiming for the teams from that level.	No answer
8	*I started playing in high school*, that's when I really started to have the qualities to be at university team levels.	My father was a coach and his work made me feel confident to practice.
9	I was playing in the street. and I had the opportunity when I was in fifth or sixth grade to start.	The university league made me feel that I could play at a good level.
10	In secondary school, when I started playing fast football and I continued all through secondary school, then high school and finally in undergraduate school.	No answer

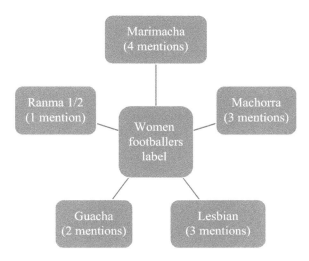

Diagram 10.1   Representation of the labels applied to women footballers

The stereotyping of gender and social transformations in the lives of female football players is inscribed in their own representation of gender, feminist empowerment and female leadership (see Diagram 10.2). A binary sex-gender perspective is observed in their definition of gender (Butler, 2007), and only four players came close to the social structure of masculine or feminine. In the case of feminism, the relationship that can be seen is closer to a social movement with an ideology that seeks equity as well as equal rights and opportunities (Ordonez, 2011). This vision is connected to the representation achieved through empowerment and leadership: feeling rebellious, outstanding, free, intelligent, autonomous, persistent and with rights, which makes the woman determined to continue seeking development opportunities for younger generations.

The perception of change that university women footballers construct with respect to sports is underwritten by the visibility of achievements and a greater presence of public policies for women and opportunities in decision making (see Table 10.2). These achievements do not indicate that a gender policy is being followed in sport, rather several of these progressive advances are driven mainly by global feminist movements (Klavenes et al., 2020) and, to a lesser extent, the development of policies

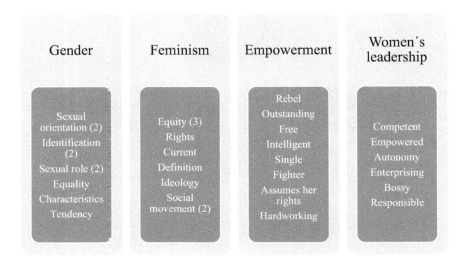

Gender	Feminism	Empowerment	Women's leadership
Sexual orientation (2)	Equity (3)	Rebel	Competent
Identification (2)	Rights	Outstanding	Empowered
Sexual role (2)	Current	Free	Autonomy
Equality	Definition	Intelligent	Enterprising
Characteristics	Ideology	Single	Bossy
Tendency	Social movement (2)	Fighter	Responsible
		Assumes her rights	
		Hardworking	

Diagram 10.2 Representation of the words gender, feminism, empowerment and women's leadership

of global organisations such as the United Nations (UN), the UN Educational, Scientific and Cultural Organization (UNESCO) and the IOC.

One of the most significant achievements in the last five years has been the formalisation of the Liga MX Femenil, which brings together the best Mexican women footballers in sports affiliates that play in the top circuit of Mexican football. It initially started as a quota (Poncela, 2011), an obligation,[4] and in the second year it became an outcome with unexpected audience reach and record-breaking numbers in Internet

---

[4] In Mexico, the theory of the representation movement had a great impact on the recognition as a right for women to achieve representation and parity in various public scenarios, together with the reforms carried out by FIFA in 2016 to promote the development of women's football, which led to teams in the men's league having a women's team in the same division as a rule of participation.

Table 10.2 Women Academic Football Players' Perceptions of Change and Opportunity for Women Today

Unit of analysis	Perception of change
Sporting progress	Well, I think that there is a very drastic process of change; I think that now the exposure of women's sport has increased a lot. (I1)
	Empowering sportswomen has allowed us to demand more. (I2)
	When I started, there were no women referees; there were no women to lead the teams. (I3)
	There are very, very good female players who the world does not know as well as the men who are very famous and who even go to other foreign leagues to play. (I4)
	Progress has been made in the participation of women in sport, marketing, sales, politics, social material for politics. (I5)
	I think they already have many opportunities; you can even make a living from some sports. (I6)
	There is more openness from all the structures of sport, talking about sportswomen as such, coaches, referees, people who are in technical management. (I10)
Public policies	Some struggles and initiatives for wage differences between female and male athletes. (I1)
	I know some proposals of political parties, but not political as such. (I2)
	The Law on Physical Culture and a PILARES programme that addresses women's demands around sport. (I3)
	Little. (I4)
	No. (I5)
	Changes in the rules of the Football League that protect women with their salary if they become pregnant. (I6)
	I don't really know much about public policy; I don't know much about this. (I10)

(continued)

Table 10.2 (continued)

Unit of analysis	Perception of change
Decision making	There are more women directors of sports institutes. (I1)
	In the MX League, women have arrived at the head of sports projects and teams. (I2)
	There is a lack of women leaders. (I3)
	The cases I know of do not know the core of sport; they have got to know it when they are put in that sporting or administrative position. (I4)
	They have been very good; the first director of sports institutes at a national level lasted 12 years, which has allowed the openings for other women. Currently, there are 7 out of 32 in states and a national director. (I9)
	There are women directors who were sportswomen, who trained in the area and who are also academics and researchers, which indicates enormous progress and offers certainty about decisions. (I10)

I = Informant

broadcasting,[5] stadium attendance and the sales of products and club shirts, indicating the increasing interest of young women footballers in following the new Mexican women's football stars. Thus, regarding the Liga MX Femenil, the women academics are of the opinion that:

I3: It is in development, it is growing, it seems to me that there are many things that can be improved … it lacks many adaptations, much more support from the directors, more exposure.

I5: Excellent project, which lacks economic support, the same conditions for women's as for men's teams.

I6: It is a growing league, with a great future if it is given the recognition it deserves … people became interested in women's football, something that the clubs did not expect. They broke so many records of full

---

[5] Women's teams in 2021 generated almost 52 million interactions across Twitter, Facebook, Instagram and YouTube, with growth in the digital environment derived from low engagement in the traditional media environment. *Source:* El Mister: https://elmister.substack.com/. Women's football fans found in digital media the opportunity to follow and be part of the Liga MX Femenil story; this is corroborated by Nielsen Sports, MX League and HR Ratings that on average there are between 257,000 and 300,000 people watching Liga MX Femenil matches every week, which gives women's football approximately 10.2 million viewers per year (only for the 34 regular season dates).

stadiums, streaming, goals, everything, and I think that the league did not expect that.

I9: Now the matches are broadcast on Facebook or on one of the team's channels because they are looking for that interaction with all the people; there are matches that have 15–20,000 viewers, 10,000 views.

I10: I have followed press releases or videos; I think it is good, the fact that I know that some of the graduates of the faculty participate there, the fact that they are young, that they have recognition beyond being athletes, as people, as professionals is what makes it extraordinary.

The effects that Liga MX Femenil has had on women footballers in the country go in two directions: the first towards the transformation to a professional profile—today, a female footballer must be dedicated to discipline, maintain optimal physical preparation, mental toughness and sporting adaptability (relying on 'invisible training') while possessing a minimum academic preparation or using media resources to further her education—— and the second corresponds to a social impact related to the deconstruction of the masculinised imaginary of Mexican football. In other words, the political impetus of FIFA and consequently FEMEXFUT, as well as media exposure, led to the normalisation and homogenisation (Butler, 2007) of women playing football, as these informants noted:

I1: Today, girls can see football as a job; we always saw it as a hobby and pastime.

I6: In the news, women's football is now being shown more and more often.

I10: It is already a possible scenario to be a professional.

Finally, women academic footballers, as a generation of transformation and empowerment, now see that the great opportunity to change the imaginary, the panorama and the showcase spectacle is possible, to the extent that:

I1: Playing at a good level of football and with values shows the physical and mental strength of this new generation.

I2: Sports projects with a high level of professionalisation.

I4: Ignore social labels; just be a woman who plays football.

I6: The new generation of football players must prepare themselves to be professionals.

I9: Congruence in sporting life, public life, to be a role model, to inspire and be a parameter.

Conclusions

The group of women who study or work in tertiary educational institutions has a very different way of seeing football than other groups of women footballers, such as those who were not able to study for a university degree and those who have reached the professional football league with degrees or just because they are very talented. When we reflect on the diversity of women footballers, it is clear that there is not a single category of women; there are university women, women from the Mexican plains, women from sports clubs, women from veteran leagues, women from the national team or those who play in professional leagues in Mexico and the world. This study's category of university women footballers is one that experiences sporting independence through the student sector, understood as the school representative space; in other words, the permissiveness of the family and society protects and approves of them when they represent their school, high school or university in events organised by educational institutions.

The social structure of their position on the playing field, with respect to their sporting and human rights, is firm and powerful; they are determined to seek conditions to improve their opportunities, and especially those of the next generations. The academics who play football understand that feminism is an ideological current and a mechanism to reinforce and intellectually train women to empower themselves to assume sporting leadership in the face of the challenges they face in the development of grassroots sport and the working and sporting conditions of the professional world.

The academics who play football emphasise the perception of progress and advancement of women in sport as great advances, but not yet enough to be transformed into tangible opportunities for themselves and the new generations. They have established a greater presence in the media and have observed that women's movements and protests are already seeing results in the modification of laws, the proposed regulations and the creation of public policies.

In five years, the Liga MX Femenil, from the perspective of academic women footballers, has led to the breaking of stereotypes of women's football (i.e., once perceived as slow, boring and unable to generate interest). Commercial brands have invested heavily in the league and its outstanding players, models of sporting success have been developed that have inspired new generations and players have gained recognition of sporting rights—for example, security during pregnancy, major medical insurance, job recognition, clothing that meets the requirements of fitness and comfort, increased presence of women in decision-making positions (38% are female coaches and 27% are female sports administrators) and protection from harassment and discrimination through a national protocol.

Nevertheless, pay equity and discrepancy in terms of awards or bonuses is one of the least advanced areas in the league; although, it is relevant that the league and the women's teams are beginning to become profitable in terms of their own income, which would generate financial autonomy (i.e., because they continue to be financed by the men's league) and better scenarios for Mexican women footballers.

Finally, feminist movements also have brought about a change in the labels of women footballers, and they, strengthened and empowered by global campaigns such as #MeToo and #8 M, have made assertions and constantly pointed out misogynistic expressions and instances of micro-machismo by managers, journalists and players in the men's league.

References

Acuna-Gomez, G., & Acuna, A. (2016). Football as a cultural product: Literature review and analysis. *Citius, Altius, Fortuis, 9*(2), 31–58. http://cdeporte. rediris.es/revcaf/Numeros%20de%20revista/Vol%209%20n2/Vol9_n2_ Acunna_Acunna.pdf

Alabarces, P. (2003). *Futbologies: Football, identity and violence in Latin America. CLASCO,* Latin American Council for Social Studies. http://biblioteca. clacso.edu.ar/gsdl/collect/clacso/index/assoc/D2295.dir/alabarces2.pdf

Angelotti, G. (2005). The dynamics of football in Mexico. The construction of collective identities around the football club in our times. *Efdeportes Digital Journal, 10* (82). https://www.efdeportes.com/efd82/pachuca.htm

Angelotti, G. (2008). *Football and identity. The historical formation of sport and the construction of collective identities around Mexican football.* Thesis. Centre for Anthropological Studies. https://colmich.repositorioinstitucional.mx/ jspui/bitstream/1016/225/1/AngelottiPasteurGabrielH%C3%A9ct or2008Tesis.pdf

Arellano, A. (2015). Natural semantic networks. A research technique for the study of meaning. In A. E. Perez Barajas (Ed.), *Techniques for Linguistic Research and Related Disciplines* (pp. 331–346).

Arnold, M. (1998). Resources for systemic/constructivist research. Moebio tape. *Journal of Social Science Epistemology, 3.* https://revistaatemus.uchile.cl/index. php/CDM/article/view/26454/27747

Baltar, F., & Gorjup, M. T. (2012). Online mixed sampling: An application in hidden populations. *Intangible Capital,* 123–149.

Blanco, J. (1993). *The Adventure of Mexican Cinema: In the Golden Age and After.* Grijalbo.

Bourdieu, P. (2000). *Things Said.* Gedisa.

Bracken, C. (2020). *The impact of NAIA student-athletes' academic and athletic motivation on academic performance.* [Doctoral dissertation, Eastern Oregon University.]

Butler, J. (2007). *Gender in Dispute: Feminism and the Subversion of Identity.* Paidós.

Ceballos, J., Ochoa, J., & Cortez, E. (2000). Depression in adolescence. Its relationship with sports activity and drug use. *IMSS Journal of Medicine, 38*(5), 371–379.

Coral-Diaz, A. M. (2010). The sexualized female body: Between gender constructions and justice and peace law. *International Law: Colombian Journal of International Law, 17,* 381–409.

Coronado, N. (2020). *University Football Enriches Women's MX League.* Udeportes.   https://puntou.uanl.mx/u-deportes/futbol-universitario-enriquece-a-liga-mx-femenil/

Eribon, D. (2004). *Insult and the Making of the Gay Self.* Duke University Press.

Ferreiro, J. P. (2003). Not even death will separate us, from heaven I will cheer you on. Notes on identity and football in Jujuy. In P. Alabarces (comp.), *Futbologies. Football, Identity and Violence in Latin America* (pp. 57–74). Buenos Aires: Latin American Council of Social Sciences.

Galeana, P. (2013). *Breaking the Glass Ceiling. Women in Science, Education and Financial Independence.* FEMU.

Glanz, M. (2013). *The Malinche, Her Parents and Her Children.* Taurus.

Gonzalez, A. D. L., & Melero, M. A. A. (2012). *Living together in equality. Preventing male violence against women at all educational stages.* UNED.

Gruber, J. (1986). Physical activity and self-esteem development in children: A meta-analysis. In G. A. Stull & H. M. Eckert (Eds.), *Effects of Physical Activity on Children.* Human Kinetics.

Hernandez-Sampieri, R., & Torres, C. P. M. (2018). *Research Methodology.* McGraw-Hill InterAmerican.

Jimenez, A. R. C. (2012). Masculinity and femininity: What are we talking about? *Educare Electronic Journal, 16*, 5–13.

Klavenes, H., Orea-Giner, A., Garcia-Muiña, F. E., & Fuentes-Moraleda, L. (2020). Gender and the #MeToo effect in Spanish professional football organisations: An exploratory qualitative approach. *Gender in Management, 35*(4)), 349–371.

Kuper, G. Z. (2015). Women in Mexico's economic and political spheres of power. *Mexicana Journal of Political and Social Sciences, 60*(223), 61–94.

Lakoff, G., & Johnson, M. (1983). *Metaphors of Everyday Life.* Catedra.

Leon, A. O. (2015). Critical discourse and the ethnographic interview. A multi-disciplinary approach. In A. E. Perez Barajas (Ed.), *Techniques for Linguistic Research and Related Disciplines* (pp. 203–232).

Loaeza, G. (1995a). *Good People's Handbook* (Vol. 1). Plaza & Janes.

Loaeza, G. (1995b). *The Good Girls.* Oceano.

Lopez, C., & Robles, K. (2019). Mexican women's football: almost half a century of history and barely three years of being a reality. CNN Sports. https://cnnespanol.cnn.com/2019/04/10/el-futbol-femenino-mexicano-casi-medio-siglo-de-historia-y-apenas-tres-anos-de-ser-una-realidad/

Montoya, M. (2012). *Other ways of being a woman: social representations of women's football in Pereira, from their grassroots organisations.* [Doctoral dissertation, Technological University of Pereira. Faculty of Health Sciences, Sports and Recreation Sciences.]

National Institute of Historical Studies of the Revolutions of Mexico. (2020). *Leona Vicario, insurgent heroine.* Secretariat of Culture of the Government of the State of Mexico.

Ordonez, A. (2011). Gender and sport in today's society. *Polemika, 3*(7).

Orozco, L., & Usuga, D. (2018). *Social representations about lesbian women, gay men, transgender women or men held by young people in grade eleven of the Arturo Velasquez Ortiz and San Luis Gonzaga educational institutions in Santa Fe de Antioquia.* Master's Degree Thesis, University of Antioquia.

Poncela, A. M. F. (2011). Gender quotas and women's political representation in Mexico and Latin America. *Arguments (Mexico, DF), 24*(66), 247–274.

Ramirez, M. C. C. (2018). *Ecuadorian women and sports journalism: Gender roles in television programmes: Estadio TV and 100XCiento Football.* Bachelor's thesis, Quito: UCE.

Rivera, E. (2005). Culture and football, the generation of knowledge from the University. *University Digital Journal, UNAM, 6*(6), 1–8. http://www.revista. unam.mx/vol.6/num6/art55/jun_art55.pdf

Rocha, M. (2019, June 4). *Amelio Robles, the first recognised transgender revolutionary.* The current. History, arts and culture.

Salazar, C., & Manzo, E. (2020). Public policy in Mexican women's sport. In L. M. Lara (Ed.), *Sports and Gender: The Margin from the Margins* (pp. 27–42). Autonomous University of Juarez City/ Autonomous University of Mexico State.

Santillan, M., & Gantus, F. (2010). *Feminine Transgressions: Football. A Look from the Press Cartoon, Mexico 1970–1971.* Scielo. http://www.scielo.org.mx/ scielo.php?script=sci_arttext&pid=S0188-28722010000200005

Soriano, A. V. (2020). *Sor Juana Ines de la Cruz, verb doncella.* Ministry of Culture and Sport of the State of Mexico.

Terol, R. (2006). Study on university sports models in the United States, Canada and Australia. University of Alicante. http://www.planamasd.es/sites/default/ files/programas/medidas/actuaciones/modelo-deporte-universitario-eeuu-can-au pdf

Ulloa, R. D., Ciro, M. M., & Ortiz, L. C. (2017). Sports and gender equality. *Economia UNAM, 40*, 121–133.

Venegas, M., Chacon-Gordillo, P., & Fernandez-Castillo, A. (2015). *From Gender Equality to Sexual and Gender Equality. Educational and Social Reflections.* Dykinson S. L.

Yoshiharu, N. (1996). Relationship between physical activity habits and endurance fitness in college students. *Bulletin of Institute of Health and Sport Sciences, 19*, 159–166.

11

Football and Gender in Chile: Impact of the 2008 FIFA U-20 Women's World Cup on the Participation of Chilean Women in the Sport

Miguel Cornejo Amestica, Carlos Matus Castillo, and Carolina Paz Cabello Escudero

Introduction

Throughout history, women's football has faced multiple barriers, even being considered inappropriate (Hjelm & Olofsson, 2003; Knoppers & Anthonissen, 2003). Over the past few decades, however, despite

M. Cornejo Amestica (✉)
Universidad de Concepción, Facultad de Educación, Concepción, Chile
e-mail: mcornejo@udec.cl

C. Matus Castillo
Universidad Católica de la Santísima Concepción, Facultad de Educación, Concepción, Chile
e-mail: cmatus@ucsc.cl

C. P. Cabello Escudero
Pontifica Universidad Católica de Valparaíso, Instituto de Historia, Valparaíso, Chile
e-mail: carolina.cabello.e@mail.pucv.cl

187

remaining a marginal practice in relation to men's football, women's football has grown around the world in areas such as competitions and the number of female players (Mahmoud, 2017). Historically, football has been considered a male sport (Martín & García Manso, 2011; Llopis-Goig, 2010), not only a product of gender stereotypes and prejudicial categorisation of what is feminine and masculine but also establishing behavioural models that standardise gender roles (González Gavaldón, 1999; Lamas, 1999). As a result, it has been very difficult for women to occupy and build spaces for participation in this sport because of the prevailing gender stereotypes in society, the non-application of equal rights and direct and indirect discrimination in it (Yori, 2020).

To understand this issue, it is helpful to use a gender perspective, intended to contribute to the strengthening of a democratic model in which the demand for better relationships benefits both men and women in all their diversity (Fontecha, 2006). Using a gender approach implies critically analysing how the social system delimits spaces and resources for men and women and conditions their choices as well as how the symbolic and real order of gender hierarchises—what is considered masculine—over that is deemed to be feminine (Donoso & Velasco, 2013).

Despite the barriers and situations mentioned here, the Fédération Internationale de Football Association (FIFA) has identified objectives for the growth of women's football (e.g., increasing participation of girls in the sport, improving retention rates of women footballers, increasing women's participation in management positions and enhancing competitions). Through the achievement of these objectives, FIFA seeks to reduce gender gaps and promote the practice of sports by women. These initiatives can be found in the FIFA Women's Football Strategy (FIFA, 2018), which has five pillars: (1) develop and grow the sport; (2) improve competitions; (3) communicate and commercialise to broaden exposure and increase marketable value; (4) govern and start to increase women's representation in managerial positions and promote professionalisation; (5) educate and empower, building capacity and knowledge about the sport. One of the main goals is to reach 60 million female players by 2026. This is an ambitious target given that in 2019, FIFA estimated that a total of 13.36 million girls and adult women played organised football worldwide (FIFA, 2019).

Keeping this in mind, it becomes essential to understand both the current state of women's football and its development in specific contexts. Therefore, this chapter is focused on Chile, and it seeks to describe the historical development, characteristics and context of competitive Chilean women's football from the 2008 FIFA U-20 Women's Football World Cup in Chile to qualification for the 2020 Tokyo Olympic Games. It contains a contextualisation of women's sport practices in this country; a description of the historical development of Chilean women's football; an analysis of the main women's footballing events in Chile; an examination of the role of women in the development of this sport; and an identification of the differences and gaps between women's and men's football at the competitive level.

Regarding the methodology used here, heuristic work was carried out to compile sources, using gender as a category of analysis for historical study (Scott, 1986), which describes as well as orients the research towards new problematisations, offering background information that promotes academic discussion regarding the future of Chilean women's football. The methodological approach used is a balance between a documentary review with aspects of social history, particularly Chilean football, and the general history of women and gender relationships (Hernández, 2004). For this purpose, primary and secondary sources of information were selected for analysis; they were used to construct a wide range of testimonies to guide the sections of this chapter. Among the primary sources, the authors highlight historical archives of sports organisations, government documents, interviews and the national press. The secondary sources include information collected from scientific articles and books on the subject.

Chilean Women's Participation in Football

The arrival of modern sport in Chile occurred in the same way as in other European countries, as function of two concrete aspects: the British influence and the arrival of these practices through seaports, as was the case for Italy, Spain and France (Matus et al., 2018; Pujadas & Santacana, 2003). During the mid-nineteenth century, the first sporting activities in Chile began to be recorded, which were initially developed by European immigrants. These sports were then practiced by the Chilean aristocracy (Modiano, 1997). The main cities through which 'modern sport' entered were the ports of Iquique and Antofagasta in the north, Valparaíso in the centre and Talcahuano in the south-central part of Chile (Matus et al., 2018). The sports performed the most from the middle to late nineteenth century were cricket, hunting, golf, tennis and equestrian activities; the main participants were members of the upper classes and men (Santa Cruz, 2006). In this sense, Mercado (2007) pointed out that the emergence of modern English sport also served as a means of conveying masculine values.

During early Chilean sport, women's participation was low, limited to recreational and social traditions only. There is little information about whether Chilean women practiced any type of sport in a regular or competitive way, beyond the recreational ways of the two first decades of the twentieth century (Mercado, 2007). As Santa Cruz (2006) argued, the history of national sport in these first decades was eminently masculine; women only participated marginally, limiting themselves to the role of spectator and/or practitioner of an activity that would emphasise and, in any case, not undermine their femininity—or what was considered feminine from the prevailing masculine point of view.

Since the 1920s women have participated in more 'popular' sports such as boxing and cycling, revealing the popular origins of the practitioners (Marín, 2007). In the following years and decades, women began to participate in competitive sports, registering important outcomes at the international level, even though mainly in individual sports. Although Chilean women's participation in sports at the elite level increased significantly during the twentieth century and the beginning of the twenty-first century, their participation has always been lower than that of men (Azócar et al., 2012).

This was not only the case in Chile but also it was seen in other countries and contexts given the multiple barriers that have affected women's development in sports (Hartmann-Tews, 2006; Scheerder et al., 2005; Van Tuyckom et al., 2010). It is possible to consider, for example, the male models of physical education as well as the historical sexual division between men and women, gender stereotypes and social roles attributed to women (Macías, 1999). Additionally, women's sports have received limited media coverage, which has made its characteristics, growth and needs invisible (Calvo & Gutiérrez, 2017; Sainz de Baranda, 2014).

In the case of Chile, there are barriers associated with gender stereotypes and roles that affect the participation of women in physical activity and sports (Cornejo-Améstica et al., 2019). Furthermore, a factor that could influence lower female participation in sport in general has been physical education in schools. The research indicates that this subject was taught with an androcentric approach—where sexist behaviours and activities were observed as exclusive for girls and boys—and content focused on sporting competitions, often leading to the self-marginalisation of girls from physical education classes (Hidalgo & Amonacid, 2014; Poblete & Moreno, 2015; Rodríguez et al., 2017).

Currently, the results of surveys on sporting habits from 2006 to 2018 in the Chilean adult population (Ministerio del Deporte de Chile, 2019) indicate a significant increase in women's participation and interest in sport, although these levels were always lower than with men. More specifically, the following aspects also were observed among Chilean women:

- Greater participation in historically male sports (e.g., football)
- A preference for individual sport practices
- Motivations for sport participation associated with health and training
- Greater attendance at public sporting venues
- Less spending on sports than men spent
- Lower participation rates in sporting organisations than men
- Motherhood and lack of time as the main reasons for abandonment of physical activity

This information about female participation in Chilean sports can be understood through feminist and gender theory as a historically naturalised manifestation in a society where, at a cultural and structural level, power has been unequally distributed between men and women.

Following the renowned anthropologist Gayle Rubin (1986), the sex/gender system ought to be understood as the 'set of arrangements by which a society transforms biological sexuality into a product of human activity, and in which these transformed human needs are satisfied' (p. 97). Thus, the sex/gender system impacts all social practices, including football and sports. For historian Joan Scott (1986), gender is the social organisation of sexual difference—a social and historical construct—that has varied meanings across cultures, social spheres and time. In this way, history also acts as a mechanism for the production of knowledge about sexual difference. Therefore, the lack of historical legitimacy in the development of women's sport also affects female sport participation in the present.

On the other hand, authors, such as Pierre Bourdieu (2000) and Michael Foucault (1984), intensified their analysis of the power of the State in perpetuating processes of male domination, the reproduction of gender roles and the omission of women from history. An example of this is the National Policy of Physical Activity and Sport 2016–2025 of Chile (Ministerio del Deporte de Chile, 2016) that includes, among its structural approaches, a specific focus on '[g]ender, where sport is recognised as a tool that can collaborate in the reduction of gender gaps, which is materialised in the "Principles and Purposes"' of this policy (Cornejo-Améstica et al., 2019). As Cabello (2018) pointed out, however, it is necessary to know the real implications of this approach—that is, how it will materialise, what its objectives are and how the identified gaps will be addressed.

This analysis is important because the national policy (Ministerio del Deporte de Chile, 2016) indicates that, through physical activity and sport, women can (1) optimise health, (2) improve self-esteem and self-care, and (3) access leadership positions. Nevertheless, these objectives perpetuate stereotypes of women in sport and do not take into account other gender identities, thus becoming a binary policy and reproducing the hegemonic patriarchal order in all the structures of the Chilean State and national sport.

Development of Women's Football in Chile

During the early twentieth century, Chilean women's football burst onto the scene as a sporting practice with the creation of women's football clubs, thus initiating a complex path in a sporting tradition that has been dominated by men (Cabello, 2020). In 1919, a group of women's sports clubs met at the offices of the newspaper *El Mercurio* in Santiago, creating the first Women's Football Association in the country; it was made up of the following clubs: Flor de Chile, Delicias del Sport, Progreso Femenino, Unión Teatral, Flor del Sport, Bélgica Star and Compañía Chilena de Tabacos. The latter club emerged from the organisation of the female workers of the tobacco company and was created specifically to play football. The increased participation of women in the workforce during the first decades of the twentieth century—mainly in industries related to the production of clothing, as seamstresses or laundresses—led to both recreational activities and new popular sports that expanded rapidly among the female population living mostly in urban cities. The magazine *Los Sports*, which circulated between 1923 and 1931, categorised women's sports primarily as athletics, basketball, table tennis and cycling. It is very likely that some of the women of the aforementioned clubs also played these sports before playing football.

It should be noted that after the founding of the first Women's Football Association in Santiago, women's sports began to be recognised by the sports press of the time. It reported on a match between the clubs Flor del Sport and Delicias del Sport, describing them as 'nice women's clubs' (Reyes, 2019). Almost 10 years later, in 1928, the Aurora Porteña sport club of the coastal city of Coquimbo was founded and was made up of 11 players. At the same time, this was a period of struggles and demands by women for the attainment of civil and political rights—for example, the right to vote in political elections (Salazar & Pinto, 1999). Parallel to this context, women were always playing football,even though these traditions were kept within the limits of socially acceptable behaviour of the patriarchal structure and culture then (Cabello, 2020).

During the 1950s, the teams Las Dinamitas and Las Atómicas were formed in the capital city of Santiago, both of which were composed of women from the working classes and played the preliminary matches of men's clubs. These 'doubleheaders' captured the attention of the spectators. To the north of the capital, women's teams were also created, including the Colo-Colo club in Iquique, an amateur club that acquired the name of the professional soccer club of Santiago; Las Malulas and the Latino. The last two were from Vallenar (Cabello, 2020; Elsey & Nadel, 2020; Retamal, 2018).

In the second half of the twentieth century, some major milestones stand out (e.g., a 1972 international match at the National Stadium played by the Colo-Colo men's team and the Panama national team) as reported by the magazine *Estadio*. Here, the preliminary match was played between the Colo-Colo women's team and Mary Clair of the district of Las Condes. The magazine noted that 'the fans enjoyed the football graces of the girls' (Revista Estadio, 1972).

The National Amateur Football Association (ANFA) organised the Metropolitan Women's Football Cup during the 1980s. Then, in 1984, the Central Football Association expressed interest in planning a professional Women's Championship, but this idea never came to fruition. Nevertheless, the participation of women's teams in events became more frequent and evident. For example, in 1987, the Estrellas de California team was crowned champion in an international tournament in Mendoza, Argentina (Retamal, 2018).

The core of the first Chilean women's national football team was created from these championships. This team played in the Copa América of Brazil in 1991, achieving second place, with a prominent participation of Ada Cruz who won the golden ball. In this tournament, however, the Chilean team was unable to qualify for the first Women's World Cup in 1991 held in China (Castelblanco & Jara, 2007). The team had 18 players and was coached by Bernardo Bello. Some challenges pointed out by the coaching staff include the players' lack of tactical knowledge and fitness, which could be explained by their lives outside of football, together with the improvisation in the management of the team by the Chilean Football Federation. With the intention of complying with international pressures and showing itself at an global competition, the federation accepted an invitation to participate, without Chile even having a national women's league.

Milestones of Chilean Women's Football and Its Impact

Women's football has been played in Chile over the last 100 years, mainly at an amateur and recreational level. Despite the lack of support from sporting authorities, the sport's growth has not been impeded (Castelblanco & Jara, 2007). In this context, the participation of the senior women's national teamin the various versions of the Copa América between 1991 and 2018 has been a factor of great influence for the development of competitive football in this country.

Concerning this development process, a key element for the expansion of women's football was the organisation of the 2008 FIFA U-20 Women's World Cup in Chile, in addition to the recruitment of Spanish coach Marta Tejedor to as lead coach of the national team. At the same time, President Michelle Bachelet's administration, characterised by policies of gender equality, firmly supported this event (La Tercera, 2008).

During the same year, the National Professional Football Association (ANFP) organised the Women's First Division tournament called 'Copa Entel PCS', with the objective of enhancing the development of women's football. A total of 14 teams participated in this competition. Another action that joined forces in the promotion of competitive women's football was the Copa Chile SERNAM (National Women's Service), carried out in 2009–2010 with teams from all over the country participating, including a club from Easter Island (Pardo, 2009).

On the other hand, the Copa Libertadores Femenina de Futsal, organised in Chile by the ANFP in 2013, 2015 and 2016, helped make women's participation in the sport visible. In 2015, the director of SERNAM announced that more than 200 athletes participated in this competition, which highlighted the need to promote women's rights in Chile (Puranoticia.cl, 2015). In 2018, the Campeonato Sudamericano Femenino Sub-20 de Futsal (South American Women's U-20 Futsal Championship) was held in Chile with the 10 teams from the South American Football Confederation (CONMEBOL) participating (ANFP, 2018c). In this process of development and validation of women's football, the ANFP started a program in 2018 called 'CRECE', the objective of which was to promote investment in youth football for boys and girls (ANFP, 2018a).

Around this 'support' for women's football and as a way of promoting women's participation, CONMEBOL incorporated a new rule for its member associations; it states that men's clubs that participate in the Copa Libertadores de América and Copa Sudamericana must also have a women's team as of 2019. To comply with this new regulation, clubs must incorporate a first team and a women's youth category, which should participate in official tournaments. In the same way, clubs are required to have adequate facilities for women's teams, although this last requirement is less easily implemented (Marketing Registrado, 2018).

Following this development logic, the organisation of the 2018 Copa América Femenina de Fútbol represented a push towards the massification of this practice, where various actors, both governmental and private, supported this event. For example, the matches were broadcast on free-to-air television. Chile was crowned vice-champion of the tournament, allowing the country to qualify for the first time for a FIFA Women's World Cup held in France in 2019 (ANFP, 2019). The participation of the national team in the 2019 World Cup, alongside countries where women's football had already been developed significantly, represented a qualitative leap in the evolution of Chilean women's football, giving a boost to women's participation in professional and amateur teams.

Nevertheless, significant gaps in working and sporting conditions between women's and men's football still existed. In addition to the previous milestones that marked women's football in Chile, the authors must add the qualification of the national team to the Olympic Games (Tokyo, 2020), another first for the nation. This process of growth and sporting achievements has made Chilean players visible and positioned them in international leagues (i.e., France, Spain, Australia, among others), transforming them into sporting icons for girls and women who play this sport.

Women's Role in Football's Development in Chile

Even though 2019 marked 100 years since the establishment of the first Chilean Women's Football Association (Cabello, 2020), there are numerous examples that denounce the exclusion of women in the sport sector on a daily basis, not only for those associated with its practice but also with the political power, institutionality, decision making and presence in the media, among others. These factors make the participation and distribution of power, particularly in football, unequal between men and women. Faced with this situation, football players and women's groups have configured strategies to make their position visible within the national football landscape.

In 2016, groups of women footballers decided to come together and form two organisations that would eventually be key to the dissemination, positioning and recognition of women's football. The first of these is the COFFUF (Women's Football Development Corporation), which was created with the goal of bringing exposure to and supporting the work of the Chilean women's national team, as well as promoting the development of the sport in the country (Flores, 2018). The second key organisation is ANJUFF (the National Association of Women's Football Players), through which high-performance football players seek to regularise and improve the conditions of women's football, protecting and defending their rights (ANJUFF, 2020). These organisations include players and leaders (e.g., Iona Rothfeld, Javiera Moreno and Fernanda Pinilla (ANJUFF) as well as Daniela Pardo (COFFUF), all recognised for their demands for the professionalisation of women's football. In this sense, although women's participation in football has increased, this growth has not been accompanied by increased participation in political, management or decision-making spaces, which remain hegemonically male.

It should be noted that in the administrative structure of the ANFP, women make up only 0.8% of the organisation (1 out of 128 people). A similar situation is observed in professional football clubs, where the participation gap is also massive. In 2019, women composed only 4% of the boards of directors across Chilean clubs (Cabello, 2020). Faced with this reality, members and fans have articulated demands for more female participation in the sport's administration, creating associations of fans, gender commissions and feminist groups that question machismo and violence in clubs and boards. In 2020, these organisations created the *Coordinadora Feminista de Mujeres y Disidencias en el Fútbol* (Feminist Coordinator of Women and Dissidence in Football), which works toward the eradication of gender-based violence in the sport (Torres, 2020).

It is also important to highlight the opening of media towards women's participation. Historically, the media has been a reproducer of masculinising culture, largely responsible for the invisibility and stereotyping of sportswomen (Hooks, 2004; Ramos, 1995; Vélez, 2017). Thus, a privileged place has been generated for men in terms of sports (Vélez, 2017). An attempt has been made to bring this reality to light through communication campaigns and social networks aimed at demanding, for example, the broadcast of the women's championships. In this way, the 2018 Copa América (ANFP, 2018b) and Chile's matches at the 2019 World Cup in France were televised nationally on free-to-air channels (Álamos, 2019). Following a successful social media campaign in 2020, most of the National Transitional Championship matches were televised.

In terms of content and female participation in the sports media, although there are still exclusively male television and radio programmes that could be characterised as sexist, the presence of female commentators is becoming more frequent. These women face a double challenge: on the one hand, they dispute a public space, questioning stereotypes and gender roles and on the other hand, they demonstrate that it is possible to disseminate sport content with a gender perspective, without the need to resort to the use of violent or discriminating language. In 2020, women sport commentators created the Agrupación de Comunicadoras Deportivas (Association of Sport Communicators), which aims to be a safe space for them in the development of sport communication, in addition to providing educational content on gender equity and promoting strategies to eradicate sexism and machismo in the media (zonamixta. cl, 2020).

Conditions of the Practice of Chilean Women's Football

Despite progress made in recent years regarding women's participation in football, in competitions and the institutional organisation of the sport, professionalism is still considered to be a distant goal. Precarious conditions persist, although from 2018 the ANFP was selected by FIFA and CONMEBOL to develop the pilot plan for the licensing of women's football clubs. This is a certification system for professional clubs that mandates obligations to the board of directors about requirements for their teams/women's sections (Fuchslocher, 2018). As of 2021, 12 clubs have received a license, among them are Audax Italiano, San Luis and Santiago Wanderers, though in practice their conditions are not audited.

Moreover, the National Championship is not recognized by FIFA as a professional competition, which leads to issues with federal, formative and even economic rights involving the sale or transfer of players, limiting clubs' ability to invest in training and development. In terms of the organisation of women's players, this situation also poses an obstacle because the lack of contracts and status as workers (only 50 of 870 women's players have a contract), by law, ANJUFF cannot be recognised as a union (Ministerio del Trabajo y Previsión Social, 2016). Therefore, ANJUFF is not in a position to negotiate collective rights nor to be considered as a worker's organisation that ensures the defence of their members' labour rights.

The year 2020 marked the 12th anniversary of the National Women's Soccer Championship, which despite the COVID situation was able to carry out a competition for the First Division, named the ' 2020 Transition Championship' because of its short duration and the absence of relegation. The Primera B (second division), however, did not have the same planning, which was also the case for the youth football competition (Molina, 2021). At the same time, 2021 also brought uncertainty regarding the development of these championships. This is in addition to the precarious working and sporting conditions of some professional clubs, which to comply with the obligations of the ANFP and CONMEBOL, 'outsource' their women's teams. That is to say that these clubs provide their name and federative rights to amateur clubs to represent them (Labrín, 2017). Thus, the professional clubs cede responsibility for the women's area to external entities, a reality that remains in First Division clubs.

Gradually and thanks to the sporting milestones (e.g., the historical participation in the FIFA Women's World Cup in France 2019 and the qualification for the Tokyo Olympic Games) of the senior national team, along with pressure from fans, the conditions of women's football have been improving. For example, in the 2020 Transitional Championship, it was common to play matches in official stadiums, responding to a historic demand. The most significant demand from players, however, has been the provision of professional contracts, which has yet to be accomplished.

Unlike the professionalisation process in other South American countries (e.g., Argentina, where to participate in the first division it is mandatory to have a percentage of players with contracts), in Chile, regularising the employment of footballers is still a voluntary process, subject to the management of mostly male boards of directors. Only 3 of 32 clubs in Chilean professional football have contracts with their entire women's team. These contracts imply minimum wages, evidencing the extreme wage gap between men and women.

Women's football players without contracts also must reconcile this role with other employment, studies and housework. The situation is so precarious that it is common for women footballers to carry out aid campaigns to pay for medical or psychological treatments. The ANFP offers health insurance that covers only injuries during matches and/or training; therefore other injuries or sicknesses must be covered by the footballers themselves.

Finally, a potential opportunity to accelerate the development of women's football is in the separation and independence of the National Football Federation from the National Professional Football Association. Both institutions were unified in the early 2000s, in a process that was intended to facilitate the incorporation of businesses into Chilean football (Cabello, 2020). Since then, both entities have been unified in terms of representation, attributions and interests, which has generated a conflict noticed by various actors. CONMEBOL indicated in a letter to the

ANFP that the situation corresponds to a legal irregularity (Radio Cooperativa, 2020). Likewise, the same situation was warned against by the former president of the ANFP, Sebastián Moreno (Contragolpe, 2021), and by Ian Mac Niven, former manager of the Chilean men's team. In this context, it is evident that within patriarchal structures, such as the ANFP, where there are limited to no channels of communication and spaces for women to negotiate, the development of women's football has had to advance through alternative pathways.

Reflections

Considering the background presented in this chapter, it can be concluded that every milestone in the development of Chilean women's football, especially those evidenced in the last two decades, has been a consequence of the struggle and consistency of women footballers to conquer and defend their right to practice professionally in a society and football culture characterized by male hegemony, machismo and sexism. The most significant growth of women's football begins with the 2008 FIFA U-20 World Cup, starting a process of formalising women's football. This event was a key impulse that involved a shift from amateurism to incorporation into the structure of Chilean professional football, but without adequate conditions.

Despite the barriers described in this chapter, the development of Chilean women's football was evidenced by the regularity of the national championships and the increase in the number of women players, which has generated greater visibility and participation of clubs in international competitions like the Copa Libertadores de América. These experiences came to fruition at the national team level with the Chileans' historic qualification for the 2019 FIFA Women's World Cup in France and subsequent qualification for the 2020 Tokyo Olympic Games. These results have increased women's interest in football; however, the COVID pandemic exposed the precariousness faced by women's teams. With these issues in mind, the main objectives of national women's football are: improving practice (i.e., training and competition) and working conditions (i.e., professionalism); access to decision-making positions in sport organizations; and greater female participation in the media.

Undoubtedly, the growth achieved by women's football in Chile is remarkable, considering the multiple barriers in organisations that have been historically and traditionally masculine. In this sense, the proposal by Hall (2004), Puig (2007) and Moragas (2014) that organisations are not neutral from a 'gender' perspective—that is, they are 'gendered' (through forms of male socialisation: politics, structure, practices)—is very relevant; in other words, given that it is consistent with the structure and organisation of Chilean football in which a clear male hegemony has been observed. This is a situation that generates barriers and gaps, thus affecting the development of the women's game.

To conclude, and in accordance with Fontecha's (2006) approach to gender relations, Chilean women's football requires prompt (re)construction and development using a gender perspective as a basis for its management, thus ensuring the establishment of better relationships and conditions for both women and men who play football in Chile.

References

Álamos, M. (2019). *Con comentarios y despachos de mujeres: Así será la cobertura del Mundial Femenino en CHV*. EMOL. https://www.emol.com/noticias/Espectaculos/2019/05/30/949575/Con-comentarios-y-despachos-de-mujeres-Asi-sera-la-cobertura-del-Mundial-femenino-en-CHV.html

ANFP. (2018a). *ANFP inicia 'Programa CRECE' para clubes asociados*. ANFP. https://www.anfp.cl/noticia/31098/anfp-inicia-programa-crece-para-clubes-asociados

ANFP. (2018b). *La Copa América Femenina 2018 se verá en las pantallas de Chilevisión*. ANFP. https://www.anfp.cl/noticia/30333/la-copa-america-femenina-2018-se-vera-en-las-pantallas-de-chilevision

ANFP. (2018c). *Memoria 2018. Asociación Nacional de Fútbol Profesional*. ANFP. https://www.anfp.cl/documentos/MEMORIA%202018%20WEB%20v2.pdf

ANFP. (2019). *Memoria Anual 2019*. ANFP. https://anfpfotos.cl/notas/memorias/MEMORIA-2019.pdf

ANJUFF. (2020). *Primera Asamblea de Fútbol Femenino*. National Association of Women's Football Players. https://anjuff.cl/project/primera-asamblea-de-futbol-femenino/

Azócar, F., Revilloud, M., & Guzmán, M. E. (2012). *Mujer y deporte en Chile: Carreras y desafíos*. Comité Olímpico de Chile.

Bourdieu, P. (2000). *La Dominación Masculina*. Anagrama SA.

Cabello, C. (2018). El deporte está en disputa. Reflexiones en torno al «Enfoque de Género» de la Política Nacional de Actividad Física y Deporte 2016–2025. *Revista de Ciencias Sociales, 27*(40).

Cabello, C. (2020). El fútbol femenino en Chile: Estrategias políticas feministas para discutir el deporte nacional. *Ensambles, 7*(12), 32–56.

Calvo, E., & Gutiérrez, B. (2017). El deporte femenino en los informativos deportivos de televisión. Un estudio de caso sobre la noticia de la victoria de Garbiñe Muguruza en Roland Garros. *Estudios sobre el Mensaje Periodístico, 23*(2), 747–758. https://doi.org/10.5209/ESMP.58013

Castelblanco, R., & Jara, M. (2007). *Participación femenina en organizaciones de fútbol: «mujeres a la ofensiva»* Tesis de licenciatura, Universidad Academia de Humanismo Cristiano. http://bibliotecadigital.academia.cl/xmlui/handle/123456789/841

Contragolpe. (2021). *Sebastián Moreno en exclusiva con CONTRAGOLPE explica la necesidad de separar la ANFP y la FFCH*. Nota de prensa. https://www.contragolpe.cl/sebastian-moreno-en-exclusiva-con-contragolpe-explica-la-necesidad-de-separar-la-anfp-y-la-ffch/

Cornejo-Améstica, M., Tello, D., Matus, K., Vargas, C., Poblete-Valderrama, F., & Matus-Castillo, C. (2019). Participación, roles y visibilidad de la mujer en talleres de actividad física públicos en Chile. Un enfoque cualitativo. *Espacios, 40*.

Donoso, T., & Velasco, A. (2013). ¿Por qué una propuesta de formación en perspectiva de género en el ámbito universitario? Profesorado. *Revista de Currículum y Formación del Profesorado, 17*(1), 71–88. https://recyt.fecyt.es/index.php/profesorado/article/view/41565

Elsey, B., & Nadel, J. (2020). La lucha histórica de las mujeres en el fútbol. In C. Cabello & C. Vergara (Eds.), *Gol o Penal: Claves Para Comprender y Disputar el Deporte en el Chile Actual* (pp. 23–30). CLACSO. https://doi.org/10.2307/j.ctv1gm025w.5

FIFA. (2018). *Estrategia de Fútbol Femenino*. Zurich. https://img.fifa.com/image/upload/jor8jikrnmjulndmyoip.pdf

FIFA. (2019). *Women's football. Member associations survey report.* https://img. fifa.com/image/upload/nq3ensohyxpuxovcovj0.pdf

Flores, S. (2013). *La lucha de la Coffuf, la organización que levantó a la Roja femenina cuando nadie daba un peso por ella.* eldesconcierto.cl. https://www. eldesconcierto.cl/deportes/2018/04/16/la-lucha-de-la-coffuf-la-organizacion-que-levanto-a-la-roja-femenina-cuando-nadie-daba-un-peso-por-ella.html

Fontecha, M. (2006). *Intervención didáctica desde la perspectiva de género en la formación inicial de un grupo de docentes en educación Física.* Tesis doctoral, Departamento de Didáctica de la Expresión Musical, Plástica y Corporal, Universidad del País Vasco. https://repositorio.minedu.gob.pe/handle/20.50 0.12799/1831?show=full

Foucault, M. (1984). *La Historia de la Sexualidad* (Vol. I). Siglo XXI.

Fuchslocher, W. (2018). *FIFA elige a Chile y apuesta por la competencia del Fútbol Femenino.* ANFP. https://www.anfp.cl/noticia/30858/fifa-elige-a-chile-y-apuesta-por-la-competencia-del-futbol-femenino

González Gavaldón, B. (1999). Los estereotipos como factor de socialización en el género. *Comunicar, 6*(12). https://www.redalyc.org/articulo. oa?id=15801212

Hall, M. A. (2004). Gestión de la diversidad en las organizaciones deportivas. Un acercamiento crítico. *Apunts. Educación Física y Deportes, 4*(78), 19–25. https://raco.cat/index.php/ApuntsEFD/article/view/301523

Hartmann-Tews, I. (2006). Social stratification in sport and sport policy in the European Union. *European Journal for Sport and Society, 3*(2), 109–124. https://doi.org/10.1080/16138171.2006.11687784

Hernández, E. (2004). *Tendencias Historiográficas Actuales. Escribir Historia Hoy* (pp. 437–555). Ediciones Akal.

Hidalgo, T., & Almonacid, A. (2014). Estereotipos de género en las clases de educación física. *Journal of Movement and Health (JMH), 15*(2), 85–96. https://dialnet.unirioja.es/servlet/articulo?codigo=6348118

Hjelm, J., & Olofsson, E. (2003). A breakthrough: Women's football in Sweden. *Soccer & Society, 4*(2–3), 182–204. https://doi.org/10.108 0/14660970512331390905

Hooks, B. (2004). Entender el patriarcado. In Simon & Schuster (Eds.), *The will to change: Men, masculinity, and love.* Gabriela Adelstein.

Knoppers, A., & Anthonissen, A. (2003). Women's soccer in the United States and the Netherlands: Differences and similarities in regimes of inequalities. *Sociology of Sport Journal, 20*(4), 351–370. https://doi.org/10.1123/ssj.20.4.351

La Tercera. (2008). *Bachelet y blatter inauguraron el mundial femenino sub 20.* La Tercera. https://www.latercera.com/noticia/bachelet-y-blatter-inauguraron-el-mundial-femenino-sub-20/

Labrín, R. (2017). *El drama y la discriminación que sufre el fútbol femenino chileno.* Economía y Negocios (Online Journal). http://www.economiaynegocios.cl/noticias/noticias.asp?id=418524

Lamas, M. (1999). Usos, dificultades y posibilidades de la categoría género. *Papeles de Población, 5*(21), 147–178. https://www.redalyc.org/articulo.oa?id=11202105

Llopis-Goig, R. (2010). Masculinidades inductoras. La construcción de la masculinidad en el fútbol español. Sistema. *Revista de Ciencias Sociales, 217,* 61–76. https://dialnet.unirioja.es/servlet/articulo?codigo=3246656

Macías, V. (1999). *Estereotipos y deporte femenino. La influencia del estereotipo en la práctica deportiva de niñas y adolescentes.* Tesis Doctoral, Universidad de Granada.

Mahmoud, M. (2017). *El fútbol femenino en los clubes deportivos de la ciudad de Barcelona: Un análisis de su gestión.* Tesis Doctoral, Universidad de Barcelona. http://diposit.ub.edu/dspace/handle/2445/115424

Marín, E. (2007). *Historia del deporte chileno. Entre la ilusión y la pasión* (1st ed.). Cuadernos Bicentenario.

Marketing Registrado. (2018). *¿En qué consiste la política de la Conmebol que obliga a los clubes a tener planteles femeninos?* La Comunidad del Marketing Deportivo. https://www.marketingregistrado.com/py/futbol/2018/08/22556_en-que-consiste-la-politica-de-la-conmebol-que-obliga-a-los-clubes-a-tener-planteles-femeninos/

Martín, A., & García Manso, A. (2011). Construyendo la masculinidad: fútbol, violencia e identidad. *Revista de Investigaciones Políticas y Sociológicas, 10*(2), 73–95. https://revistas.usc.gal/index.php/rips/article/view/828

Matus, C., Vilanova, A., Puig, N., & Vidal, J. (2018). Las etapas del asociacionismo deportivo en Chile y su relación con el contexto histórico (finales siglo XIX-2012). *RICYDE. Revista Internacional de Ciencias del Deporte, 14*(53), 280–296. https://www.cafyd.com/REVISTA/ojs/index.php/ricyde/article/view/1306/571

Mercado, H. (2007). *La Mujer y el Deporte en Chile, Una Perspectiva de Género.* Ediciones Universidad de La Frontera.

Ministerio del Deporte de Chile. (2016). *Política nacional de actividad física y deporte, 2016–2025.* Santiago.

Ministerio del Deporte de Chile. (2019). *Encuesta nacional de hábitos de actividad física y deportes 2018 en la población chilena de 18 años y más.* Santiago.

Ministerio del Trabajo y Previsión Social. (2016). *Ley 20940. Moderniza el sistema de relaciones laborales.* Santiago. https://www.bcn.cl/leychile/navegar?idNorma=1094436

Modiano, P. (1997). *Historia del Deporte Chileno. Orígenes y Transformaciones. 1850–1950.* General Directorate of Sports and Recreation (DIGEDER).

Molina, G. (2021). *La división fantasma: ¿Qué pasa con la Primera B Femenina?* Contragolpe. https://www.contragolpe.cl/la-division-fantasma-que-pasa-con-la-primera-b-femenina/

Moragas, M. (2014). *Les Dones que presideixen els clubs esportius a Catalunya: factors que incideixen en l'accés i l'exercici del càrrec, i l'estil de lideratge.* Tesis Doctoral, Departamento de Ciències de l'Activitat Física i l'Esport, Universitat Ramón Llull, Barcelona. https://www.tdx.cat/handle/10803/145029

Pardo, O. (2009). *La gran final Copa Chile-Sernam de fútbol femenino.* https://diarioiquique.wordpress.com/2009/12/18/la-gran-final-copa-chile-sernam-femenina/

Poblete, C., & Moreno, A. (2015). La mirada del género femenino en la educación física. Génesis de una historia en Chile. *Géneros, 22*(17), 150–166.

Puig, N. (2007). Mujeres, puestos de decisión y organizaciones deportivas: Barreras y propuestas. In *Diputación General de Aragón* (Ed.), Actas de las Jornadas Sobre Mujer y Deporte (Proceedings of the Conference 'Women and Sport'), Zaragoza.

Pujadas, X., & Santacana, C. (2003). El club deportivo como marco de sociabilidad en España. Una visión histórica (1830–1975). *Hispania, 63*(214), 505–521. https://doi.org/10.3989/hispania.2003.v63.i214.222

Puranoticia.cl. (2015). *Ministra del Sernam Apoya Copa Libertadores Femenina de Fútbol Salón.* Puranoticia.cl. https://www.puranoticia.cl/noticias/deportes/ministra-del-sernam-apoya-copa-libertadores-femenina-de-futbol-salon/2015-07-16/132731.html

Radio Cooperativa. (2020). *Conmebol pide separar la Federación de la ANFP.* alairelibre.cl. https://www.alairelibre.cl/noticias/deportes/futbol/anfp/conmebol-pide-separar-la-federacion-de-la-anfp/2020-05-18/081603.html

Ramos, C. (1995). Los medios de comunicación, agentes constructores de lo real. *Comunicar: Revista científica Iberoamericana de Comunicación y Educación, 5*, 108–112.

Retamal, R. (2018). *La Batalla de las Pioneras: Crónica de la Primera Selección Chilena Femenina.* Trayecto Comunicaciones.

Revista Estadio. (1972). *Tarea Para los Varones, 15.*

Reyes, F. (2019). *A 100 Años de la Primera Asociación Femenina de Fútbol de Chile.* EMOL. https://merreader.emol.cl/2019/09/14/content/pages/img/pdf/LC3LP5SU.pdf?gt=050001

Rodríguez, F., Curilem, C., Berall, F., & Almagià, A. (2017). Evaluación de la educación física escolar en Enseñanza Secundaria. *Retos, 31*, 76–81. https://doi.org/10.47197/retos.v0i31.49097

Rubin, G. (1986). El Tráfico de mujeres. *Revista Nueva Antropología, 30*, 95–145.

Sainz de Baranda, C. (2014). Las mujeres en la prensa deportiva: Dos perfiles. *Cuadernos de Psicología del Deporte, 14*(1), 91–102.

Salazar, G., & Pinto, J. (1999). *Historia Contemporánea de Chile. Estado, Legitimidad y Ciudadanía* (Vol. 2). Ediciones LOM.

Santa Cruz, E. (2006). Los comienzos de nuestro Olimpo. Los deportistas como nuevas figuras públicas en Chile en las primeras décadas del siglo XX. *Comunicación y Medios, 17*, 141–148. https://doi.org/10.5354/rcm.v0i17.11514

Scheerder, J., Vanreusel, B., & Taks, M. (2005). Stratification patterns of active sport involvement among adults: Social change and persistence. *International Review for the Sociology of Sport, 40*(2). https://doi.org/10.1177/1012690205057191

Scott, J. (1986). Gender: A useful category of historical analysis. *American Historical Review, 91*, 1053–1075.

Torres, M. (2020). Nace histórica coordinadora de organizaciones feministas ligadas a las hinchadas del fútbol. *Revista Obdulio*. https://revistaobdulio.org/2020/09/23/nace-historica-coordinadora-de-organizaciones-feministas-ligadas-a-las-hinchadas-del-futbol/

Van Tuyckom, C., Scheerder, J., & Bracke, P. (2010). Gender and age inequalities in regular sports participation: A cross-national study of 25 European countries. *Journal of Sports Sciences, 28*(10). https://doi.org/10.1080/02640414.2010.492229

Vélez, B. (2017). Una socio-antropóloga interroga el fútbol y el género. In *¿Quién raya la cancha? Visiones, Tensiones Y Nuevas Perspectivas en los Estudios Socioculturales del Deporte en Latinoamérica*. CLACSO. https://www.clacso.org.ar/libreria-latinoamericana/buscar_libro_detalle.php?id_libro=1209

Yori, G. H. (2020). Las mujeres en el fútbol profesional: la difícil carrera contra la discriminación. *UNA Revista de Derecho, 5*, 63–93. https://una.uniandes.edu.co/images/Volumen5/20202%2D%2D2.HernndezYori.pdf

zonamixta.cl. (2020). *Contra el machismo en los medios: Comunicadoras deportivas se unen por el respeto y la equidad*. Zona Mixta. http://zonamixta.cl/contra-el-machismo-en-los-medios-chilenos-comunicadoras-deportivas-se-unen-por-el-respeto-y-la-equidad

Part III

Latin American Conversations:
Pasado, Presente y Futuro

12

'*Femina sana in corpore sano*' (As long as they don't play football): Football and Womanhood in the 1920s' Argentine Capital

Pablo Ariel Scharagrodsky and Magalí Peréz Riedel

Introduction

After the British imperialist commercial expansion in Argentina, some sports arrived at the La Plata River (River Plate) in an international context of a robust and intense process of globalisation, circulation, exchange, appropriation, imposition and normalisation of objects, ideas, people and practices. Football was one of those bodily practices, and highly regulated sports games, introduced by the British community in Argentina. Gradually, this activity became a regular and legitimate practice in the heterogeneous landscape of Argentine cities. At first, a large portion of the creole community and the most numerous groups of European settlers in Argentina (i.e., the Italians and the Spanish) saw football as a strange, exotic and semi-violent practice of dubious morality. In just a

P. A. Scharagrodsky (✉) • M. Peréz Riedel
Universidad de Quilmes (UNQ), Bernal, Argentina
e-mail: pas@unq.edu.ar

© The Author(s), under exclusive license to Springer Nature Switzerland AG 2022
J. Knijnik, G. Garton (eds.), *Women's Football in Latin America*, New Femininities in Digital, Physical and Sporting Cultures,
https://doi.org/10.1007/978-3-031-09127-8_12

few decades, however, football became a widespread and socially accepted phenomenon (Archetti, 2003).

In regard to the practice of football and its dissemination, the period that extended between the last decade of the nineteenth century and the first decade of the twentieth century was key in the city of Buenos Aires, the Argentine capital. In those decades, with steps forwards and backwards, the formal and official practice of football began thanks to the formation of a league and an association linked to that sport. Initially practiced by the wealthier sectors (e.g., British residents, British business executives or business representatives, students from educational institutions of the British Empire, the Argentine upper classes and so on), football quickly made its way to other social sectors—the consolidated urban strata, middle strata and medium-low classes created by urbanisation (Archetti, 2003). The popularisation of football boosted the economic, social and political interests of various social actors. One of these actors was the press, which stood out because it contributed to the creation of a commercial scene, sports as entertainment, as well as the creation of a new modern figure—the spectator. All this materialised as a series of consumer rituals and generated new spaces for socialisation: football stadiums. By the 1920s, according to Frydenberg (2011):

> … football had ceased to be a trend for young people and had become part of the life of almost all social institutions and corporations, which organised their own tournaments. Simultaneously, the spectacle, incipient during the first decade and spasmodic in the concentration of large crowds, was enriching and expanding (p. 125).

The consumption of football developed massive and popular dimensions. The sport slowly became a space for the strengthening of local, regional and national identities, as a country and even as a neighbourhood or *barrio*, for example. It also became a significant commercial business in a decade when the real wage growth was 19% (1922–1929), which promoted new types and forms of consumption. Some social actors started to stand out in this huge commercial, identitarian and cultural spectacle: fans, coaches or managers, players and club members.

Across the country, the accelerated growth of football generated mixed reactions. Some politicians saw it as an ingredient of the welfare state that they wanted to promote. Club executives highlighted football's hygienic and virile virtues while visionary entrepreneurs prioritised its economic profit. Pedagogues warned about the physical and moral violence that this practice generated. Sports doctors and physical educators had varied reactions that changed over time (Armus & Scharagrodsky, 2014). There were critical voices that fervently opposed the growing professionalisation of football. Some left-wing segments, speaking on behalf of the workers, encouraged the creation of alternative football leagues (Barrancos, 2011; Martínez Mazzola, 2014); although other sectors on the left fiercely fought against the sport because they saw it as some sort of opium that diminished the revolutionary potential of the working class (Camarero, 2004).

In this context, on October 13, 1923, an outstanding sporting event occurred: the first football match between two teams of women; it was covered by the most important and influential media outlets in Argentina. This was the first time that several media outlets wrote and published articles about a commercial match between women's teams in the Argentine capital. The match took place at the former field of Club Atlético Boca Juniors, which at the time was, and still remains, one of the most popular clubs in the capital. It was open to the public, and visitors had to pay an entrance fee to watch the two teams made up entirely of women. This match was announced and promoted by the press as an encounter between the *'Argentinas'* [Argentine women] and the *'Cosmopolitas'* [Cosmopolitan women].

In many ways, it became an unprecedented and original event. On the one hand, during those years, recreational and semi-professional football had already become a practice that was highly consumed and experienced by a predominantly male sector. Football in Argentina was a homosocial practice for men, distant from the female universe (Archetti, 2005).[1] On

---

[1] This does not mean that there were not any women playing football. In Argentina, in the first decades of the twentieth century, although they were not the majority, nor was there much interest in stimulating or publicising these types of experiences, women played football in various cities. For example, in 1913, a football match between two teams of women took place in the Rural Society of the city of Rosario, Santa Fe.

the other hand the commodification of the female workforce (Barrancos, 2007) in a public football sporting event was rare, especially in a context in which this commodification was common in other areas and low-paid jobs; it generated conditions of intense exploitation of numerous groups of girls and women. In short, the spectacle of football was historically a male-dominated space, especially in regard to its practice and the sale of the sport's 'male labour force'.

Using the contributions of social and cultural history and gender studies, this chapter's research seeks to analyse how the general and specialised press described and, at the same time, fabricated and interpreted the first commercial women's football match to be recorded in the Argentine capital. The specificity of this event evoked and consolidated various meanings (e.g., socially accepted conventions, fantasies, fears, phobias, concerns, prejudices and so on) that were widely spread by the Argentine press. For the purposes of this investigation, the authors selected articles from national newspapers and media outlets with the highest circulation and prestige (e.g., *La Nación*, *La Prensa*, *La Razón*, *Crítica* and *La Vanguardia*) and magazines with great dissemination and presence— *Caras y Caretas*, *Fray Mocho* and *El Gráfico*. The research focused on discursive meanings, thematic recurrences and semantic patterns, as well as their nuanced and diverse representations related to this event and its participants.

According to Kircher (2005), the press is both a social and political actor, serving as a performative space of cultural production, transmission and circulation. It is also a source of information about historical events. Thus, this study used a hermeneutical approach to analyse a 'text' together with its historical and contextual conditions of production (Fairclough, 2003), accepting that 'sexual difference seems to be already present in how we construct meaning: it is already part of the logic that presides over writing' (Laqueur, 1994, p. 43). The following sections analyse the types of arguments that questioned women's football as well as the nuances and contradictions that circulated in the Argentine press during the 1920s.

Sports and Femininity During the 1920s: The Place of Football

Starting in the decade of 1920, although slowly and with a certain resistance, a new public figure emerged in Argentina—modern sportswomen as role models (Bontempo, 2016). This ideal was influenced by the arrival and circulation of several paradigmatic cases of physical–moral archetypes of European and North American athletes. The proliferation and spread of the women's sports crusade was attributable to a varied set of reasons in the context of social, cultural, sexual, legal and political changes in relation to women.

Some of the rationale behind this movement stemmed from the propagation and allure of the eugenic discourse, the importance of the female body in the future of the race and the fight against certain diseases deemed 'feminine', such as hysteria, nervousness, dyspepsia, scoliosis, muscular weakness or tuberculosis (Armus, 2007, 2016). Other reasons included the dissemination of an aesthetically desirable feminine body ideal for the modern hetero-normative gaze, fears about the fertility rate in the country, the association between a healthy female body and the improvement of the quality and quantity of the population and its genetics; this was combined with growing fears around the ambiguity of certain female bodily behaviours.

Specifically, 1923 was a year of great visibility for the Argentine sports world. Various agonistic events transcended the national stage and made international headlines. One of the most prominent events widely covered by the press was the boxing match between Argentine Luis Ángel Firpo and American Jack Dempsey in September 1923. This was the first sporting event broadcast by radio in the country. In August, just a month before Firpo faced Dempsey in New York City, a record-breaking Italian–Argentine swimmer, Enrique Tiraboschi, made headlines when he crossed the English Channel, swimming from France to England (Scharagrodsky, 2020, 2021).

Nonetheless, 1923 was also a significant year for female athletes as several women's sporting events were widely covered by the media, although to a lesser extent than those featuring male athletes. For example, Lilian Harrison, born in Argentina and of British descent, became the first person to swim across the River Plate. In just over 24 hours of uninterrupted swimming, she made her way from Colonia, Uruguay, to Punta Lara, Argentina (Scharagrodsky, 2019). This accomplishment was featured on the cover of numerous national and international newspapers and magazines, and the media continued to write about Harrison's feat for several weeks.

The First International Women's Athletics Tournament was held in Buenos Aires; it was organised by the General Directorate of Squares and Physical Exercise of the Argentine capital, drawing public participation and media coverage. Moreover, the media disseminated other sports activities carried out by women, including the River Plate Championship at the Buenos Aires Lawn Tennis Club (Deportes: Campeonato, 1923) and women's sports tournaments (e.g., *cestoball*, tennis, certain athletic events, and so on) organised by the National Higher Institute of Physical Education (INEF).

In 1923, the most influential weekly sports magazine of Argentina, *El Gráfico*, featured sportswomen on its covers. Created in 1919 and primarily focused on topics related to the male sports universe, *El Gráfico* published several articles about the growing female physical culture and its undeniable and necessary hygienic–moral benefits; this showcased the ideal of the new modern Argentine woman and brought it into the social imaginary. During 1923, about 10% of their covers alluded to women.[2] Throughout the 1920s, approximately 27% of their covers made references to women, but of that 27%, about 60% were published between 1920 and 1921. Many of the covers in these early years were linked to female faces or silhouettes from the foreign entertainment industry, although they did not refer explicitly to any sports.

---

[2] The first cover of the magazine *El Gráfico* on women's football was published in 1925. It showed two female players wearing their sports attire, greeting each other in the middle of the playing field. The greeting was with the hand and, simultaneously, with a kiss—a clear homo-erotic image. In the background, there was a man with a ball ('La mujer', 1925). During the 1920s, there was another cover about football and women in October 1928 and a few more covers with women holding footballs, although without a clear mention of said sport, and they were not dressed in the typical sportswear. At the beginning of the twentieth century, a popular Argentine magazine published a few articles on an 'adaptation' of women's football. It was described as 'football with skates, as the new game for ladies in England' ('Un nuevo', 1905).

It was in this social and sporting context, both open and contradictory in regard to the female collective, that the capital city hosted an unprecedented sporting event: the previously mentioned women's football match at the former stadium of Boca Juniors; it was played in front of 'no less than 6000 people' (Atrajo gran, 1923). This event was covered before and after it took place, and the diverse articles, editorials, photographs and illustrations concentrated on various meanings linked to concerns, fears and fantasies of a specific male sector; they were based on both the emerging figure of the modern sportswoman and the symbolic, material, aesthetic and moral limits that women had to face in certain practices—football.

The match was held in Buenos Aires on October 13, 1923, and it was something different and new in terms of what had been organised and consumed in the world of sports entertainment in the region until that point. Nevertheless, in other countries, the reality was radically different. For example, at the end of the nineteenth century in England, the pioneers of women's football used the sport 'as a platform to make feminist demands visible, awakening great passions among public opinion' (Marinello Bonnefoy, 2018). It was during World War I, however, that women, especially workers, took up football with great interest and force. Dozens of women's football teams sprang up across the industrial north of England in factories to raise funds for charities. Although during the 1920s there were very popular female football teams, the male leaders of the Football Association (FA) quickly shut down the growth of the women's game (Marinello Bonnefoy, 2018).

In several Western countries where football, especially men's, was already deeply entrenched, national federations and much of the sports establishment questioned women's participation. Their arguments combined medical, moral and scientific issues, although many of the concerns and fears were motivated by commercial interests and by panic in the face of some sort of female empowerment. As this analysis of sports articles and media shows, with nuances and differences, and thanks to certain local translations and appropriations, Latin American women's football was interwoven, regulated and subjected to arguments originating from scientific, biomedical and moralistic discourse (Elsey & Nadel, 2019; Mallada Messeguer & Quitzau, 2020; Prates Silva, 2019; Pujol, 2019).

This complicated international context served as the backdrop for the first commercial football match between women in the Argentine capital. Before the event, the headlines of some media outlets and magazines anticipated the uniqueness of the it and the news about the foundation of the first women's football clubs: 'Women's football is practised in Buenos Aires,' adding that 'River Plate was the first club of this nature, founded in the capital' and that 'two teams, made up of young ladies, train daily to be able to present themselves in public' ('En Buenos Aires', 1923; 'Se realizará', 1923). A double-page article reported on the characteristics of the two teams, their names, clothes and names of the captains.

The '*Argentinas*' wore light blue shirts with white collars while the '*Cosmopolitas*', made up of British and German women, wore white shirts with a light blue collar. In the photographs, it is obvious that the players had caps that covered a good part of their hair, sports shoes, knee-high socks, long shorts and long-sleeved shirts. Media outlets published details of the match, the names of the team members, their captains ('En Buenos Aires', 1923), their main players ('En Buenos Aires', 1923), the highlights of the event ('Atrajo gran, 1923; El match, 1923), the final score, the profits and descriptions of some *picturesque* scenes.[3]

The Press and Voices Against Women's Football

When referring to the 1923 women's football match, Argentine journalists developed a wide array of arguments against women's football; some were based on scientific and biomedical discourses, particularly from physiology and gynaecology. Some media outlets concentrated on the dominant moral discourse on sexuality even as others focused on criticising the economic and commercial aspects.

The hegemonic biomedical discourse brought back the old and prejudiced heritage of nineteenth-century hygienism. It started to spread and

---

[3] 'Shortly after, amid lively discussions, the corresponding percentage was distributed among the players. The scene was very picturesque, due to the bid to get more than what the businessman wanted to pay' ('El match', 1923).

promote new fears about how certain sports, activities and practices could potentially be detrimental to women's bodies, especially certain areas—for example, the lower abdomen and women's reproductive organs (Anderson, 2014, 2015). An article from the newspaper *La Nación* said the following about the 1923 women's football match: 'Let us first discuss the physiological argument. The woman—and they are all the same ... —does not need to subsume her delicate and fragile maternal apparatus into what is for her the rough practice of football' ('Un médico', 1923, p. 3).

Another fear was that women could contract genitourinary diseases, suffer physical injuries and have fertility problems because of intense, abrupt or violent actions that were likely to occur in a football match. The use of categories derived from the medical discourse provided an air of scientificity to the arguments and inferences made by the press while discouraging and delegitimising women's access to football and to sports (e.g., rugby or other high-intensity athletic disciplines).

Other arguments from the press, concerning the women's football match that took place at the former Boca Juniors field, focused on how football could negatively affect the social customs and traditions that were defined by the hetero-patriarchal order, especially in terms of moral deviation. In some instances, the press emphasised the immorality of the game and warned of the dangers of the loss of the footballers' femininity: 'Today's match showed how improper it is for ladies to practise football' ('Match de fútbol', 1923, p. 4). One of the main concerns about the match in 1923 was related to the possible loss of the alleged natural femininity during sports practice: 'We are not supporters of women's football ... because we do not think that this excessively energetic and essentially virile game is the most suitable for women's activities in terms of physical culture' ('El 12', 1923). According to Reggiani (2019), in the

[19]20s, women's sports were not frowned upon. Girls and women of the elite and urban areas were encouraged to move their bodies to practise physical exercise and sports. However, there was a symbolic and material limit that they were advised not to cross, a limit defined by a set of customs and traditions, and crossing such limits could lead to an erasure of their 'femininity', [their beautiful] 'curves'' [and their] 'reproductive capacity' (p. 209).

Moreover, these sportswomen could become a doorway for a dangerous and misconstrued form of feminism:

> This game is for men and that's it. There are many reasons, simple and complicated reasons (physical, physiological and aesthetic reasons) that are more than enough to make favourable arguments in this sense. ... Think a little and you will notice that this novelty of football being played by women is one element of the many that make up the outcome of what 'progressive men' and 'progressive women' have wanted to call the advancement of women. It is a tiny part of that feminism that is so misunderstood and, unfortunately, so tolerated. ('Un médico', 1923, p. 3).

One of the main Argentine experts in sports medicine, Gofredo Grasso (1924), supported the previously mentioned moral arguments in regard to certain sports practices. He strongly promoted a female physical culture to develop certain qualities such as dexterity, coordination and greater body control; combat muscular and functional deficiencies in unhealthy girls and women; and improve procreation, feminine aesthetics and self-esteem. Still, Grasso believed women should not practice some sports:

> A woman does not need to resort to certain overly virile sports such as wrestling, boxing, football or rugby, which, by their very nature, hurt the sense of femininity that should prevail in her. Naturally, it will be necessary to know how to distinguish the highly moral public manifestations of athletics—connected in that sense to those of tennis, swimming, skating, horse riding, etc.—from those of female boxing, football or wrestling, which are inappropriate for the sex and that, in all fairness, are criticised by public opinion and reasonable people (1924, pp. 101, 104).

Important authors and icons from the world of sports and physical culture that were popular in Argentina agreed on the idea of '*femina sana in corpore sano*' if they did not play football. This same thought was reinforced in the educational field. One of the leading figures of physical education in the country, Dr. Enrique Romero Brest (1873–1958), said that football was a pedagogical practice for children.

Terms, such as 'inappropriate' or 'improper', were often used to describe women's football in mainstream media. Yet, some left-wing newspapers like *La Vanguardia* offered more nuanced interpretations regarding the 1923 women's football match. Generally speaking, the newspapers objected to girls and women playing football. It was only acceptable if women did it without brusqueness or violence, respecting the rules of the game and with the sole objective of playing selflessly for the love of the game.

> Football is certainly not an appropriate sport for the weaker sex, but perhaps it could be accepted as a manifestation of vigour if it was practised exclusively as a hobby, and if the players maintained the standard that we stated of integrity in their actions, without using brusqueness ('El match', 1923, p. 3).

Apart from that, when referring to the women's football match that took place in 1923, some local newspapers published drawings and cartoons to ridicule, censor or make fun of those women who dared to play a sport previously, and unfairly, defined as exclusively male. For the patriarchal imaginary, women's football became one of the many practices and situations used to parody and satirise the alleged physical–emotional and moral inabilities of girls and women to kick, pass, head pass or defend the ball; mark their opponents; fall on the ground or score a goal. The press also sought to ridicule and normalise women's alleged difficulties when it came to controlling their intense, unstoppable and ungovernable emotions. For example, one of the most important newspapers at the time, *La Razón*, published a drawing of four women hugging the crossbar and goal posts, seemingly expressing fear and nervousness, and calling for 'help' after seeing a mouse sitting on a soccer ball ('Las mujeres', 1923).

In some cases, sports journalists who wrote articles about the *Argentinas vs. Cosmopolitas* match used a mocking and sarcastic tone to report on the skills, ability and expertise of the players:

> The female football players showed us that the weaker sex can play football and that it is possible to get something good out of it, despite the bad habits they may develop to win conjugal fights. ... Pulling hair, breaking a plate over the head, a blow with the rolling pin, these are more or less tolerable. But a good kick cannot be received with indifference ('Atrajo gran', 1923).

Still, there was no mention of the difficulties, stigmas and impossibilities caused by the social, political, pedagogical and family context with regard to experiences such as playing football.

The critics highlighted the immorality of the semi-professional and public game, warning about the potential loss of femininity of the football players. Nonetheless, the real fear behind many of these statements was that women's football could become a space for subversion or erosion of the socially accepted conventions transmitted by the hetero-patriarchal order. Some social actors had reactions that were derogatory, discriminatory and, in some cases, humiliating. These reactions were partially a result of the potential loss of certain symbolic and material privileges.

In sum, to criticise female football players, the Argentine press used and spread 'scientific' arguments, particularly from the biomedical discourse, together with certain patriarchal discourses of feminine sexual morality. On the other hand, there were also criticisms and objections to the sporting event as a strictly commercial event. These objections arose from some media (e.g., the socialist newspaper *La Vanguardia*), which particularly denounced the true purposes of the 1923 match—business, financial gain, commercial exploitation and profit:

> But the game played yesterday on the pitch of Boca Juniors, apart from the lack of skill shown by most of the female players, was far from a match between foo-ball enthusiasts. Instead, they were women who had been employed by a businessman to supply the show and who, after the game, received payment for their services, from yesterday's total income of 2192 pesos. In this way, it has been irrefutably demonstrated what the purpose was for the organisers of this parody: to conduct business (El match, 1923, p. 3).

La Vanguardia was aligned with the socialist discourse that opposed the capitalist, corporate and corrupt commercialisation of sports. Although the newspaper mainly questioned the sad spectacle, it also maintained the assumption that football was not an appropriate sport for women. Barrancos states that: 'Socialism did not explicitly express any kind of preferential gender in regard to most sports, but it is evident that their football also had men as its only performers. ... It was a male struggle, and the socialists did not fight the stereotype (2011, pp. 436–437).

Although socialists did not support women's football, they did greatly encourage them to practice swimming, athletics and basketball, among other sports. From 1923, other leftist groups, such as the Communist Party, promoted football in their workers' clubs. By 1926, there were 50 clubs around the Capital and Greater Buenos Aires and 20 more in Santa Fe, Córdoba and Tucumán (Camarero, 2004, pp. 16–22). Left-wing parties wanted to promote matches among workers to foster feelings of brotherhood and working-class solidarity as opposed to the football matches from the bourgeois leagues that were losing their nature to rivalry (Camarero, 2004, p. 23). Nevertheless, none of them encouraged women to practice football.

Press Coverage and Nuanced Views About Women's Football

During the 1920s, media coverage of women's football matches was mainly negative. Media outlets either portrayed it as a rarity and a surprising event, rejected or mocked the players or were more cautious about their disapproval and focused on other topics instead. For example, the newspaper *El Argentino* focused less on the criticism of football and the female players and more on the need to stimulate physical and sports culture among Latin girls. The Latin identity or *latinidad* became a signifier that condensed various meanings about a type of womanhood that was linked to traditional customs, with regressive and not particularly modern ideas about women's bodies, aesthetics and physical care.

> The proverbial decency of the Latin woman, which … has been defined by her adversity to sports, has not only given up ground in that way but also, judging by its recent growth, it is easy to predict that soon our female sportsmen (*sic*) will score at the level of the foreigners ('La mujer argentina', 1923, p. 5).

Although the media questioned the supposed Latina 'decency', it also set a high standard: Argentine women should be like foreign female athletes, if not better than them. According to *El Argentino*, this was the goal, despite some ambivalence and sometimes contradictory meanings about what the football match represented. An article said: 'The football match that will take place this Friday on Boca Juniors' field signals the culmination of women's activities in sport, due to the nature and characteristics [of the sport] to be practised, which seem to be inappropriate for our girls' ('La mujer argentina', 1923, p. 5). The newspaper congratulated Club Estudiantes de La Plata for accepting the request to let local girls play football on its pitches to see for themselves the advantages of this practice.

Other well-known newspapers, such as *Fray Mocho*, also advertised the women's football match of 1923 ('En Buenos Aires', 1923). They published large photographs and lacked the burlesque, ironic or derogatory tone of other media. Although the names of the women who played in this match are known,[4] the thoughts and feelings that players had in the face of the almost inquisitive or sarcastic gaze of the press and their contemporaries (e.g., the public, family, friends) are unknown. We also do not know the type of symbolic and material support that they had, or why they dared to play in a football stadium, whether for money, pleasure or curiosity. Apart from the criticism and ridicule received from the media, the articles, illustrations and cartoons, the match took place and it even attracted significant media coverage. Whether because of economic, political and ideological reasons or simply the pleasure of competitive sports, these footballers played the game in front of an audience, ignoring, discounting and resisting the androcentric and heterosexual gaze of the broader social imaginary regarding sports (El match, 1923). It also is recognised that there were audience members, although their reactions or opinions are not known.

Beyond that, it is possible to infer that the materialisation of this match generated a micro-resistance or new meanings among those more conservative voices that argued the inadequacy, impertinence and impropriety of women's football. Although this resistance was temporary, the event was a novelty and possibly disruptive. Yet, this resistance must have not

---

[4] Their names were Elsa Martínez, Josefa Beguerie, Nélida Martínez, Margarita Iriarte, Alicia Tisset, Emma Meyer, Estela Solari, Lidia López, Lucía Reyes had, Margarita Silva and Estrella Villegas or Silvia Pilnick, Elena van der Beck, Ana Schwartinsky, Erna Vollnas, Frida Bisicamp, Elisa Bulat, Elly Bisimcap, Elisa van der Beck, Elsa Schwartinsky and Mizzi Baurer.

grown greater because, as far as is known, this match was followed by other sporting events, with more participation from football clubs and even the creation of the Women's Football League (*Liga de Fútbol Femenina*).

In conclusion, according to the hetero and male sports gaze from the Argentine press of the 1920s, the bodies of female footballers did not fit within the sexual morality, aesthetics, socially accepted movements and sex/gender binary of the time. Consequently, theirs were likely to be considered abject bodies. Nonetheless, the materialisation of the event caused contradictory reactions. In other words, the abjection of certain bodies and their visibility also could have momentarily subverted the sex/gender system by revealing bodies and discourses that were different from the gender logic, from a certain feminine aesthetic and the normative sexual morality. As Butler (2002) argues, abjection allows one to ponder the possibility of other bodies. It also contributes to breaking the hegemonic limits of the body, making room for a radical rearticulation or disruption of the symbolic horizon where bodies come to matter (Butler, 2002). Symbolic cracks were caused by the match and the news articles, which questioned, enabled and invited one to think about other bodies, aesthetics, dress codes and movements. Nonetheless, it would take several decades for women to become politically visible in the world of football in Argentina.

Conclusions

The purpose of the current study was to analyse how local newspapers and magazines represented the first women's football match to be recorded in Argentina. Although there was an increasing number of Argentine girls and women who practiced sports during the 1920s, research has shown that the press put into circulation a series of arguments against women playing football. These arguments were supported by the biomedical discourse and a set of patriarchal discourses, social customs and traditions that exceeded the biological discourse itself. At the same time, the arguments defined and excluded certain feminine sexual aesthetics and moralities. Some media outlets criticised how the match from October 1923 was a strictly commercial event with the end goal of making a profit. The national and local press treated the women's football match with a tone of strangeness and exoticism. They used words and images that expressed rejection, disapproval and mockery. A minority of media outlets were less disapproving and focused on other topics, even though they still questioned the match between the two women's teams.

Not even less-conservative media outlets, such as socialist ones, mentioned the very social, political, pedagogical and family contexts that made it difficult for women to have access to play certain sports such as soccer. The predominant patriarchal tone of the press won by a landslide. Consequently, Argentine women had to wait until the end of the twentieth century to participate in football events as players, not just as spectators, either for money, for pleasure, out of an interest or out of curiosity.

References

Anderson, P. (2014). Mens sana in corpore sano: deportismo, salud y feminidad en Argentina. 1900–1945. In P. Scharagrodsky (Comp.), *Miradas Médicas Sobre la Cultura Física en Argentina, 1880–1970* (pp. 83–100). Buenos Aires: Prometeo.

Anderson, P. (2015). Sporting women and machonas: Negotiating gender through sports in Argentina, 1900–1940. *Women's History Review, 24*(5), 700–720. https://doi.org/10.1080/09612025.2015.1028210

Archetti, E. (2003). *Masculinidades. Fútbol, Tango y Polo en Argentina*. Buenos Aires: Editorial Antropofagia.

Archetti, E. (2005). El deporte en Argentina (1914–1983). *Trabajo y Sociedad, 7*(6), 1–30. https://dialnet.unirioja.es/servlet/articulo?codigo=2792152

Armus, D. (2007). *La Ciudad Impura. Salud, Tuberculosis y Cultura en Buenos Aires, 1870–1950*. Edhasa.

Armus, D. (2016). Eugenesia en Buenos Aires: discursos, prácticas, historiografía. *Histórea, Ciências, Saúde—Manguinhos, 23*(16), 149–169. https://doi.org/10.1590/S0104-59702016000500009

Armus, D. & Scharagrodsky, P. (2014). El fútbol en las escuelas y colegios argentinos. Notas sobre un desencuentro en el siglo XX. In S. Rinke & D. Armus (Coords.), *Del Football al Fútbol/Futebol. Historias Argentinas, Brasileras y Uruguayas en el Siglo XX. Cuadernos de Historia Latinoamericana* (pp. 85–99). Madrid/Frankfurt: Edit. Iberoamericana-Vervuert.

'Atrajo gran'(1923, October 12) Atrajo gran concurrencia el primer partido de football disputado por mujeres, *Crítica*, p. 2.

Barrancos, D. (2007). *Mujeres en la Sociedad Argentina. Una Historia de Cinco Siglos.* Editorial Sudamericana.

Barrancos, D. (2011). Ideas socialistas en cuerpos sanos (Argentina 1920–1930). In P. Scharagrodsky (Comp.), *La Invención del 'Homo Gymnasticus'. Fragmentos Históricos Sobre la Educación de los Cuerpos en Movimiento en Occidente* (pp. 423–440). Buenos Aires: Prometeo.

Bontempo, M. P. (2016). El cuerpo de la mujer moderna. La construcción de la feminidad en las revistas de Editorial Atlántida (1918–1933). In P. Scharagrodsky (Comp.), *Mujeres en Movimiento. Deporte, Cultura Física y Feminidades. Argentina, 1870–1980* (pp. 329–348). Buenos Aires: Prometeo.

Butler, J. (2002). *Cuerpos que Importan. Sobre los Límites Materiales y Discursivos del 'Sexo'.* Paidós.

Camarero, H. (2004). Los clubes deportivos comunistas. *Todo es Historia, 448*, 16–25.

'Deportes: Campeonato' (1923, May 19) Deportes: Campeonato Río de la Plata en el Buenos Aires Lawn Tennis Club. Jugadoras y jugadores que toman parte en los partidos de eliminación, *Caras y Caretas*, p. 75.

'El 12' (1923, October 7) El 12 se jugará un match de football entre mujeres, *La Nación*, p. 3.

'El match' (1923, October 12) El match femenino de football. Argentinas 4, Cosmopolita 3. *La Vanguardia*, p. 3.

Elsey, B., & Nadel, J. (2019). *Futbolera. A History of Women and Sports in Latin America.* University of Texas Press.

'En Buenos Aires'(1923, October 2) En Buenos Aires, se practica football femenino, *Fray Mocho*, p. 22.

Fairclough, N. (2003). El análisis crítico del discurso como método para la investigación en ciencias sociales. In Wodak, R. and Meyer, M. (Comp.), *Métodos de Análisis Crítico del Discurso* (pp. 179–204). Barcelona: Gedisa.

Frydenberg, J. (2011). *Historia Social del Fútbol: Del Amateurismo a la Profesionalización.* Siglo XXI.

Grasso, G. (1924). *Acción del Médico en la Cultura Física.* Establecimiento Gráfico A. de Martino.

Kircher, M. (2005). La prensa escrita: actor social y político, espacio de producción cultural y fuente de información histórica. *Revista de Historia, 10*, 115–122.

'La mujer' (1925, June 13) La mujer y el football, *El Gráfico*, n. 310.

'La mujer argentina' (1923, October 9) La mujer argentina en la práctica de todos los deportes. El torneo del 12 en el field de Boca Juniors será un digno exponente atlético, *El Argentino*, p. 5.

Laqueur, T. (1994). *La Construcción del Sexo: Cuerpo y Género Desde los griegos Hasta Freud*. Cátedra.

'Las mujeres' (1923, September 30) Las mujeres juegan al football. *La Razón*, p. 5.

Mallada Messeguer, A. N., & Quitzau, E. A. (2020). Elegantes siluetas femeninas y las varoniles formas armoniosas: primeros acercamientos históricos sobre mujeres y cultura física en Montevideo. *Movimento, 26*, e26028. https://doi.org/10.22456/1982-8918.90527

Marinello Bonnefoy, J. C. (2018). Fútbol Femenino: Breve historia de un deporte prohibido. *Ser Histórico. Portal de Historia*. https://serhistorico.net/2018/07/17/futbol-femenino-breve-historia-de-un-deporte-prohibido/

Martínez Mazzola, R. (2014). Gimnasia, deportes y usos del tiempo libre en el socialismo argentino (1896–1916). In P. Scharagrodsky (Comp.), *Miradas Médicas Sobre la Cultura Física en Argentina, 1880–1970* (pp. 275–299). Buenos Aires: Prometeo.

'Match de fútbol' (1923, October 12) Match de fútbol entre mujeres, *La Razón*, p. 4.

Prates Silva, K. (2019). É uma coisa indecente, imoral e escandalosa: os primeiros relatos sobre football feminino na imprensa do Rio de Janeiro (1910–1920). *Recorde: Revista de História do Esporte, 12*(2), 1–10. https://revistas.ufrj.br/index.php/Recorde/article/view/30991

Pujol, A. (2019). *¡Qué Jugadora!, Un Siglo de Fútbol Femenino en la Argentina*. Editorial Planeta.

Reggiani, A. (2019). *Historia Mínima de la Eugenesia en América Latina*. El Colegio de México.

Scharagrodsky, P. (2019). ¿Cruzando fronteras? El primer cruce a nado del Río de La Plata, Uruguay-Argentina, 1923. *Claves. Revista de Historia, 5*(8), 211–233. https://doi.org/10.25032/crh.v5i8.9

Scharagrodsky, P. (2020). Las peleas económico-comerciales más allá del box. Prensa, avisos publicitarios y radio en Argentina en los años '20. *Pensar la Publicidad, 14*(1), 89–103. https://doi.org/10.5209/pepu.68435

Scharagrodsky, P. (2021). Nacionalidad, masculinidad y política en la natación. La prensa argentina y el primer cruce a nado del Canal de la Mancha, 1923. *Historia y Sociedad, 41*, 93–119. https://doi.org/10.15446/hys.n41.84920

'Se realizará' (1923, September 28) Se realizará en Buenos Aires el primer match femenino de football, *La Razón*, p. 16.

'Un médico' (1923, October 14) Un médico habla del football en un sentido nuevo. Lo condena acerbamente como sport practicado por mujeres, *La Nación*, p. 3

'Un nuevo'(1905, June 24) Un nuevo deporte para mujeres, *Caras y Caretas*, n. 351, p. 4

13

Transgression and Resistance: An Approach to Mexican Women's Football History through the Case of Alicia Vargas (1970–1991)

Giovanni Alejandro Pérez Uriarte

The International Federation of Football History & Statistics (IFFHS) recognises Alicia Vargas as one of the best players of the Confederation of North, Central American and Caribbean Association Football (CONCACAF). A member of the Mexican national team from 1970 to 1991, Vargas was also an outspoken advocate for the equal treatment and competitive salaries that she and her teammates deserved, fighting against abuse by football promoters and administrators. During her professional career, which took place in the context of second-wave feminism, Vargas challenged gendered discourses that rejected the presence of women in football and became one of the most recognised players in Mexico (Elsey & Nadel, 2019; Carreño, 2006).

In 1970, without the support of the Mexican Football Federation (FMF), the country's first women's national team was formed. This new team played in the 1970 Women's World Cup in Italy, where the host

G. A. Pérez Uriarte (✉)
Instituto de Investigaciones Dr. José María Luis Mora, Mexico City, Mexico
e-mail: gperez@institutomora.edu.mx

© The Author(s), under exclusive license to Springer Nature Switzerland AG 2022 **231**
J. Knijnik, G. Garton (eds.), *Women's Football in Latin America*, New Femininities in
Digital, Physical and Sporting Cultures,
https://doi.org/10.1007/978-3-031-09127-8_13

team as well as England, Austria, Switzerland and Denmark also participated. That year, Mexico's team achieved a third-place finish and would finish as runners-up in the next year's World Cup held in Mexico. Neither event was sanctioned by the Fédération Internationale de Football Association (FIFA); however, both set an important precedent in the history of women's football.

Despite this early success, it would take more than two decades for another national team to be organised, this time to participate in the qualifying rounds for the first FIFA Women's World Cup held in China in 1991, although the Mexicans were unable to achieve qualification. In this sense, the history of Vargas's life is a window through which we can approach this important era in women's football and analyse how Mexican women transgressed and resisted gendered discourses that imposed a model of domesticity on them (Santillán & Gantús, 2010).

This author considers Alicia Vargas, along with her fellow players, to be a transgressive character in two senses. First, by playing football she entered a space historically reserved for the expression of hegemonic masculinity. It was common for women to approach this sport as spectators or even as 'trophies' for the most virile winners, but not as players (Torrebadella-Flix, 2016). In this way, when Alicia began to play football on the streets, eventually playing in teams and leagues, she contributed to the transformation of football into a field of dispute, in which female players challenged the social values and gender stereotypes that defined them as tender, fragile and passive (Espinosa, 2016; Santillán & Gantús, 2010). Second, by demanding recognition as professionals, Alicia Vargas and her teammates incorporated an element that made their struggle more complex: the labour dimension, or their status as workers. In this sense, they fought to receive fair remuneration for their service, equal to that of their male counterparts.

This chapter is divided into three sections that follow Alicia Vargas's career. The first explores her approach to amateur sports and how she joined organised football. The second section deals with her experience as a national team player and her participation in the first and second Women's World Cups. Finally, the third part explores her return to amateur teams and her final involvement with the national team in 1991.

This investigation relied on structured interviews and unstructured conversations with Alicia Vargas during March 2021. A lot of attention was given to the words and, especially, the silences she used while remembering her life story. It was also very important to cross-reference her testimony with hemerographic resources from that period; thus, journals (e.g., *El Heraldo de México, La Prensa* and *Novedades*) as well as magazines like *Balón* were consulted. This contrastive method allowed the author to fill information voids and broaden the perspective on the women's football phenomenon in Mexico.

Origins: From the Streets to the Fields

Alicia Vargas (born February 2, 1954, in Guanajuato, a state in central México) moved to Mexico City with her family at a very early age. During her childhood, she used to play with her four sisters and two brothers, the latter avid football fans. The relationship with her siblings gave her an early insight into football. Between the ages of 10 and 12, family and friends grew increasingly surprised at her game skills in the parks and streets of her neighbourhood. Nevertheless, some neighbors were not happy about the girl who practiced this sport. Alicia remembers that 'it was very frowned upon. Sometimes they would say things to my mother, that she should force me into the kitchen, that I looked *fea* (ugly) playing with the boys. They felt it was an invasion; they did not understand how a woman was going to play a 'male sport" (Vargas, personal communication, March 16, 2021). Comments of this nature were not limited to neighbours. Individuals who enjoyed a certain prestige within the community were also opinionated; for example, during his Sunday sermon, the local priest reprimanded mothers who allowed their daughters to play with boys (Vargas, personal communication, March 16, 2021).

Despite the rejection in some sectors and the insults she had to face, Alicia defended her right to practice her favorite sport. In addition, she was not the only girl in the mid-1960s who exhibited a deep passion for football. Mexican women had already formed amateur teams as early as the 1930s (Añorve, 2019), and countries (e.g., England, Australia, China, France, Chile and Argentina) also had women's teams (Williams, 2007;

Elsey & Nadel, 2019; Franzini, 2005) So, it can be presumed that, although it remained hidden, women's football was present and survived through hardships. Historiographic evidence indicates that the first matches were met with resistance, some segments diminished their importance, rejected them or outright banned them. Examples of the latter include the bans of women's football in England from 1921 to 1971 and in Brazil from 1941 to 1979 (Williams, 2007; Knijnik, 2014; Votre & Mourão, 2003).

Nevertheless, it was towards the end of the 1950s when the sport earned attention in several states of Mexico; for example, in Jalisco and Tamaulipas, several exhibition matches were organised (Carreño, 2006). In that sense, the tours of foreign female teams in Mexico became a major source of its popularisation. Among them, América of Costa Rica and Costa Rica FC held several friendly matches in Mexico in 1963 (Elsey & Nadel, 2019).

Likewise, the growth of women's football in Mexico occurred within a framework of drastic social and cultural transformations. During the 1950s, Mexico was mainly a rural country, but by the 1970s 60% of the nation's population lived in urban areas (The World Bank, 2018). In this context, women's participation in the workforce increased dramatically as well as their access to educational opportunities (Sánchez, 2002). For example, in the 1970s, women represented 17.6% of the total labour force, while 65% of women had at least finished elementary school (Instituto Nacional de Estadística, Geografía e Informática, 2007). Although fewer women than men benefitted from these opportunities, they were able to study and work in greater proportions than their mothers and grandmothers of prior generations.

These changes coincided with the momentum of second-wave feminism that, during the 1960s and 1970s, defended the right of women to develop beyond the domestic sphere, called for labour equality and defied the notion of motherhood as a social imperative, among other changes. In other words, as these adjustments took place, gender identities also underwent a transformative process: women's life plans emphasised their satisfaction related to professional development. This was a break with traditional gendered discourse which placed a universal obligation for marriage and motherhood on all women (Espinosa, 2016).

In this context, Alicia Vargas entered football, first playing in the streets of her neighbourhood. When she was 15, she heard that the women's teams of the América and Guadalajara clubs were playing a friendly match near her. She attended eagerly, hoping to play despite not being part of any team. The match took place on the field at the *Tribunal para menores* (Juvenile court). After watching the first half, she approached both José Morales, Guadalajara's coach, and Elsa Salgado, the team captain. Alicia asserted herself so much that both parties allowed her to play. At the end of the match, Alicia also convinced them to let her join the team. In this way, she became a player for Guadalajara, a club that was in the process of joining the only women's league in the country—the América League (Vargas, personal communication, March 16, 2021).

Alicia Vargas's entry into organised football would not have been possible without the effort and organisation of the enthusiasts who created this tournament. The América League had its roots in the passion of cheerleaders from Club América who also wanted to play. By November 1969, there were 16 independent teams in Mexico City and nearby cities; thus, Efraín Pérez decided to organise the First Amateur Women's Football Championship of Mexico City, also known as the América League. Pérez was a coach who had recently graduated from the *Escuela Nacional de Educación Física* (ENEF) and became involved in the training of the women soccer players of Club América.

Ten teams from Mexico City and six from nearby states, such as the State of Mexico, Morelos and Puebla, participated in the América League (Carreño, 2006). In the following months, more women were organising new teams and applying to enter the competition. The growth in popularity enabled the formation of the Asociación Mexicana de Futbol Femenil A.C. (Mexican Association of Women's Football, AMFF) in February of 1970 (Carreño, 2006). This association was very important for Alicia Vargas's sporting career; at that time, she could never have foreseen that football would take her to another continent.

The First Women's Team and Job Offers

In April 1970. the Federation of Independent European Female Football (FIEFF) invited AMFF to participate in the first Women's World Cup, sponsored by the alcoholic beverage company Martini & Rossi. The AMFF held a thorough local selection process, after which a team of 16 players was formed, among whom was Alicia Vargas (Carreño, 2006). Alicia and her teammates attended the training sessions thanks to the financial assistance of their families, and after just two months of training, they traveled to Italy.

The national team did not have the FMF's support, and the players went through several hardships to complete the journey. The women met at the Mexico City airport without uniforms, shoes, flags or emblems that identified them as national representatives. A few moments before boarding the plane, they received uniforms from an anonymous sponsor. Alicia recalls that they were not sure, but, from the labels on the jackets, they assumed that the uniforms came from Enrique Borja, a famous Mexican football player and owner of a sporting goods store (Vargas, personal communication, March 16, 2021).

The hardships suffered by the Mexican team mirror the ones their Argentinian counterparts experienced a year later. According to Ayelén Pujol (2019), the Argentinian women's team also lacked uniforms, equipment, a medical team, a masseuse or a coach. This reveals two facts: the dismissiveness of the sport's governing bodies in both countries and the bravery of the athletes who defended their right to play despite facing major adversities.

In Italy, Alicia dazzled the European press. After winning their opening match against Austria 9 to 0, the Mexicans reached the semi-finals, and, despite losing to tournament hosts, they later took third place by defeating England. Vargas's abilities earned her the recognition of tournament most valuable player (MVP). The European press compared her playing style with that of the Italian Angelo Domenghini and the Brazilian superstar Edson Arantes Do Nascimento, better known as 'Pelé'. Back in Mexico, coach Efraín Pérez stated to the Mexican press that some players, including Alicia Vargas, had received offers from Italian teams, but the players declined them citing 'family reasons' (Carreño, 2006). Yet, in reality, Alicia did not receive a formal offer on that occasion (Vargas, personal communication, March 16, 2021).

When she returned to Mexico City, she discovered that more teams and women's football leagues had emerged; some of them included the Iztaccíhuatl League, Xochimilco League, National School of Physical Education League and Naucalpan League (Carreño, 2006). Women were attracted to the sport by Mexico's good performance in the World Cup. Later that year, sports promoter, Jaime de Haro, saw a business opportunity if a second world championship were to be celebrated in Mexico. The project came to fruition when the Mexican delegation, composed of Efraín Pérez, journalist Manelich Quintero and Jaime de Haro himself, traveled to the FIEFF congress in Italy to win the bid to host and formalisd the tournament for September 1970.

Nevertheless, organising a team for the second World Cup became even more complicated. The appearance of new teams and leagues triggered bureaucratic mishaps. Every league and team made their own decisions and a consensus was unreachable. Alicia recalls that originally it was established that the players would be picked after the celebration of a *selectivo*—a tournament where more players would be oberved as a kind of trial. This new roster would be reinforced with players from the team that played in the 1970 World Cup, most of whom were members of the América League. By then, Guadalajara, Alicia's club, had already left that league in favor of the Iztaccíhuatl League, so despite her participation in the prior World Cup, she had to participate in the *selectivo* (Vargas, personal communication, March 16, 2021).

Even though the *selectivo* did take place, in a last minute decision the coaches decided that the national team would be the same one that traveled to Italy, but the players had to be part of the América League. Only three footballers from the rest of the leagues would be included as reinforcements. Alicia's participation was in doubt because of this administrative confusion; just a week before the tournament, coach Víctor Manuel Meléndez finally called her in as a player (Vargas, personal communication, March 16, 2021).

It is possible to confirm, thanks to reports in the press, that the 1971 Women's World Cup in Mexico was a sporting and commercial success.

Even though the total profit generated is unknown, some newspapers estimated it to be around 8-million Mexican pesos (4.2 million in today's US dollars, adjusted for inflation), but this estimate did not include the broadcasting fees for Mexico and several countries in Europe (*El Heraldo de México*, 1971; *La Prensa*, 1971). According to *El Heraldo de México* (1971), the event included musical intermissions, folk dance numbers, acrobats and an exhibition match played by local actresses and singers. Manelich Quintero, Teodoro Cano, Hugo Sanmontiel and Juan Acevedo are some of this newspaper's journalists who gave great details about the competition while also pointing out the impact it had on its audience. *El Heraldo de México* reported 90 thousand people in Estadio Azteca for the opening ceremony, an important indicator of the tournament's success.

Alicia Vargas once again showed her skills, and this time she and her teammates reached the final. Thanks to coverage in newspapers, one also knows that the matches were broadcast on television and that many businesses organised publicity campaigns around the competition, such as the department store El Palacio de Hierro (*Novedades*, 1971). Television broadcasting of women's football was not a novelty because matches of the first female leagues of Mexico City were shown on Channel 8 a few years earlier. The Mexican case was not an exception; other countries, like Argentina, also organised friendly tournaments of women's football that were also broadcast on television (Pujol, 2019).

In the 1971 World Cup, the Mexican team's matches filled the Azteca Stadium with eager fans. Vargas attributes this attendance to a lewd curiosity because, despite the success achieved the year before, various sectors of society still considered it improper for women to play football, arguing that it was a 'rough' sport (Vargas, personal communication, March 16, 2021). In this sense, it is important to remember that throughout the twentieth century and as women entered the sports field with greater force, the limits of their infiltration were redefined by differentiating sports practices between those considered 'feminine' and 'masculine'. Those of the latter category were understood as practices in which physical expressions of violence and aggression were developed, assumed as characteristics of masculinity (Moreno, 2007). For this reason, some sectors of society viewed sports (e.g., gymnastics, tennis, swimming, volleyball or basketball) as better suited for women; football was not among them (Moreno, 2007).

This vision was also shared by the tournament organisers, who modified the game regulations and presented them as 'concessions' that would make football a sport suitable for women. One of these changes, enforced during the World Cup, reduced the playing time of each half from 45 to 35 minutes. Likewise, 'feminine' details were added to the stadium. For example, the goalposts were painted with pink stripes, and pots of yellow chrysanthemums were placed behind the goals and on the players' benches. Similarly, the media declared that the dressing rooms were transformed into 'beauty salons' (Espinosa, 2016).

In the same vein, the Mexican press actively objectified the players through chronicles and cartoons; their presence on the football field was associated with sexual issues, as though being an object of longing for the male gaze was an obligation and an inherent female quality (Santillán & Gantús, 2010). Alicia was no stranger to these gazes, and she remembers that the fans 'were lewd; they wanted to see how we lowered the ball with our chest or how our legs looked' (Vargas, personal communication, March 16, 2021). The sexualisation of football players by the media and fans alike was not an isolated case. The same phenomenon occurred in other regions and still lingers. According to Goellner (2005), Brazil had built a discourse of eroticism around female players since the 1970s, which emphasised the sensuality of their bodies above their qualities as players; this is similar to what the Mexican players experienced around the same time.

Despite the hardships that arose as the tournament progressed, Vargas's talent and bravery led the Mexicans to the final match. It was then that the women challenged the organisers; they demanded remuneration for their services: two million pesos (1.055 million US dollars adjusted for inflation) divided equally between all the players and staff members, 20 people in total. Alicia Vargas was 17 years old at the time, and most of her teammates were her age or even younger. According to her statement, the request was not an agreement among players, and most of them did not find out about it until it was published in the newspapers. Nonetheless, she sympathised with the request: Alicia was one of the most vocal advocates in the media as we can see in the newspapers of the time.

In an interview with Bernardo Vargas García, from *Balón* magazine, she declared: 'It is improper that the organisers keep all the money and they do not give us anything because we are the most important part of the show. But we are going to speak up' (1971). Despite the demands, the event promoters and organisers refused to pay; they argued that the players were amateur. Alicia remembers that '[the tournament] gave them a lot of money and we did not receive anything. Sometimes we did not even have enough money to buy the newspaper. We bought one and shared it to read the news. We depended [financially] on our families' (Vargas, personal communication, March 16, 2021). When the press questioned her, she answered that if this were an amateur tournament, then they should not charge the fans an entrance fee. Likewise, she did not hesitate to point out that it was unfair that players did not receive any remuneration despite being the stars of the show while the organisers profitted from their image and work (Vargas, personal communication, March 16, 2021).

Alicia Vargas's position can be explained from what Hollander (2002) calls gender resistance. This is a set of intentional or unintentional acts, which are opposed to conventional expectations or beliefs about roles and behaviors that, in a certain vision, each gender should perform (Hollander, 2002). According to Hollander, it is unlikely that individual actions by themselves produce a determining social change, but by developing alternative discourses based on them, they acquire greater impact and become key elements that allow confrontation against hegemonic models of masculinity and femininity. When Alicia played football, she clearly exemplified a form of gender resistance in Hollander's terms. In the same way, by articulating discourses that criticised the decisions of the organisers and the unequal treatment to which the football players were subjected, she transgressed the dominant patterns regarding femininity (Hollander, 2002), according to which a woman had to dedicate herself to housework and, of course, in no way could claim a fair payment—one that any man would receive for performing the same job.

Still, after the organisers refused to pay them, some players suggested a resistance tactic: not playing in the final until their demands were met. In this situation, the young women were coerced by promoter Jaime de Haro and by the federal authorities of Mexico City. After several days of agitated discussions, they convinced the players to play the last match against Denmark. The Mexican team showed up, and although they did not win, they achieved one of the most important results in the history of Mexican women's football—World Cup runners-up. As part of their recognition, the players received financial support from a group of Mexican actresses and singers who raised money outside the stadium and distributed it among the players. On the other hand, Jaime de Haro, motivated by the scandal and with the intention that the players desist from the request, gave around 10 000 pesos (5275 in today's US dollars) to each one of the players once the tournament ended (Vargas, personal communication, March 16, 2021).

After the championship, most of the women returned to their teams and leagues as amateur footballers. Martha Espinosa (2016) has emphasised that, despite how transgressive their participation in the second Women's World Cup was, most of the players saw their foray into football as just another stage in their lives. For most of them, this was a moment of transition between adolescence and adulthood, which would be marked by marriage (Espinosa, 2016). Yet, Alicia Vargas went beyond this and defended her football career as a legitimate profession. Her performance in both the Italy and Mexico World Cups was an important showcase for her abilities, which piqued the interest of European teams. Italian club Real Torino contacted her in 1971 to offer her an opportunity to join, along with a scholarship for her studies, guaranteed accommodations and a salary. She accepted under two conditions: first, that they allow her to reach the age of majority—18 years of age in Mexico—and second, that the offer be put in writing, in a duly signed contract, which should be validated by the Mexican and Italian authorities (Vargas, personal communication, March 16, 2021).

When she turned 18, a representative of the Italian club went to Alicia's house in Mexico City with the plane tickets to Italy. Vargas inquired about the contract and received an unexpected answer: she could review it when she was in Europe, not before. 'We are not accepting that. If you are not serious about your contracts, I am not leaving. Take your tickets with you', the player declared (Vargas, personal communication, March 16, 2021). 'You are going to regret it', snapped the representative, but Alicia ignored him.

This episode is very indicative of Vargas's ideals. When she requested that the offer be duly placed in a contract, she demanded the same dignified and serious treatment male football players received. With her actions, Alicia entered a struggle that continues to this day, that of equal pay. Even though women's football has undergone a global process of professionalisation through the years, the pay gap between male and female players is still one of the most visible aspects of gender discrimination in sports, especially when female players are forced to quit their profession at an early age because of economical hardships caused by low or nonexistent salaries (Aliendre & Contreras, 2019). Thus, when Alicia demanded recognition for her work under dignified conditions in the 1970s, she took the first steps in defending a cause that still is one of the main demands of current female footballers.

Return to Amateur Leagues and Alicia's Last National Team Experience

During the 1970s, Alicia was actively playing for teams of various amateur tournaments, such as Guadalajara and Jalisco of the Iztaccíhuatl and Independiente leagues, respectively (Vargas, personal communication, March 16, 2021). Like several of her former teammates in the national team, she studied physical education and went on tours with the national women's team to various cities in Mexico. These itinerant exhibition matches were organised by sports promoters who pitted national team players against local clubs. Still, Alicia remembers that travel conditions were not always the best, and she never received any kind of payment for the tours. The promoters' argument, as they had stated before, was that the footballers were amateurs and thus they should not charge a playing fee.

For this reason, the tours only covered the transportation and accommodations of the players. Alicia remembers that 'at the end of the matches the promoters always told us that they had not earned much, that it was all spent on the hotel and what we had eaten'. She recalls that when they returned to Mexico City, they were always abandoned. 'We had to wait as a group until the subway opened because they abandoned us on the street regardless of the time of the night; they did not even give us money for a taxi fare' (Vargas, personal communication, March 16, 2021).

Despite the difficult circumstances, Alicia was part of the team that in 1976 toured Costa Rica, marking the official debut of the Costa Rican women's national team (Hinojosa, 2016). The Mexican's second-place in the 1971 Women's World Cup motivated more and more women to form amateur teams in several regions of the country. For example, Mercedes Rodríguez Alemán entered the national team a few years later; she recalls being inspired by the success of the Mexican team in 1970 and 1971, and those matches also motivated women in her native Coahuila to form teams (Elsey & Nadel, 2019).

Notwithstanding this growing interest, Alicia noticed that the support for women's football and the national team was not increasing. For this reason, she decided to quit the tours. Her companions, on the other hand, organised a team called Mundialistas that participated in the Cabeza de Juárez League, which they won between 1973 and 1980 (Elsey & Nadel, 2019). Vargas continued her football career in the Jalisco team until 1991 when she, already a veteran player, received a peculiar proposal: a return to the national team.

To understand how unexpected this proposal was, we must remember that the FIFA did not yet recognise the 1970 and 1971 World Cups as official tournaments. In addition, for several years, they were indifferent to the development of women's football. It was not until the late 1980s and 1990s that this position began to change; this led to the organisation of the first FIFA Women's World Cup in China in November 1991 (Williams, 2007). The qualifying round offered only two places for CONCACAF teams. Alicia Vargas received the offer to return to the national team after the FMF hastily improvised the organisation of a team to participate in the qualifying playoffs in Port-au-Prince, Haiti.

Twenty years had passed since the Mexican women were runner-up World Champions. Alicia's conditions were no longer the same. She had a stable job that could not be neglected to join the national team, so she was hesitant to accept. Still, the FMF insisted, and, after acquiring the necessary work permits, she joined the team. This was the only intervention by the FMF that Alicia witnessed: 'We did not receive support; we had no field, no balls and we did physical conditioning at Alameda Central Park', a public space in the heart of Mexico City (Vargas, personal communication, March 16, 2021).

With the same abandonment they experienced two decades ago, the Mexican women's national team prepared for the regional playoffs. A few days before traveling, the team received flags and uniforms. The former player recalls that when the press interviewed her about their chances, she gave a hopeless response; given the poor preparation of the football players and the nonexistent support of both the team managers and the federation, the probability of qualification was minimal (Vargas, personal communication, March 16, 2021).

The veteran football player was not wrong because the Mexican team failed to qualify for the 1991 FIFA Women's World Cup, which also marked the end of Alicia's participation in the national team. After playoffs, she returned to her work and her daily life. That last experience was enough for her to understand that women's football was ignored by Mexican managers and promoters while in other countries (e.g., the United States), it was growing fast. Back in Mexico, Vargas faced health problems; she had to undergo surgery after suffering a fracture in her fibula during a match. After recovering, she returned to the fields, played for a couple more years and retired. 'Being a professional footballer was my dream. I could have even played in a men's team', Alicia recalls; she was aware that certain circumstances were the reason her plans never came to total fruition.

Several years later, Irma Chávez, a teammate from the 1971 national team, called Alicia on the phone. She convinced her to buy the local newspaper. 'You are the best', she told her joyfully, knowing that Alicia's triumph was the triumph of a whole generation. In the newspaper, Alicia discovered that the IFFHS had named her the third-best CONCACAF player of the twentieth century, tied with United States' national team player Julie Foudy and just under Foudy's compatriots Michelle Akers and Mia Hamm. At that moment, Alicia knew that the world had not forgotten them.

Conclusions

The life experiences of Alicia Vargas are a valuable window into a vital period in Mexican women's football between 1970 and 1991. Her case allows one to see that, despite difficult circumstances, women communicated forms of resisting and transgressing hegemonic models of femininity. At the same time, they articulated discourses and took action against the conditions they faced. Alicia, with courage and dignity, demanded recognition as a professional football player, a worker who deserved a fair salary and decent treatment. The support and solidarity from other women, such as actresses and singers, showed Alicia's cause, and that of her teammates, was based on a structural problem suffered by women in various professional activities. In this sense, her stance and her actions contributed to a struggle that continues to this day: that of labour equity and the defence of every woman's right to develop professionally in any chosen field.

References

Aliendre, C. R., & González, M. C. (2019). La discriminación de género en el deporte. El caso del futbol femenino. *Scientiamericana. Revista Multidisciplinaria, 6*(2), 81–90.

Añorve, D. (2019). El desarrollo del futbol femenil en México: entre la policía y la política en los procesos de inclusión y exclusión (1970–2017). *Ponta Grossa, 27*, 9–26.

Carreño, M. (2006). *Futbol femenil en México, 1969–1971* (Tesis de Licenciatura en Historia). Universidad Nacional Autónoma de México.

Elsey, B., & Nadel, J. (2019). *Futbolera. A history of women and sports in Latin America*. University of Texas Press.

Espinosa, M. L. (2016). *Género y cultura de masas en el proceso de modernización de México en la década de 1970: El II campeonato mundial de futbol femenil (1971) y el concurso de belleza Miss Universo (1978)* (Tesis de Maestría en Estudios de Género). El Colegio de México.

Franzini, F. (2005). Futebol é 'coisa para macho'? Pequeno esboço para uma história das mulheres no país do futebol. *Revista Brasileira de História, 25*(50), 315–328.

Goellner, S. (2005). Mulheres e futebol no Brasil: entre sombras e visibilidades. *Brazilian Journal of Physical Education and Sport, 19*(2), 141–151.

Hinojosa D. (2016). *El fútbol femenino profesional. Una perspectiva de género desde Argentina, Costa Rica y México* (Tesis de Maestría en Estudios Latinoamericanos). Universidad Autónoma del Estado de México.

Hollander, J. A. (2002). Resisting vulnerability: The social reconstruction of gender in interaction. *Social Problems, 49*(4), 474–496.

Instituto Nacional de Estadística, Geografía e Informática. (2007). *Mujeres y Hombres en México*. Instituto Nacional de Estadística, Geografía e Informática.

Knijnik, J. (2014). Gendered barriers to Brazilian female football: Twentieth-century legacies. In J. Hargreaves & E. Anderson (Eds.), *Routledge handbook of sport, gender and sexuality* (pp. 121–128). Routledge.

Moreno, H. (2007). Mi última pelea. *Debate Feminista: Cuerpo, 36*, 11–29.

Pujol, A. (2019). *¡Qué Jugadora! Un siglo de Fútbol Femenino en la Argentina*. Ariel.

Sánchez, A. R. (2002). *El feminismo mexicano ante el movimiento urbano popular. Dos expresiones de la lucha de género (1970–1985)*. Universidad Nacional Autónoma de México, Plaza Valdés.

Santillán, M., & Gantús, F. (2010). Transgresiones femeninas: futbol. Una mirada desde la caricatura de la prensa, México 1970–1971. *Tzin Tzun. Revista de Estudios históricos, 52*, 143–176.

The World Bank. (2018). *Urban population (% of total)*. https://data.worldbank.org/indicator/SP.URB.TOTL.IN.ZS?locations=MX

Torrebadella-Flix, X. (2016). Fútbol en femenino. Notas para la construcción de una historia social del deporte femenino en España, 1900–1936. *Investigaciones Feministas, 7*(1), 313–334.

Vargas, B. (1977, Septiembre 2). Nosotros hicimos el negocio y no nos pagan un céntimo / Alicia Vargas entrevistada por Bernardo Vargas García. *Balón. Fútbol Mundial, 5*.

Votre, S., & Mourão, L. (2003). Women's football in Brazil: Progress and problems. *Soccer and Society, 4*(2/3), 254–267.

Williams, J. (2007). *A beautiful game. International perspectives on women's football*. Berg.

14

An Oral History of Women's Football in Colombia: Building Tools for Collective Action

Gabriela Ardila Biela

Introduction

The history of football practiced by women in Colombia has not been a particularly researched field in historiography, sports and football. This author wants to clarify why it is imporant to write about 'football practiced by women' and not 'female football' as it is called in Spanish—it is the same sport played by various people. One should not believe there is women's football and men's football, separately (Rial, 2013). Apart from some journalistic texts and a few articles, such as Watson's (2021), the only book on the subject was published in February 2021 by the social communicator Carolina Jaramillo Seligmann (2021); it is entitled *'Balón de Cristal': A History of Women's Football in Colombia*. The book is constructed on interviews to explain a story that focuses mainly on the last

G. Ardila Biela
University of Hamburg, Hamburg, Germany

© The Author(s), under exclusive license to Springer Nature Switzerland AG 2022
J. Knijnik, G. Garton (eds.), *Women's Football in Latin America*, New Femininities in Digital, Physical and Sporting Cultures,
https://doi.org/10.1007/978-3-031-09127-8_14

247

20 years of football practiced by women in Colombia, not claiming that this is where its history begins, but rather exploring this era in more detail.

This chapter argues that women have been playing football since its origins in England. In Colombia there are journalistic records as early as 1949, in which various matches are reported ('La reina caleña', 1949; 'Solteritas y a la Orden', 1949). Nevertheless, why are there so few studies on the subject? Why is there so little talk in the media about football practiced by women? Why is it that when people think about football, they usually think about men playing football?

Colombia has had a women's national team since 1998, as well as regional amateur leagues since the 1980s, and women in the country have been interested in the sport and playing it at least since the late 1940s. This chapter seeks to reflect on the possible reasons for the erasure of women football players in the history of football in the country and which tools are useful to make them visible, and using these tools to begin the path toward visibility. To accomplish this, the chapter focuses on experiences of women playing football in Bogotá, Bucaramanga, Cali and Medellín. First, the role that football has played in the construction of 'feminine' and 'masculine' binary bodies is analysed, each with their specific characteristics without the possibility of existing outside this binarism and the imaginaries of the nation. Then, using a feminist perspective, the chapter reflects on the place attributed to women in this construction and the spaces of escape they have built (Müller, 2009). Finally, it presents and analyses the reflections of women on their experiences, using the methodology of oral history. This chapter's objective is to visibilise the stories of women who play football and contribute to current knowledge of their history, struggles, achievements and difficulties.

Body Politics

Sociological studies have investigated the uses of sport in the construction of national identity, recognising that its usefulness is not based on sporting achievements, but rather on the processes of differentiation and exclusion that can be generated through sporting practices (Patiño, 2010). Since the late nineteenth and early twentieth centuries, the

Colombian bourgeoisie, which was beginning to consider a capitalist development project to be a republic, was nourished by sports practices imported from Europe and the United States for this socio-political project (Patiño, 2010). For example, clubs were created to promote urban sports practices exclusively for the bourgeoisie as well as to discuss politics and literature in those spaces, building a material and symbolic differentiation from the rest of the population (Patiño, 2010):

This exclusionary practice of differentiation gained momentum in two directions: on the one hand, building exclusive spaces and, on the other hand, aiding in the search for national policies to control the population, based on racist reflections of a eugenic hygienist nature (Patiño, 2010). This exclusionary 'geographic' practice was accomplished through the creation of elite clubs in the cities, so the upper classes and their families could enjoy and play tennis, golf, and other elitist and new sports while practices of social control grew through the development of public policies in schools and sport spaces (Patiño, 2010).

Thus, Law 80 of 1925 created the National Commission of Physical Education, which received a budget to regulate sports events, the use of public spaces for sports, sports presentations during national holidays and anthropometric measurements (*Ley 80 de 1925. Sobre educación …*, 1925). This law rather than a practical reality exemplifies a discourse that was being expanded because it was only in 1933, with the approval of Decree 1734, that sport became regulated by the state and along with it the search to control and shape bodies (Patiño, 2010). In theory, this law and decree should have popularised sport in Colombia, not just making it accessible for more people but also by controlling the measurements of the people who practiced sports through medical, health and anthropometric records (Gómez, 2011).

Along with the institutionalisation of sports entities, the discussion on the 'degeneration of the race', guided the eugenicist pedagogical discourse on the body and the need for physical work to combat this alleged degeneration (Roldán, 2013). Emphasising 'race' as a biological construct, these discourses reinforced the need for homogenisation with the white European population, using sports as a medium to achieve this. These media strategies were strengthened at the national level, and thus nurtured nationalist discourses entrenched in sports practices, particularly between 1948, when football practiced by men was professionalised, and 1951, when the first round of Colombia cycling practiced by men took place (Roldán, 2013). These two events were used by the State in the construction of a specific idea of a nation: strong, competitive and masculine.

This is evidenced by the advancement of the professionalisation of football practiced by men, which sought to alleviate the popular uprisings resulting from the assassination of popular political leader Jorge Eliécer Gaitán on April 9, 1948 (Racines, 2011). Gaitán was the first political leader who talked in a language that the Colombian people could understand. His assassination resulted in the historical period known in Colombia as 'The Violence'. In other words, Colombia was facing a difficult time in which the two political parties found themselves in a violent war and Colombian ideas were divided into liberal and conservative thought. The government used sports, specifically football and cycling, to create an idea of unity across the political positions that fuelled the two-party war and used physical education in schools to construct bodies according to gender, class and racial stereotypes (Racines, 2011; Gómez, 2011).

Building the Feminine Body: Control and Exclusion in Colombian Sports

At the time, women were not thought of as citizens; they had no right to vote and thus feminised bodies were assigned the specific task of reproduction. This control over feminised bodies was framed in terms of reproductive capacities and was a central argument for the supposed need to regulate, dominate and exploit these bodies. In the field of education, in the first half of the twentieth century, schools guided the education of girls towards the service of their family and community. Later, other pathways were opened that allowed them to go to university while maintaining the role of mother, wife and educator (Báez, 2011). That is to say, although new opportunities appeared, control of bodies by the State was maintained.

The antropologist Zandra Pedraza takes up the specificities during the educational reforms of the first half of the twentieth century around sports. It is worth noting that one of early physical education's main characteristics was division according to social class, age and sex. Specific exercises were exclusively for upper-class men while mechanical forms of gymnastics were intended for other people, such as the popular classes and women (Gómez, 2011). Among women, class also mattered because, before the State had eugenic interests in maternity and childcare, only upper-class women could practice what was called physical culture.

The gynaecological discourses that inspired the country's sport and educational policies affirmed the need to subdue the typical 'irritability' of women through adequate physical education. These were also discussed during the first National Pedagogical Congress, where medical doctors reinforced the differences between sexes, and so the fragility of women's bodies. This encouraged the prioritisation of the pedagogical use of exercises for women that exalted feminine beauty and grace (Gómez, 2011).

Thus, by the 1940s, sports became part of women's education through the specification of which disciplines were acceptable and how women should practice them. Therefore, they were permitted to participate in those disciplines that revered delicacy while rejecting the exhaustion and masculinisation of the female body, which should embody elegance. Thus, sports such as basketball, volleyball and other ball sports (a list in which football was not mentioned), were regarded positively for the development of women's bodies. This sort of sports segregation also happened in other South American countries, as pointed out by Brazilian researcher Silvana Goellner (2005), who reflects on the discourse about the masculinisation of female bodies in football. There are similar investigations in the same direction on Mexico (Nadel, 2014) and other countries in Latin America (Elsey & Nadel, 2019) and Europe (e.g., Germany), where some studies highlighted the argument of masculinisation of women's bodies as a primary obstacle to their access to football (Selmer, 2013).

Other sports were accepted for developing specific body parts, such as swimming, rowing, skating and even cycling. The main goal was to develop an elegant body and protect the reproductive organs (Gómez, 2011). This last argument was also used in other places:

> In the 1920s, invigorated efforts began to exclude women from football within physical education programs. In part this was due to the perceived physicality of the game, in part due to its supposed masculinizing nature. Moreover, the increasing identification of football as the national sport heightened its representative power. The process of professionalization of men's football in the early 1930s and its perception as violent, … created new market approaches to the sport that increased its penetration into social life. (Elsey & Nadel, 2019, p. 66)

Overcoming Body Control and Colombian Football's Pioneers

Sport represented the institutionalised construction (at least through discourse) of sexualised bodies through physical education in public and private schools with differences of class, sex, gender, racialisation and ability. Although bodies were stereotyped and acceptable activities for each were limited in public education and state discourses, however, many people bypassed these spaces of control and actively practiced the sports they chose (Elsey & Nadel, 2019). After overcoming stereotypes, the challenge has been to overcome erasure. Because sports are builders of bodies and nations, as stated earlier, deletion of women in football from the field of historiography, as well as the study and analysis of the sport, has been the subsequent way to maintain control. This is why, even though there are numerous studies on football, almost all of them refer to football practiced by men.

It could then be considered that the Colombian State's controls were successful and women did not practice football, but this argument is easily refuted by a quick review of press articles from the late 1940s. This author's research of the Colombian press included analysing two national magazines, *Semana* and *Cromos*, specifically, as well as some national and local newspapers according to tips given by interviewees and other academics (Watson, 2019). is The first year in which it was possible to find something about football practiced by women was 1949 in the form of references to some matches played in Cali and Barranquilla. Also, there are articles that appear in 1951 about two Costa Rican women's teams that toured Colombia and encountered obstacles, mainly in Bogotá with the criticism of the league's decency—that is, a group of conservative politicians' wives questioned the morality of the event (Zeledón, 1999).

Although there are some newspaper articles on the topic during the 1950s, 1960s and 1970s, there are less than 15, which seems to signify a low interest on the part of women to practice this sport. This absence is why it is necessary, from a feminist perspective of historiographic analysis, to resort to oral history to glimpse the developments of historical agents that have been made invisible—in this case, women who practice football.

Oral Histories of Colombian Women's Football

Oral history is characterised by the fact that it is done in practice; in addition, it confronts debates about objectivity and subjectivity, memory and the present. The historian Carmen Collado Herrera asserts that there are two ways of doing oral history: through oral archives and through the collection of sources and consulting testimonies (Collado Herrera, 2006). The latter is the method used in for this investigation. Thus, the author understands oral history as a tool that creates, among other things, sources, which are the joint result of the articulation of the oral discourse that emerges in the encounter between interviewer and interviewee.

Based on this, in this work interviews were conducted with the objective of learning about the experiences lived by the women players in the development of football. The interviews reflect the subjectivity of the interviewees in the reconstruction of their memory as well as subjectivity in the formulation of the questions. The systematisation of these interviews allows one to reflect on the possibility of collective memories of football practiced by women in diverse cities and also on the various interregional sports encounters.

Women players have appeared and disappeared from football history. Their existence has been thought of as exaggerated or monstrous and their exclusion has been justified by the supposed lack of female sporting tradition (Elsey & Nadel, 2019):

> Women's soccer in Latin America, however, was not simply overlooked. National leaders sought to suppress it. Sports authorities systematically closed down options for women to play the game with the support of public health 'experts' who claimed that soccer damaged women's reproductive capacities. Ultimately, the reason for banning women's soccer had little to do with the game itself and much more to do with the meaning of soccer and womanhood for Latin American nations. While men's soccer was—and remains—the national game throughout much of the region, women's soccer was seen as the threat, making the game almost antinational. The idea that women soccer players violated national ethos led to the near dismissal of the sport. (Nadel, 2014, pp. 209–210)

Understanding that the erasure of women players is framed in social, political and economic structures, this author sought to dismantle this imaginary of women players without a football career. Using their voices, the aim was to build narratives that can nurture the past and thus strengthen the present towards a future where women and dissidents can practice the sports they want to practice in a dignified manner.

To challenge the dominant history and reflect on the narratives of women players, we understand them as an important part of oral history. As Dora Schwarzstein proposes:

> Oral history by—reflecting on the nature of the process of remembering as a key element in the compression of the subjective meaning of human experiences and by trying to explain the nature of individual and collective memories—allows for the construction of an innovative and different modality of dialogue between memory and history. (2002, p. 489)

This chapter discusses the conversations and interviews with 20 different people involved with football in Colombia, including women players and male coaches of football practiced by women. The interviews were semi-structured and took place in the Colombian cities of Medellín, Cali, Bucaramanga and Bogotá. The data was collected between 2018 and 2021. The women players interviewed had diverse experiences and expectations within the sport. Seven of the interviewees were part of the first official national team and some of them have been coaches. Some of the interviewees visualised and imagined a life as a football player while others played football as a hobby. The times in which the players have been active range from 1970 to the present. This diversity is intentional, because the author sought to investigate football practiced by women in dissimilar spaces, both institutional and self-organised.

The Beginning: Influence of Brothers and the Streets

From the narratives of the players, there are common factors in most of the accounts regardless of the interviewee's age. The players' entry into football was mainly through their siblings, cousins or parents—mostly male family members—either because they watched them play, they played together or they were fans of teams. This is a factor that is seen both in the countryside and in the city, in the players who had economic resources and those who did not and throughout the various regions of the country. Most of them explained that they started playing with their brothers or cousins or that they used their brothers' equipment (e.g., gloves or balls) despite the fact that typically they were not supported. They might not have been prohibited and some were validated, but most did not have the support of their families.

Former national team player Ruth Ortiz said: 'Well, as I think [it] is the story for all of us, I started playing football because of my brothers, because it was easier for me to play football than for them to start playing dolls with me. I only had one brother, so from a very young age I played with him'. From the narratives, the street emerges as a central place to begin in this practice. Most started in the street, either in their neighbourhoods or in towns. Myriam Guerrero, former national team player said:

> …I am a daughter who shared life with her three brothers, with a single mother who was abandoned when I was very young, so the economic limitations were extreme, and we did not know anything about toys, we did

not know anything that other children could have known. So, as a result of that, life begins to make sense in the street, it begins to make sense with a ball of paper, it begins to make sense to have a bag at your disposal, fill it with paper and kick it around.

So, the streets were central, and neighbourhood tournaments were spaces of struggle for the players. Although some founded or created mixed or women's competitions, others had to fight for the chance to play in tournaments for men and boys. The street is a common space that does not disappear when players enter other spaces. Some started playing in the street and, after passing through more institutional spaces, returned to street tournaments. There is also the example of Amparo Maldonado, a Colombian football player since 1970, who in a very particular way, entered 11-a-side football directly after a call from the Valle del Cauca league and several media outlets in 1970. She began to play, but when the league stopped supporting her, the street was the space she and other women found to continue playing.

The space of the street appeared repeatedly within the interviewees' narratives along with self-organisation. In all generations, female players have organised their own spaces for practice. On one hand, most of them created their own teams and even tournaments. They sought funding in more formal spaces such as schools or universities. In most cases, the autonomous initiatives of the players were their only opportunities to play. These were identify as emancipatory practices that are the basis for the existence of football played by women. Thus, self-organisation is a transversal characteristic of the experiences recalled by the players. Reaching institutional spaces did not mean ceasing self-organisation; many returned to self-organisation after being unable to continue in institutionalised spaces.

Official women's 11-a-side football teams (e.g., Águila Roja, Independiente Cali, Marmar and *Formas Íntimas*) were built on the foundations of self-organisation. This shows the interest of women in playing football, which is also evident in diverse places of the world; as Jorge Knijnik observes in Brazil, '[d]espite the forces that push them from one point to another on the gender continuum, and despite their compliance with or resistance to orthodox gender rules, the women are all clearly passionate and strongly committed to playing' (2015, p. 67).

The interest of women in playing football has existed since the beginning of this sport, but it has been made invisible. In 1885, the British Ladies Football Club was called Football Club, although there are records of football matches played by women as early as 1881 (Hoffmann & Nendza, 2011). In the Federal Republic of Germany, between 1950 and 1970, it was forbidden for women to play football, but during that period at least 150 games were played illegally (Heibel, 2011). Women have practiced football regardless of prohibitions or discrimination and have found and created various strategies to do so.

Practicing Gendered Football: Growing as a Footballer in a Masculine Field

Most players did not have other women as role models in football. Nevertheless, figures—such as Margarita Martinez, one of the best-known coaches who was also part of the coaching staff of the first Colombian women's national team; Amparo Maldonado, a player since 1970 and current coach; Myriam Guerrero, captain of the first women's national team and recognised coach; and Liliana Zapata, president of one of the best known Colombian women's clubs, *Formas Íntimas*—have become references for various generations and among themselves. Still, several interviewees were not aware of women playing football in their region, even from more recent generations than those mentioned before.

All the interviewees played with boys and men in their early days and for a large part of their sporting careers. Some of the players were given nicknames of male players as a sign of respect and recognition of their abilities—for example, Myriam Guerrero was called 'Sequi' and Margarita Martínez, 'Tarantini'. In other words, they were respected because they could be compared with men and thus accepted as football players. Women who played football were only accepted if they could be identified with men. Various players said this, which on the one hand goes along with the idea that football masculinises bodies. As seen earlier, in

Colombia, national educational policies at the turn of the century rejected the practice of certain sports, such as football, for women because of the potential masculinisation of their bodies (Gómez, 2011).

The idea of the masculinisation of women's bodies was based on understanding female and male bodies as necessarily distinct (as well as the only ones in existence), which created a hegemonic masculinity and femininity that had to be maintained (Faust, 2019; Müller, 2009). The masculinisation of these women made it possible to understand their participation in a sport that represented masculinity, and thus they were able to be recognised on the field. At the same time, by only accepting them as peers if they represented masculinity, the argument of football as a dangerous sport for femininity, and therefore for women, was strengthened (Elsey & Nadel, 2019; Goellner, 2005).

Regardless of whether the interviewees sought football as a career option or not, they all remember that practicing it was difficult, and they were questioned in diverse spaces for doing so. Amparo Maldonado, for instance, felt ashamed for a long time and did not invite her mother to see her play. All of them remember being insulted while playing, often about their physique but they were also attacked for their sexuality and told that their place was in the kitchen and/or having babies. Their stories are similar to what has happened in other places in Latin America (Elsey & Nadel, 2019). Similarly, most of them explain that to play football they often needed arguments beyond the desire to do so. From demonstrating that they could play, to accepting that they would put up with the conditions imposed by boys' and men's teams, to having the support of their brothers and/or friends.

Another aspect narrated repeatedly was the issue of equipment, particularly uniforms. They all remembered having to play with men's old uniforms; or, for example, the first official national team in 1998 had to fight to be allowed to keep their uniforms after competing because they were asked to return them. Sonia Chala, former national team player in 1998 voiced:

> …The bad thing is that they gave us a uniform, it was a blue and a yellow jersey. First of all, the uniforms of that time were uniforms for men, so those jerseys were like that, those were the jerseys! And when the tournament

was over, Mr. Alvaro said: 'No, I need the jerseys for the U17 team', I don't know who was going to use them … but we: how can we give back the jerseys? So, nothing, Myriam, as captain, showed up and said 'No, we are not going to give you the jerseys, so 'take one and leave us one'. So, they left us the yellow one, they let us have one, otherwise they would have taken our jerseys. So, it was a very bad, very bad, very bad, very complicated situation.

As for football shoes, or boots, many had to play barefoot to avoid damaging their own boots, and access to goalkeeper gloves was difficult. Lucila Marín, who played for the Santander leagues' team for 12 years, said: 'I played at school, and I played with the boys and they didn't hit me, but I did hit them hard and barefoot because if I damaged my shoes, they would hit me at home. Our football boots were our barefeet'.

Another memory shared by all the players, especially in the regional leagues, was the terrible conditions in which tournaments were played. Not only did they have inadequate uniforms and gloves but also, during the league tournaments, they had to stay in dirty places, sleep on buses, struggle for food, play and train on fields in poor condition and struggle with difficult schedules (e.g., midday games, in hot weather, or at night without any lighting). Ruth Ortiz remembered:

…Yes, as always, we were the Cinderellas of the sport, in the league of Bogotá. Bogotá took us, the first time I was in the Bogotá team in 1992, it was in Granada Meta, that was terrible. We arrived at a house there, and it was a residence. It was terrible, the beds were turned over, the sheets were stained, in some there were even something like tablecloths to cover the beds, and the administrators left for a better hotel. We then took our things and we sat there on the sidewalks of the town to wait for them to change our hotel.

More research needs to be done on the transformation of these conditions for the league players of subsequent generations, but those interviewed for this study all recall outrageous conditions and little recognition for their sports practice. The mistreatment of women who practice football has been part of the polarisation that has been created functionally between the genders. Although since the late 1800s there has been criticism from medicine on the feminised structure of bodies; sports have also strengthened the binary construction of bodies (Faust, 2019). Thus, a body that refuses to fit into this binary is punished socially, economically and politically. Also, the way women are seen in sport depends on class and race, whether seen as athletes or as ridiculous. As has been shown, historically sport was permitted as a practice for health and the construction of a specific type of femininity (Elsey & Nadel, 2019). Football was not this kind of sport, so the women who dared to practice it were punished, or at least ignored.

Early Matches, Exhibition Football and Professionalisation by Women

Most of the players interviewed participated in small-sided football in the street, at school or at university as a pathway to 11-a-side football. Although their desire was to play this type of football, these versions of the game, with fewer players and reduced spatial requirements, allowed them to initiate, or at least continue, their footballing career.

A practice that appears repeatedly in several generations is that of exhibition matches. The game organised by the Queens in Cali in 1949 was presented as an exhibition as were the matches played by the Costa Rican players in 1951; it was the match for which Amparo Maldonado was called by the league of Valle del Cauca in 1970 and the matches the national team played in the tour of Ecuador in the mid-1970s. Since the mid-1980s, Myriam Guerrero also organised exhibition matches as well as in the early 90s with the Universidad Nacional de Colombia (UNAL) team. Recognising these recurrences allows us to see how women football players sought at various times in history to build strategies not only to play the game but also to earn recognition. Nevertheless, these strategies have been repeated with little success. For 40 years, women practicing football revealed themselves to demonstrate their abilities, in circus-like and self-organised spaces, but nonetheless, all generations reported that they have experienced violence and discrimination for playing football. In Brazil, during the 1930s and 1940s, circuses became a central stage for the practice of sport by women who were welcomed in these spaces that housed 'strange and exotic' talents (Bonfim, 2019).

From diverse experiences, the research also shows that women have participated in all areas related to football: as players, coaches, technical directors and referees. Amparo Maldonado was a player and a coach; Margarita Martínez was a player and part of the coaching staff of the first national team; Myriam Guerrero was captain of the first national team and later became a coach; Liliana Zapata was the president of the club *Formas Íntimas*; Elizabeth Oviedo has been a referee since the 2000s; and Nancy Mora was a player and also a coach of the League Santander. The fact that they have managed to occupy these spaces at certain times, however, has not resulted in more broadly opening these spaces for women. Within the social transformations evidenced over time, during the 1990s and early 2000s most women's teams had female coaches, but by 2020 in the 'professional' teams there was only one woman in a coaching role (Seligmann, 2021).

In a 1949 article in *Semana* magazine, the referee was a woman (*'La reina caleña'*, 1949); similarly, *El País*, a Cali newspaper, reported on a tournament in 1971–1972, with some articles noting the intention of using women referees for the competition, advertising that there were referee courses available for women who were interested in participating ('Mañana: cierre de inscripciones para tomar parte en el torneo femenino de fútbol', 1971). Yet, subsequent matches have had mostly male referees, although it is not a topic that has been discussed extensively or that the players have felt the need to mention in their interviews.

In the narratives of the footballers interviewed, it is evident that the attainment of certain positions did not imply a linear development towards greater possibilities. Opening spaces in small-sided and 11-a-side football did not expand possibilities after institutionalisation. On the contrary, as Amparo Maldonado recalls in her interview, even though the players on her team were registered in 11-a-side football and small-sided football, they were sanctioned and had to withdraw from small-sided football to participate in 11-a-side football. The recurring exhibitions are another example.

It is also fundamental to mention that the existing clubs, which had been conducting grassroots work with women and girls for years, were not allowed to register in the league when the 'professionalisation' of football practiced by women began in 2017. In large part this was because of the South American Confederation's (CONMEBOL) requirement for men's clubs to incorporate women's teams. The new requirement led to the traditional professional men's clubs poaching players without giving recognition to the clubs where they had been trained for years. There was no financial recognition, no purchase of sporting rights and no transparent transfers of the players. Liliana Zapata explained that in the first professional tournament in 2017:

> The men's football clubs created the teams, but did so reluctantly. There was a lot of mistreatment from the men's football clubs. The men's clubs stole the players, and at 3 a.m. the Federation gave them the Comet passwords. The Colombian Football Federation has the passwords of all the clubs. The Federation used the passwords of the women's clubs to give the players to the different teams; this was done with all the players of all the clubs. *Difútbol* was upset but in the end nothing happened. The training fees were not paid.

Developments in professional football practiced by women are underway. Considering what has happened so far, however, this professionalisation has not recognised the historical trajectories of female players, coaches, technical directors and referees; it has simply fulfilled the call of the most important regional institution of football practiced by men—CONMEBOL. Faust (2019) argues that the lifting of the ban on women playing football in Germany was because of a fear of autonomous football practices. In this analysis, professionalisation seems like more of a quest for control of football practiced by women rather than listening to the needs and desires of the players and a recognition of the women who historically have made the practice of the sport possible for women in Colombia.

New Segregations

Therefore, the trajectory over time has not meant a gradual linear opening of spaces for women, but rather constant struggles for participation and recognition. In the same way, institutionalisation has not led to the recognition of the work of those who historically have fought for spaces; instead it has signified an element of loss of participation for women by preventing self-organisation. Some players were also coaches, but since professionalisation in 2017, there is just one female coach. Although for players professionalisation has meant the promise of a career in the sport—which has not yet been fully fulfilled—as indicated by Selmer citing Müller, the process of women's exclusion from football has been historical and institutionalisation has often also in reality been a search for control by patriarchal institutions (Selmer, 2013). Historical developments do not demonstrate a process of gradual interest and introduction of women in football, but rather perpetual interest and struggle to open spaces that have been closed to them. Thus, it is actually a gradual process of exclusion, which could not take hold, foiled by the passionate struggles of those interested in women's participation in football. This last point is fundamental because all the interviewees recognise their achievements as well as the later achievements of women in football as the result of their struggles.

Most of the players perceive this historical process as one of social and cultural transformation, of struggles they have won, of hope for a professional future and, at the same time, of frustration at the exclusion from spaces beyond that of a role as a player. Many affirm that they would like to be players now, to have a 'professional' tournament, although they recognise the precariousness of this supposed 'professionalisation'. Nevertheless, it is evident that the opportunities to fill spaces as coaches, technical directors and members of a coaching staff have largely been lost. As the institutionalisation and recognition by sports entities (e.g., *Difútbol* and *Dimayor*[1]) have become more consolidated, even fewer spaces within coaching staffs have become available for women. Patricia Vanegas asserts

---

[1] The *Difútbol* is the Amateur Division of Colombian Football. The *Dimayor* is Major Division of Colombian Professional Football.

that during the 1990s it was relatively normal to see female coaches, just as Liliana Zapata remembers Margarita Martínez as a coach and Amparo Maldonado as both creator and coach of her team in the late 1980s.

Most of the interviewees consider that the latter generations have 'had it easier' than them, and that their own struggles have been difficult and painful. Despite the conditions they faced, however, the practice of football has been gratifying. They recognise the spaces, the friends and the sociability as successes and reasons why it was worthwhile to practice this sport. Still, they also relate their experiences with a lot of pain and shame. They were never presented with spaces freely offered to them, but always as spaces they had to earn, according to Elsey and Nadel:

> History telling can confer legitimacy on its subjects, just as it can deny it in the same instance. The neglect of women's historical participation in Latin American sports has served to naturalize [*sic*] gender differences in society more broadly and to justify the denial of resources to women athletes. Focusing on women's activities within sports illuminates a site of women's creativity and community. The media's disinterest in women's sports has given historians a difficult track to follow. Frequently, the athletes themselves preserve the history of women's sports, offering up their memories, photographs, jerseys, and press clippings to journalists and historians. (2019, p. 2)

In Colombia, women have been practicing football intermittently since the end of the 1940s and then continually after 1970, as evidenced by journalists' reports from the 1970s and mainly by the stories of the players interviewed for this study. During this time, female football players have been discriminated against, had their sexuality questioned, either facing insults for being lesbians or through lesbophobic practices. In this author's interviews, all the interviewees recall being insulted while playing and having their sexuality questioned. It is not necessary to go that far to see examples of this. In 2018, a technical director, arguing against supporting football played by women in Colombia, asserted that it was a 'hotbed of lesbianism' ("'Caldo de cultivo del lesbianismo', el ataque del presidente de un club al fútbol femenino que causa indignación en Colombia", n.d.).

Regarding lesbophobia, Elsey and Nadel (2019) consider that '[t]he history of sexuality within sports also deserves much greater attention, both regionally and globally. In oral histories, queer sportswomen explained that they found a supportive community among their fellow athletes. Questions remain about how vigilance of women's sexuality and violence against lesbians affected women athletes' (p. 6). Moreover, Goellner (2005) also reflects on the questions surrounding the experiences of Brazilian female players in terms of sexuality. On the other hand, there also have been cases of the homogenisation of black women, as observed in newspaper reports from the 1970s, when several black female players were called 'The Colombian Pelé' ('América y Águila Roja, líderes', 1971). These aspects, along with classism and ableism are fundamental to understand the experiences of women players and to work to make the sport a liberating space and not a replica of football practiced by men.

Conclusions

Recognising the narratives of the players as present reflections of their past makes it evident that the lack of historical references about their practices has forced them to start over repeatedly, return to exhibition tournaments, reestablish teams, demand spaces in technical direction, and so forth. Thus, by compiling their experiences, supporting their reflections with journalistic documents, capturing their life stories and bringing to light the disinterest of sports institutions, one can provide the players with the tools to organise themselves. In this way, they can argue that they are not just starting out, but rather their sporting experience is more than 70 years old. They have history, the skills and the knowledge to occupy all kinds of sporting spaces, whether as players, coaches, referees or administrators. In this way, it is possible to seek to transform the continuity of exclusion from the spaces these women have fought for in the past, giving the female football pioneers a place in history by to recognising their experiences and showing, from their narratives, the paths they have taken to be able to practice football in spite of all the difficulties they have faced.

References

'América y Águila Roja, líderes'. (1971, Diciembre 15). *El País*, p. 15.

Báez, L. A. P. F. (2011). La educación femenina en Colombia y el inicio de las facultades femeninas en la pontificia universidad javeriana, 1941–1955. *Revista Historia de la Educación Colombiana, 14*(14), 121–146.

Bonfim, A. F. (2019). Football Feminino entre festas esportivas, circos e campos suburbanos: uma história social do futebol praticado por mulheres da introdução à proibição (1915–1941) (Master's thesis). Centro de Pesquisa e Documentação de História Contemporânea do Brasil (CPDOC).

Collado Herrera, M. del C. (2006). ¿Qué es la historia oral? En C. De Garay (Ed.), *Historia con micrófono* (13–32). Instituto Mora.

"'Caldo de cultvo del lesbianismo', el ataque del presidente de un club al fútbol femenino que causa indignación en Colombia." (n.d.). *BBC News Mundo*. Retrieved April 23, 2021, from https://www.bbc.com/mundo/deportes-46647690

Elsey, B., & Nadel, J. H. (2019). *Futbolera: A history of women and sports in Latin America* (1st ed.). University of Texas Press.

Faust, F. (2019). *Fußball und Feminismus eine Ethnografie geschlechterpolitischer Interventionen*. Budrich UniPress.

Goellner, S. V. (2005). Mulheres e futebol no Brasil: Entre sombras e visibilidades. *Revista Brasileira de Educação Física e Esporte, 19*(2), 143–151. https://doi.org/10.1590/S1807-55092005000200005

Gómez, Z. (2011). *En Cuerpo y Alma: Visiones del Progreso y de la Felicidad; Educación, Cuerpo y Orden Social en Colombia (1830–1990)* (2nd ed.). Universidad de los Andes, Facultad de Ciencias Sociales, Departamento de Lenguajes y Estudios Socioculturales-CESO.

Heibel, M. (2011, June 10). *Die Geschichte des Frauenfußballs in Deutschland*. https://www.netzathleten.de/. https://www.netzathleten.de/lifestyle/sports-inside/item/2235-die-geschichte-des-frauenfussballs-in-deutschland

Hoffmann, E., & Nendza, J. (2011). *Verlacht, verboten und gefeiert: Zur Geschichte des Frauenfußballs in Deutschland*. Liebe.

Knijnik, J. (2015). Femininities and masculinities in Brazilian women's football: Resistance and compliance. *Journal of International Women's Studies, 16*(3), 18.

'La reina caleña'. (1949, Octubre 29). *Estadio*.

Ley 80 de 1925. Sobre educación física, plazas de deportes y precio de becas nacionales. (1925, Noviembre 18). On physical education, sports places and price of national scholarships. http://www.suin-juriscol.gov.co/viewDocument. asp?id=1625996

'Mañana: Cierre de inscripciones para tomar parte en el torneo femenino de fútbol'. (1971, September 14). *El País*, p. 8.

Müller, M. (2009). *Fussball als Paradoxon der Moderne: Zur Bedeutung ethnischer, nationaler und geschlechtlicher Differenzen im Profifussball* (1. Aufl.). VS Verlag für Sozialwissenschaften.

Nadel, J. H. (2014). *Fútbol! Why soccer matters in Latin America*. University Press of Florida.

Patiño, J. H. R. (2010). *La Política del Sport: Élites y Deporte en la Construcción de la Nación Colombiana, 1903–1925* (1st ed.). Carreta Editores; Pontificia Universidad Javeriana-Bogotá.

Racines, R. J. (2011). El fútbol de el dorado: 'El punto de inflexión que marcó la rápida evolución del 'amaterismo' al 'profesionalismo''. *Alesde, 1*, 111–128.

Rial, C. (2013). El invisible (y victorioso) fútbol practicado por mujeres en Brasil. *Nueva Sociedad, 248*, 114–126.

Roldán, D. L. Q. Q. (2013). Deporte y modernidad: Caso Colombia. Del deporte en sociedad a la deportivización de la sociedad. *Revista Colombiana de Sociología, 36*(1), 19–42.

Schwarzstein, D. (2002). Memoria e historia. *Desarrollo Económico, 42*(167), 471–482. https://doi.org/10.2307/3455848

Seligmann, C. J. (2021). *Balón de Cristal. Una Historia del Fútbol Femenino en Colombia* (1st ed.). Planeta.

Selmer, N. (2013). Der andere Fußball. Pferderennen mit Eseln? En *Frauenfußball in Deutschland Anfänge—Verbote—Widerstände—Durchbruch* (pp. 49–62). Verlag W. Kohlhammer.

Solteritas y a la Orden. (1949, Agosto 27). *Revista Semana, 7*, 27.

Watson, P. (2019). *#UnPaísEnUnaCancha?: Football and nation-building in Colombia during the presidency of Juan Manuel Santos (2010–2018)*. University of Sheffield.

Watson, P. J. (2021). Superpowerful but superinvisible? Women's football and nation in presidential discourse in Colombia, 2010–2018. *Movimento (ESEFID/UFRGS), 27*, e27004. https://doi.org/10.22456/1982-8918.109246

Zeledón, C. E. (1999). *Deportivo Femenino Costa Rica F.C: Primer equipo de fútbol femenino del mundo, 1949–1999 (Reseña Histórica)*. Ministerio de Cultura, Juventud y Deportes, Editorial de la Dirección de Publicaciones.

15

Has Latin America's Title IX Arrived? Impact of the CONMEBOL Institutional Incentive Regulations on South American Football

Fernando Augusto Starepravo, Giovanna Xavier de Moura, and Felipe Canan

Introduction

Created in 1972, Title IX is federal legislation that established that no person in the United States (US) should be excluded or discriminated against based on sex in any educational program or activity that receives

F. A. Starepravo (✉)
Departamento de Educação Física, UEM—Universidade Estadual de Maringá, Maringá, Brazil

G. X. de Moura
Departamento de Educação Física, UEM—Universidade Estadual de Maringá, Maringá, Brazil

Ingá University Centre (Uningá), Maringá, Brazil

F. Canan
University of the State of Amazonas, Boca do Acre, Brazil

© The Author(s), under exclusive license to Springer Nature Switzerland AG 2022
J. Knijnik, G. Garton (eds.), *Women's Football in Latin America*, New Femininities in Digital, Physical and Sporting Cultures,
https://doi.org/10.1007/978-3-031-09127-8_15

federal financial assistance. Therefore, the law enabled equal opportunities and funding for sport programmes between men and women (Gregg & Fielding, 2016). The law significantly increased women's participation in sports as athletes particularly in university sport, intramural sport, intercollegiate sport and high school programmes in the United States.

Almost 50 years later, this type of initiative, which was very successful in the North American context, has reached the South American continent through the Club Licensing Regulation of the South American Football Confederation (CONMEBOL). The initiative meets, Knijnik's (2015) claims, the need for a gender equality policy in sport when discussing inequalities in Brazilian football.

CONMEBOL is an international sport institution that organises, develops and controls football competitions in South America, including the Copa América, in which the national teams compete, and its major club tournaments such as the Copa Libertadores de América, which is the continent's principal football competition, and the Copa Sudamericana. In 2016, CONMEBOL launched its new club license regulations that introduced a new series of rules. The document complies with Article 23 of the International Federation of Association Football (FIFA) statute, which obliges national federations and football bodies to have governance measures—for example, political and religious neutrality, antidoping control and, key for the discussion in this chapter, the incorporation of legal dispositions that provide for gender equality.

With this new regulation, to obtain a CONMEBOL license, a club must have an adult female team and at least one female youth category (under 15) or be associated with a club that has such teams. In both cases, the candidate must provide technical support and all equipment and infrastructure necessary for the development of the women's teams under suitable conditions. Both teams also are required to participate in national and regional competitions, authorised by their respective local federation (Confederação Sul-Americana de Futebol, 2016). This initiative can be interpreted as a multicentric sport policy of a regulatory and redistributive type for gender equality (Canan et al., 2019), a type of policy that will be conceptualised and discussed further in the following and that bears similarities to Title IX—part of Public Law 92-318 of the United States.

This type of multicentric policy presents an attempt to reduce the historical gender inequality that affects society and, in this specific case, football in South America. Under the management of CONMEBOL, for example, the 2019 Copa Libertadores da América provided prize money of US$12 million to Brazilian club Flamengo, the champions of the men's tournament, 141 times more than the US$ 85,000 awarded to the winning women's team, Corinthians from Brazil (Lance, 2019).

Still, the case of the difference in prize money between genders for CONMEBOL competitions is not an isolated case, but it portrays a chronic sport and social issue. For example, women have played football in Latin America for more than 100 years, despite legal restrictions in some countries. In Brazil (Brasil, 1941), women were not allowed to play football because it was considered non-feminine or masculine and supposedly had negative effects on women's reproductive capacity (Nadel, 2015). Likewise, according to Nadel (2015), such discourse was defended by public health experts, whereas other critics questioned players' sexuality, suggesting that the women who played football were homosexual and that football served as a 'recruiting place' for lesbians. These ways of thinking served and, to some extent, continue to serve to marginalise women's football in Latin America.

It is important to highlight that there are multiple realities of women's football within South America. While Mexico, Brazil and Chile are at the forefront on the continent, despite the difficulties faced by women and the wage gap between men and women, in other South American countries, women footballers still experience unfavourable conditions. Miryam Tristán, top scorer for the Peruvian national team, says that in Peru, those who play football do because they really like it, not because they want to earn money; even though in Argentina, a female player from the first division receives the same minimum salary as a male player from the fourth division, although some players do not even receive a salary (Mancera et al., 2021).

While in the widely studied North American case, it is certain that the regulatory and redistributive legislation has had a great impact on women's sport, there are still no data on the scope and effect of the changes in the licensing regulations for CONMEBOL clubs. In this sense, the present study intends to identify multicentric sport policies of a regulatory and redistributive type of gender equality in relation to women's football in South America and their respective developments. To this end, the policies adopted by CONMEBOL are analysed, as well as the national federations of South American countries in relation to women's football. Analysis and discussion are supported by two essential theoretical references: public policies, particularly in the duality of statism and multicentrism, and gender inequality, its motivations and effects (Marks et al., 1996; Höfling, 2001; Secchi, 2012).

Theoretical Approach: State and Multicentre Public Policies

A public policy can be understood in several ways. In the state-centric model, governments are the ultimate decision maker, and a multi-level governance does not reject the view that the State is important, but it no longer monopolises policymaking. Decision-making competencies are shared by actors at different levels rather than monopolised by State executives (Marks et al., 1996). In this scenario, non-state organisations (e.g., CONMEBOL itself and the national football federations) influence and promote policies.

Secchi (2012), in a similar sense, points out that public policy is a guideline designed to solve a society problem—that is, a socially relevant need. This need can be general, serving society as a whole, or specific, serving a part of society and/or a particular area; in this case, known as sectorial policy (Starepravo et al., 2019). Thus, public policy does not only mean the action of the State but also the regulations made by it; public policy seeks to solve not only general but also specific problems. This perspective allows one to understand that, even though they are public—that is, in the public interest of society or part of it—policies do not necessarily have to be state-owned. According to Höfling, 'the State cannot be reduced to the public bureaucracy, to the state bodies that would conceive and implement public policies' (2001, p. 31).

Because many public problems are specific, or sectorial, it is important that social groups directly associated with such problems be involved in their resolution. The State is responsible for regulating, guiding and encouraging this social participation, although not necessarily responsible for resolving it entirely. In this sense, Secchi (2012) didactically advises that there are two approaches to understanding public policy: the statist and the multicentric. In the first, public policies are fully developed by state actors, by the public bureaucracy, the so-called public administration (i.e., state agencies and agents). On the other hand, in the multicentric approach, institutions and non-state agents assume the lead, or at least, the important roles in the implementation of public policies, contributing to the resolution of the social problems that directly affect them.

The typology presented by Frey (2000) and reinforced by Secchi (2012), which classifies public policies as: (1) distributive, which privileges certain social groups or regions, with costs distributed across the whole society; (2) redistributive, which privileges certain social groups, but with costs concentrated on other social groups; (3) regulatory, establishing or guiding standards of behaviour or action for public and private agents; and (4) constitutive, structuring state or public organisations in general. Considering this typology, multicentric policies typically are more strictly related to regulatory ones.

This suggests that the State and civil society understand something as a public problem—in the sense that it is something that deserves attention and collective action—but instead of taking full responsibility for its resolution (i.e., to act so that the social issue is focused on fully), recognise its (e.g., budgetary, human, institutional, bureaucratic) limits and include civil society to act in partnership. So, often if one is interested in such a problem, the State may simply abstain or even allow assumption of a certain role in helping to resolve it. This is the case, for example, of sport laws (i.e., rules of sport and its competitions) from which the State abstains, leaving it to the responsible governing bodies (e.g., confederations, federations, associations).

On the other hand, the analysis of governmentality suggests that the emergence of policy communities represented not a diminution of government power, but a more subtle exercise of power and, in fact, an extension of State power. According to this analysis, the governmental power in relation to sport is less a matter of imposing constraints on organisations and their leaders than constructing or shaping organizations capable of bearing a kind of regulated freedom. The key objective is to encourage federations and sport clubs to become malleable partners in the implementation of government policy (Houlihan, 2005).

Canan, Rojo and Starepravo et al. (2019), seeking to understand possibilities for guaranteeing the right for sport beyond State policy, presented examples of multicentric and regulatory policies in three spheres:

1) Gender equality, recognising the historical gap between sport (and other social spheres in general) for women and for men, as noted by Moura (2018).
2) The equalisation of sport disciplines (e.g., football, basketball, athletics, weightlifting and so on) and age groups, recognising the historical gap between elite spectacularised sport and non-spectacularised sport and/or aimed at social groups other than the main athletes, as highlighted by Bourg and Gouguet (2005), and Bueno (2008).
3) The division of powers between the State and the private sector, with the former offering means (i.e., permission, incentive) to earn profits in the exploitation of services of public interest to the latter, provided that minimum guidelines are met, recognising the inability of the State to attend exclusively to every and any social demand, as pointed out by Höfling (2001).

In the case of equalisation between genders in the field of sport, which is of particular interest to this research, Canan, Rojo and Starepravo et al. (2019) examined the example of Title IX, a US law that requires gender equality in any educational program funded by federal resources; and the example of the CONMEBOL licensing regulations, which require clubs participating in men's competitions organised within CONMEBOL's scope also have women's football programmes.

The first example is a typical case of regulatory policy whereas the second illustrates an interesting multicentric policy. Even without specific State guidelines—this does not mean that it is not important to the State—gender equality, with the consequent development of women's sport, has been a public concern highlighted by international organisations at least since the 1970s. This is the case, for example, of the

UNESCO International Charter for Physical Education and Sport of 1978, or more recently the CONMEBOL club regulations, which have regulatory policy characteristics.

Gender Inequality in Sport

Difficulties faced by women in sports have been noticed for a long time. Since the beginning of their participation in this environment, which is socially recognised as masculine, questions about the masculinisation of their bodies and the dangers to their health emerged, especially regarding the risks to maternal functions—considered women's main social contribution (Goellner, 2006; Knijnik, 2003).

This limiting vision of women's participation in sport, based on medical discourses, lasted for many years, leading, for example, to the creation of a Brazilian legislation that reinforced the idea that women could only practice physical activities and sports that were compatible with what was considered maternal and feminine (Brasil, 1941). This relationship of limitation in the practice of sport was narrowed years later with the prohibition of modalities with physical contact, including football (Brasil, 1965).

Even after the repealing of the football-related legislation in Brazil and the expansion of activities aimed at women's football (Goellner, 2005), not only in this country, but throughout the Americas, women continued experiencing difficulties in accessing the sport. The idea that football was a sport that valued the aspects of being a man, of virility and strength, were perpetuated, and women who practiced this sport were thus still seen as transgressors of the social norms of femininity; this went far beyond the actions of the game per se and also were related to their bodies and clothing. The inequality was also reflected in women's difficulties in accessing areas, training materials, salaries and funding for the modalities as well as in a lack of space and inadequate coverage in the media (Knijnik, 2015).

The previously mentioned inequalities between men and women connected with the sport sector, not only in football, but in various disciplines, meant that the project and laws were created in an attempt to break the historically created imbalance. It is in this sense that the US Title IX law, presented in the following, was created.

Title IX, part of US legislation, is one of the most well-known public policies in gender and sport studies because it has significantly changed the reality of women's sport in the United States. The law, created in 1972, states that 'no person shall, on the basis of sex, be excluded from participation in, be denied the benefits of, or be subjected to discrimination under any academic, extracurricular, research, occupational training, or other education program or activity operated by a recipient which receives Federal financial assistance' (US Department of Education, 2015).

It is interesting to note that during the discussion period regarding the approval of the law, the debate about women's sport was not present, considering that the legislation was focused on education. Yet, by addressing discrimination—a common issue in sport because this is a gendered space from which women have often been excluded—led advocates of women's sport to recognise the applicability of the law in the field (Theune, 2019). Additionally, because the US sporting system has a solid foundation in the educational sector, whether in schools or universities, sport was inevitably affected by the law.

The law enabled equal opportunities and funding for sport programmes between men and women (Gregg & Fielding, 2016) with equal levels of competitions considering the interests and abilities of both sexes, as well as equipment and supplies, training conditions, travel, remuneration, changing rooms, sport facilities, medical services, accommodations and advertising (Francis, 2016). Moreover, there is an obligation to have teams of men and women in all sports. In the absence of women's teams, they could play on men's teams and vice versa (Senne, 2016; McDowell et al., 2016).

As stated earlier, the law significantly changed women's participation in sport as athletes. According to McDowell et al. (2016), within four years of the legislation, there was an increase of 55% in the participation of girls in sport clubs and 108% in intramural sports events. In intercollegiate sport, the participation of women increased from 16,000 to 200,000 in 2014, and in high school sport programmes, from 294,015 to 3.3 million in 2016 (Lane, 2016). In general, in 40 years of legislation, there has been a 600% increase in the participation of women in sport in the United States (Yanus & O'Connor, 2016). Advances at the micro-level also have enabled changes at the macro-level in such a way that, in 2012, at the London Olympics, the US delegation was comprised of more female than male athletes.

Outside the sport sector, the law also allowed for a greater presence of women employed at US colleges and universities, an end to discriminatory policies in admissions to undergraduate and graduate courses and access to teaching materials. Besides, the legislation also was applied to issues, such as access to scholarships and financial resources and the prevention of sexual harassment in the academic environment (Yanus & O'Connor, 2016; Lane, 2016; Druckman et al., 2018).

Methodology

This chapter is based on exploratory qualitative research using documentary analysis. The exploratory research focuses on objects that are still little studied, seeking to clarify, develop or even modify ideas and concepts (Gil, 2008). The qualitative approach does not point at numerical representation, but rather at an in-depth understanding of the topic studied, considering patterns, as well as details. The document analysis procedure uses materials that have not yet been explored and described following scientific standards as a source for analysis (Silveira & Córdova, 2009). Thus, the source documents were: (1) CONMEBOL's Club License Regulations; and (2) Club License Regulations of the national football federations of the CONMEBOL member countries: Argentina, Bolivia, Brazil, Chile, Colombia, Ecuador, Paraguay, Peru, Uruguay and Venezuela.

In the absence or unavailability of this type of document on the website of the respective federations, the authors sought to obtain information regarding the existence of this kind of document on the Internet in general. Furthermore, we looked for other documents issued by the respective federations, which dealt in some way with the development of women's football. Data were collected in May 2021.

All documents were read in full, highlighting the excerpts that contained information related to women's football. Based on the documents' content analysis, the assessment of the impact of the license regulations of CONMEBOL clubs in national confederations was separated into four categories:

1) The existence or not of a regulation like that of CONMEBOL's within the scope of the national football federation.
2) The extension of the criteria for granting a license to participate in internal (national) competitions organised by the federation itself.
3) The competitions to which the license requirements apply within each federation (or competition level), such as national, State, first division, second division, and so on.
4) Specific criteria for the development of women's football programmes by clubs participating in professional men's competitions to verify whether they are identical, extensive or restrictive in relation to those of CONMEBOL, with regard to the license to participate in national competitions.

After proceeding with the documents' coding, we tried to establish a discourse between the documents, categories and the theoretical framework of multicentric gender equality policies such as Title IX.

Impact of CONMEBOL Club License Regulations on National Confederations Across South America

Since 2016 CONMEBOL has adopted a Club Licensing Regulation that establishes conditions for clubs participating in their professional competitions for men (Canan et al., 2019). These conditions are programmatic, sporting or related to infrastructural, administrative, legal or financial issues and must be progressively implemented by national football federations and clubs. At the end of the term or during the fulfilment of the conditions, a new regulation, the current one, was published by the entity in 2018 (Confederação Sul-Americana de Futebol, 2018).

Within the scope of sporting criteria, according to Article 90 (Confederação Sul-Americana de Futebol, 2018), the clubs that participate in CONMEBOL's official competitions for men must develop a football program for women, including the establishment of an adult team or, at least, a grassroots team (i.e., a youth team composed of young players up to 15 years of age). Obviously, the club may have more than one team from other age groups, but it is not on a 'sine qua non' requirement to obtain the license. The club itself can either develop the program for women, or it can join a club that already has a women's program, as long as it effectively guarantees the conditions for this in terms of infrastructure, funding, technical support and so forth. In addition, both the adult and youth teams must participate in official, national and/or regional competitions held or authorised by the respective national federation (Confederação Sul-Americana de Futebol, 2018).

Compliance is not required of clubs that are not participating in CONMEBOL competitions, but Article 7 states that the requirement must be included in the club licensing regulations of each national football federation affiliated with the South American sporting body. According to Article 12, in their respective clubs' licensing regulations, national federations must adopt the same minimum criteria or even more (but not less) stringent criteria to be met for the participation of their clubs in CONMEBOL competitions. Still, by the same Article 12, the adoption of such criteria or any other for the participation of clubs in domestic competitions (i.e., national or regional/state championships in the first or lower divisions, and so on) is optional.

Concerning national club licensing regulations, they were found in 8 out of 10 federations that comprise the organisation (i.e., Argentina, Brazil, Chile, Colombia, Ecuador, Paraguay, Peru and Uruguay). Regarding Venezuela, a club license regulation was not found; but the Regulatory Norms of the First Division present some equivalence to the documents of other countries in relation to the development of football for women. In Bolivia, a mention was made about the creation of such a document, but it was not available on the institution's website; so for the purposes of this chapter, its existence is unknown. For example, the Bolivian media, such as the newspaper *Los Tiempos* (2019), reported difficulties for the federation and football clubs to be able to fulfill the criteria established by CONMEBOL. Nevertheless, despite the fact that no news expressly affirmed the existence or nonexistence of club license regulations in this country, the Bolivian media insinuated that they do exist. Or, least, if they do not exist, then the criteria are being met through some other means and that this is acceptable for CONMEBOL because the respective clubs continue to participate in the competitions organized by the sports entity.

Regarding the club licensing regulations of the football federations of the countries that have made them available, it appears that they all reproduce the CONMEBOL criteria pertaining to the participation in the sports entity's competitions. In other words, in this case, the national regulations subscribe to and/or reproduce those of CONMEBOL. In relation to the adoption of criteria for the participation of clubs in national competitions in each country, similarities also have been found; yet, at the same time, there are small specificities (see Table 15.1).

Although most countries reproduce the CONMEBOL criteria and some even outline more obligations for the development of women's football, some actions are softened, mainly with the intent that clubs can, somehow, figure out how to fulfill all requirements. Brazil, for example, adopted a progressive criterion. Since the publication of the regulations, clubs in the first national tier (Series A1 and A2) have had less time than tier B clubs to implement the criteria and acquire the license; tier B clubs have had less time than tier C clubs, and so on. The license for participation in other national competitions and regional/state competitions has been waived and, consequently, the fulfillment of the criteria has been as well (Confederação Brasileira de Futebol, 2019).

Colombia has not expressly mentioned the obligation of a youth team to participate in a competition organised or recognised by the national federation (Federación Colombiana de Fútbol, 2017). Nonetheless, because of the other obligations in relation to the development of the youth team (i.e., common to CONMEBOL and other national federations), this can be understood as implicit. Peru provides a provisional license to the clubs for the first year after achieving promotion to the higher division of the national leagues, which waives, among others, the requirements relating to football for women (Federación Deportiva Nacional Peruana de Fútbol, 2018).

It is unclear why many national federations only publish the version that is possibly the first of their respective regulations. This could be because they are continuing to adopt them; even if they were published

Table 15.1 National Club License Regulations and Women's Football

Country	Entity responsible for football	Document consulted	Document year	Reproduces CONMEBOL regulations	Competitions to which the license requirement is applied	Specific criteria for development of women's football
Argentina	*Asociación Del Fútbol Argentino*	*Reglamento de Licencias de Clubes*	2017	Yes	Document indicates that the criteria for participation in national competitions will be defined in a future regulation that has not yet been officially advertised	–
Bolivia	*Federación Boliviana de Fútbol*	–	–	–	–	
Brazil	*Confederação Brasileira de Futebol*	*Regulamento de Licença de Clubes*	2019	Yes	Series A, B, C and D (Divisions 1 to 4)	Requires a minimum qualification (in terms of the training criteria for coaches adopted by the national confederation itself) for the adult female team coach

(continued)

Table 15.1 (continued)

Country	Entity responsible for football	Document consulted	Document year	Reproduces CONMEBOL regulations	Competitions to which the license requirement is applied	Specific criteria for development of women's football
Chile	Asociación Nacional de Fútbol Profesional	Reglamento de Licencias de Clubes	2017	Yes	Three major divisions of its main national championship	
Colombia	Federación Colombiana de Fútbol	Reglamento de Licencias de Clubes de la Federación Colombiana de Fútbol y la Dimayor	2019	Yes	All competitions organised by the national federation	
Ecuador	Federación Ecuatoriana de Fútbol	Reglamento de Licencias de Clubes	2019	Yes	All competitions organised by the national federation	
Paraguay	Asociación Paraguaya de Fútbol	Reglamento de Licencias de Clubes	2021	Yes	License regulations for clubs participating in the country's main national competitions, including futsal (for men and women) and beach football	Requires a minimum qualification for the adult women's team coach

Peru	Federación Deportiva Nacional Peruana de Fútbol	Reglamento para la Concesión de Licencias de Clubes de Fútbol Profesional de la Federación Deportiva Nacional Peruana de Fútbol	2018	Yes	It has not accurately clarified that the championships that cover the need for a license, but it has implied they are the country's main ones	
Uruguay	Asociación Uruguaya de Fútbol	Reglamento de Concesion de Licencias de Clubes Profesionales	2017	Yes	Two major divisions of its main national championship	
Venezuela	Federación Venezolana de Fútbol	Normas reguladoras de primera division	2019	Yes	Only for clubs participating in the CONMEBOL competitions	All clubs of the first division must create a women's grassroots football team. Besides, the Federation must commit itself to organizing a Venezuelan women's super league, with at least 8 professional teams

Source: The authors, with information by National Football Federations from South America.

in the past (e.g., 2017), they are still in the process of being implemented. At the same time, it is possible that the COVID-19 pandemic adversely affected their implementation. On the other hand, it is not possible to rule out that political clashes, especially because of the fact that many clubs object to the criteria and/or have had difficulties in implementing them, as mentioned in relation to Bolivia, are leading to the softening of mandatory requirements and/or changes in the regulations.

As Canan, Rojo and Starepravo et al. (2019) pointed out, just as at the time of the creation of US Title IX, the educational institutions that developed sport programmes exclusively for men were initially opposed to regulations and imposed objections and obstacles to the mandatory development of sport for women in general, claiming that they would generate excessive expenses. A similar process of resistance and argumentation in relation to costs was carried out by South American football clubs when the CONMEBOL regulation was established, as explained by Fernandez (2017). As the author observed, however, the director of the Brazilian Football Confederation (CBF), at the time, stated that an investment of only 5% of the men's football resources would be sufficient to create a good team of women without significantly harming the men's program.

At the same time, the developments of Title IX, in addition to contributing to gender equality, leveraged rather than hindered the sport programmes of US schools and universities, including in the sense of increasing visibility and, consequently, financial resources (e.g., television, sponsors, fans and so on). By drawing a comparison with the US legislation, one can understand that the regulations of CONMEBOL and national federations can prove to be an important multicentric and regulatory policy mechanism in the quest for gender equality in sport and social development.

Conclusions

The objective of the work for this chapter was to analyse the policies adopted by CONMEBOL and the national football federations in South America in relation to women's football. By applying documentary research, checking on the existence or nonexistence of regulations in national federations and the extension of the criteria to national and State competitions, it was possible to determine that in most countries there is only the reproduction of the original text of the 2018 regulation published by CONMEBOL.

The initial text of the CONMEBOL regulations is not clear when declaring that the federations must integrate them under the same criteria, rather it could be interpreted as optional for the regulation of national competitions. Moreover, the authors did not find the amendments promised by regulations that indicated there would be future updates to the established criteria. Some countries also claim to have difficulties in implementing CONMEBOL's requirements for financial or health reasons, and clubs are sometimes allowed a provisional license of one year to adapt to the new requirements. These barriers, which range from language to the lack of documentation organisation, along with the fear of not allocating resources to women's programmes, hinder the sport's growth and visibility in some countries and throughout South America.

Despite the difficulties encountered, it is interesting to note that in some cases there is an expansion of the CONMEBOL regulations to all national competitions, with specificities such as the requirement for the technical qualifications of the coaches for women's teams. This shows the interest of these countries in developing quality women's football. There are even documents that integrate gender-inclusive language in their text, which demonstrates the intention to incorporate women and make them feel part of the entire organisational and legislative structure of the institutions.

Nevertheless, a clear need exists for greater control from CONMEBOL regarding the fulfillment of its requirements so as to support the national confederations for the creation of their own distinct and objective regulations and to provide assistance so that the clubs can structure themselves. The authors suggest that further studies be conducted to verify the programmes and the development of women's football plans in South America, with special attention to funding so that one can get a complete view of what has really been achieved by the new gender-inclusive regulations towards the growth of the sport.

References

Asociación del Fútbol Argentino. (2017). Boletín Especial n° 5378. *Reglamento de Licencias de Clubes*. AFA.

Asociación Nacional de Fútbol Profesional. (2017). *Reglamento de Licencia de Clubes*. ANFP.

Asociación Paraguaya de Fútbol. (2021). *Reglamento de Licencia de Clubes*. APF.

Asociación Uruguaya de Fútbol. (2017). *Reglamento de Concesion de Licencias de Clubes Profesionales*. AUF.

Bourg, J.-F., & Gouguet, J.-J. (2005). *Economia do Esporte*. Edusc.

Brasil. (1941). *Decreto-Lei n. 3.199 de 14 de abril de 1941*. Estabelece as bases de organização do desporto em todo o País. https://www2.camara.leg.br/legin/fed/declei/1940-1949/decreto-lei-3199-14-abril-1941-413238-publicacaooriginal-1-pe.html.

Brasil. (1965). *Deliberação nº 7 de 1965*. Conselho Nacional de Desportos. http://cev.org.br/biblioteca/deliberacao-n-7-2-agosto-1965.

Bueno, L. (2008). *Políticas públicas do esporte no Brasil*: razões para o predomínio do alto rendimento (Tese de doutorado). Escola de Administração de Empresas de São Paulo, Fundação Getúlio Vargas.

Canan, F., Rojo, J. R., & Starepravo, F. A. (2019). Direito ao esporte: possibilidades a partir de políticas multicêntricas, regulatórias e redistributivas. *Pensar a Prática, Goiânia, 22*, 1–13. https://doi.org/10.5216/rpp.v22.55426

Confederação Brasileira de Futebol. (2019). *Regulamento de Licença de Clubes*. CBF.

Confederação Sul-Americana de Futebol. (2016). *Regulamento de Licença de Clubes*. CSF.

Confederação Sul-Americana de Futebol. (2018). *Regulamento de Licença de Clubes*. CSF.

Druckman, J. N., Rothschild, J. E., & Sharrow, E. A. (2018). Gender policy feedback: Perceptions of sex equity, title IX, and political mobilization among college athletes. *Political Research Quarterly, 71*(3), 642–653.

Federación Colombiana de Fútbol. (2017). *Reglamento de Licencia de Clubes*. FCF.

Federación Deportiva Nacional Peruana de Fútbol. (2018). *Reglamento para la Concesión de Licencias de Clubes de Fútbol Profesional*. FPF.

Federación Ecuatoriana de Fútbol. (2019). *Reglamento de Licencia de Clubes*. FEF.

Federación Venezolana de Fútbol. (2019). *Normas Reguladoras de Primera División*. FVF.

Fernandez, M. (2017). Clube sem futebol feminino ficará fora da Libertadores a partir de 2019. *Globo.com.* http://globoesporte.globo.com/futebol/noticia/2017/01/clube-sem-futebol-feminino-ficara-fora-da-libertadores-partir-de-2019.html

Francis, L. (2016). Title IX: An incomplete effort to achieve equality in sports. *Journal of Philosophy of Sport, 43*(1), 83–99.

Frey, K. (2000). Políticas públicas: um debate conceitual e reflexões referentes à prática da análise de políticas públicas no brasil. *Planejamento e Políticas Públicas, 21*, 211–259. https://www.ipea.gov.br/ppp/index.php/PPP/article/view/89/158

Gil, A. C. (2008). *Métodos e Técnicas de Pesquisa Social* (p. 6 ed.). Atlas.

Goellner, S. V. (2005). Mulheres e futebol no Brasil: entre sombras e visibilidades. *Revista Brasileira de Educação Física e Esportes, 19*(2), 143–151.

Goellner, S. V. (2006). Mulher e esporte no Brasil: entre incentivos e interdições elas fazem história. *Goiânia: Pensar a Prática, 8*(1), 85–100.

Gregg, E., & Fielding, L. (2016). The implementation of title IX at Indiana University: A historical case study. *Journal of Contemporary Athletics, 10*(4), 242–255.

Höfling, E.M. (2001). Estado e políticas (públicas) sociais. *Cadernos Cedes, XXI*(55), 30–41. https://www.scielo.br/pdf/ccedes/v21n55/5539.pdf

Houlihan, B. (2005). Public sector sport policy: Developing a framework for analysis. *International Review for the Sociology of Sport, 40*(2), 163–185.

Knijnik, J. D. (2003). *A Mulher Brasileira & o Esporte: seu corpo, sua história.* São Paulo: Editora Mackenzie.

Knijnik, J. D. (2015). Femininities and masculinities in Brazilian Women's football: Resistance and compliance. *Journal of International Women's Studies, 16*(3), 53–70.

Lance. (2019, October 24). *Flamengo pode somar cerca de R$ 78 milhões em premiações caso conquiste a Libertadores.* LANCE!

Lane, J. (2016). Women are a problem: Title IX narratives in the *New York Times* and the *Huffington Post*, 1974–1975. *Communication & Sport, 6*(1), 25–40.

Los Tiempos. (2019). *Fabol denunciará a FBF ante Conmebol por licencia de clubes.* https://www.lostiempos.com/deportes/futbol/20191119/fabol-denunciara-fbf-conmebol-licencia-clubes

Mancera, D., Fowks, J., Torrado, S., & Magri, D. (2021, March 11). América Latina mantém acesa a chama do futebol feminino, apesar da pandemia. *El Pais.* https://brasil.elpais.com/esportes/2021-03-12/america-latina-mantem-acesa-a-chama-do-futebol-feminino-apesar-da-pandemia.html

Marks, G., Hooghe, L., & Blank, K. (1996). European Integration from the 1980s: State-Centric v. Multi-level Governance, *34*(3), 341–378.

McDowell, J., Deterding, R., Elmore, T., Morford, E., & Morris, E. (2016). Title IX and campus recreation: Guidelines to increase gender equity in Club and intramural sport programs. *Recreational Sport Journal, 40*(2), 133–151.

Moura, G.X. (2018). *De in-goal a in-goal: a trajetória de mulheres no Rugby no Brasil*. Dissertação de mestrado. Centro de Ciências da Saúde, Universidade Estadual de Maringá.

Nadel, J. (2015). The antinational game? An exploration of Women's football in Latin America. In H. F. In L'Hoeste, R. M. Irwin, & J. Poblete (Eds.), *Sports and Nationalism in Latin/o America* (pp. 45–65). Palgrave Macmillan.

Secchi, L. (2012). *Políticas Públicas: Conceitos, Esquemas de Análise, Casos Práticos*. Cengage Learning.

Senne, J. (2016). Examination of gender equity and female participation in sport. *Sport Journal*. http://thesportjournal.org/article/examination-ofgender-equity-and-female-participation-in-sport/

Silveira, D. T., & Córdova, F. P. (2009). Unidade 2—A Pesquisa Científica. In T. E. Gerhardt & D. T. Silveira (Eds.), *Métodos de Pesquisa* (pp. 31–42). Editora da UFRGS.

Starepravo, F. A., Souza, V. F. M., & Milani, F. G. (2019). *Políticas Públicas na Educação Física*. InterSaberes.

Theune, F. (2019). Brown, Title IX and the impact of race and sex segregation on sports participation opportunities for black females. *Sociology Compass, 13*(1), e12661.

US Departamento of Education. (2015). *Title IX and Sex Discrimination*. https://www2.ed.gov/about/offices/list/ocr/docs/tix_dis.html.

Yanus, A., & O'Connor, K. (2016). To comply or not to comply—Evaluating compliance with title ix of the educational amendments of 1972. *Journal of Women, Politics & Policy, 37*(3), 341–358.

16

'Si nos permiten jugar': Constructing a Feminist Football in Latin America

Jorge Knijnik and Gabriela Garton

No soy, no hay yo, siempre somos nosotros
(I am not, there is no I, we are always us)
(Octavio Paz)

Si Me Permiten Hablar (Viezzer, 2013)[1] is one of the most published, republished and translated Bolivian books in history. Written by Brazilian sociologist and feminist activist Moema Libera Viezzer and published for the first time in 1977, the text gives the powerful, straightforward and

---

[1] The English version was translated as Let Me Speak! Testimony of Domitila, a Woman of the Bolivian Mines.

J. Knijnik (✉)
School of Education, Western Sydney University, Penrith, NSW, Australia
e-mail: J.Knijnik@westernsydney.edu.au

G. Garton
World Players Association, Melbourne, Australia

pungent testimony of Domitilia Barros de Chungara, a Bolivian woman mining worker.

In 1975, Domitilia attended the inaugural World Conference on Women. It was held in Mexico City and was the first event organised by the United Nations with a sole focus on women's issues. When it was her time to speak, despite being intimidated by women from around the world who introduced themselves as lawyers, teachers or scholars, Domitilia courageously stood up on the stage and stated: 'Well, I am the wife of a Bolivian mine worker' (Franco, 1992). She then continued her speech by pointing to all middle-class women in the room, including Betty Friedan, questioning the arguable sorority between them around the world: 'What equality are we going to talk about among ourselves? If you and I don't look alike, if you and I are so different. We cannot, at this moment, be equal, even as women…'(Franco, 1992, p. 112).

Domitilia perhaps was one of the first women in the feminist movement to raise issues such as social class that, rather than uniting, divide women (Franco, 1992). She was giving voice to what theorists would later call 'intersectionality', the several layers of social markers that one needs to look at to understand various forms of oppression (Hancock, 2016). After the publication of *Let Me Speak!* (Viezzer, 2013) with Domitilia's testimony, she became the most famous of Bolivian women miners throughout the world.

This chapter intends to draw a parallel between Domitilia's experiences of being oppressed and silenced but finding words to push back and be heard internationally, to the experiences of women footballers across Latin America. Mirroring Domitilia's struggles and loud voice, one can say that if society 'Let us play!' ('*Si nos permiten jugar*') football, the game can drive and even lead the feminist struggle for more equitable societies across the continent.

It is possible to understand that the football game, as it was brought and implemented in Latin America, had been used as a colonising tool to disseminate the oppressors' playing culture while erasing local ones (Nadel, 2015). As shown in most of the chapters of this book, however, the same game was appropriated by local cultures, transformed and employed as means for social transformation. Thus, here the authors use sociological creativity to imagine that women's football in Latin America might also be 'an arena of resistance and conflict, a site for the development of sweeping counterhegemonic strategies' (Cusicanqui, 2012, p. 95). Moreover, the intention is to show that a renewed and empowered women's football can be a potent avenue for Latin America to display its diverse cultures to the world.

The chapter starts by briefly discussing how Western sports were used as means of colonial cultural enforcement, but how they also have been used by native populations to further their resistance against the invaders. It is argued that the game of football was transformed by Latin Americans, who brought a totally new and unknown corporeal dimension to the game (Elsey & Nadel, 2019; Maranhão & Knijnik, 2011). We bring to the discussion Paulo Freire, one of the most relevant twentieth-century thinkers of colonisation, cultural oppression and freedom, to indicate that dialogical embodied practices are key for the liberation and transformation of football within the subcontinent (Knijnik, 2018). Then the chapter tries to set up a research and activist agenda that contains the seeds that will help the transformation of the colonial and oppressive past into a future feminist football in Latin America—a decolonised game (Oxford, 2019) towards the Freirean *untested feasibility* (Freire, 1996; Knijnik, 2013) or the *Pachakuti* envisaged by Cusicanqui (2012).

Colonisation, Football and Conscientização

Many readers of Freire's philosophies argue that when discussing the means of being 'oppressed' he was just referring to communities at the bottom of the social ladder. This reading of Freire's ideas is far from being correct. Freire, in fact, states that everybody who has been colonised and/or exiled are the oppressed in current societies (Freire, 2000). According to him, colonised individuals have lost their ability to express their knowledge and wishes during the displacement or colonising process, which have been replaced by the conqueror's feelings and judgements. The oppressed struggle to discover their original mindsets. With their voices missed, their arguments and verbal expressions are unacknowledged in their new social setting. They follow a progression of self-deprecation because as either colonised or displaced human beings they fight to capture that they too not only own information but also generate it through their social enterprises. They essentially distrust themselves (Freire, 2000).

Competitive sports historically were used as colonial apparatuses of control, as several sports were and still are. Abbassi (2009) shows how the French Empire promoted such sports as a way to subjugate and govern locals during various sets of colonial occupation across their history. Conventional sports were a prevalent cultural method employed by the predominant political power to control local populations (Abbassi, 2009; Dine, 2002). This usage of competitive sports has long been associated to what Freire (2000, p. 150) called a *cultural invasion*: '[T]he invaders penetrate the cultural context of another group (…); they impose their own view of the world upon those they invade and inhibit the creativity of the invaded by curbing their expression.'

At the same time, though, one cannot consider the 'colonised' as passive beings who just submitted to the colonisers' wishes. As shown on countless occasions (Cusicanqui, 2012; Garton, 2019; Knijnik, 2013), oppressed people will contest the sports-colonial order by struggling with the sporting ideals that settlers wish to produce as well as their athletic activities and competitions (Everbach et al., 2021; Lin & Lee, 2007). People on the receiving end of oppression might try to destabilise the customs and connotations that intruders and enforcers of colonisers' sport culture and values wish to enforce on their sporting and playing cultures (Darder, 2016; de D'Amico, 2019).

These efforts by the oppressed are what Freire (2000) calls a *humanizing mission*. It is an ongoing endeavour in which the oppressed, through persistent dialogue that leads to reflection on their own social conditions, try to expose the realities of cultural control (Freire, 2000). This enduring struggle of *humanization*, which condemns subjugation while constructing innovative arrangements of community conviviality, is what can convert any footballer (i.e., coaches, players, educators, families) into cultural workers (Freire, 1996). As seen in several communities across the subcontinent (Hang, 2020; Litke, 2020), local football workers can use the power of dialogue—dialogue as a social instrument for communal change, not as a therapeutic tool for individual cure—to push for better living conditions in their communities.

Football is immersed in Latin American cultures (Bravo et al., 2016). If one sees and understands football practitioners as cultural-makers and workers, it is possible to realize that they are key actors to increase dialogue within their communities—thus, to manufacture everyday culture. The footballing dialogues may start in the proper football fields, the same social environment where coaches and instructors learn about football themselves, have also learned how to pass this culture on to other generations; they can teach them not only to understand and play the game better, but also how to use the power of football for social change (Añorve Añorve, 2021). This is relevant because in Freirean thinking, the ones who teach the cultural workers, must be in the world with the new generations, learning with them how to produce the new cultural formats (Freire, 1996).

This is how the once marginalised and expatriate navigate the *conscientização* process to renew their collective cultures, imagining a world of scenarios that goes past enduring oppression. The training and collective footballing practices, which emerge during dialogical shared moments, bring to participants what Freire called *conscientização*. This is particularly relevant for Latin American communities because their main forms of socialising and producing culture are totally connected to football; thus, the sport becomes key in the development of well-informed communal agents who will generate their own cultures, instead of just submitting to the one's of the colonisers. Football, both as an embodied practice but also as a space that allows critical dialogue, is seen as an essential tool here. It is part of a political project that points to the necessity of communities to transform the oppressive features in cultural products. That is, to express their own ways of being in the world, in search of a fairer and sustainable place to live.

Latin American Feminist Football's Agenda in Post-pandemic or Syndemic Times

During the initial years of the 1990s, the AIDS health crisis that hit impoverished communities within several cities in the United States created the conditions for the perfect storm for what Singer (1996, p. 933) theorised as a 'syndemic'. By coining this new concept, the author argued that an epidemic virus, when meeting high rates of socially unfair conditions, amplifies its actions. The lack of jobs or minimal living standards, insufficient nourishment and inadequate housing, among other abysmal social issues brought on by poverty in Latin America were the 'perfect storm' for the COVID-19 syndemic to spread in its most fatal ways (Burki, 2020). As the syndemic ran havoc through the continent and poverty became misery (Colombo, 2021), its effects could be seen in several sports leagues and especially within women's football (Biram & Martinez-Mina, 2021). Teams were destroyed, leagues abandoned and many players were left without their wages, even if those were negligible.

As one hopes that the syndemic subsides in the next few years, the following sections raise a few topics that the authors consider key points to the advancement of a feminist football on the continent. Rather than being exhaustive, this list seeks to excite the imagination of feminist researchers and activists to continue to strive for an inclusive and a fairer game for all in Latin America.

Football as a Language: Decolonising the Game

The football game arrived in South America as a colonial enterprise, created and expressed in the language of the colonisers. Nevertheless, for the native inhabitants of the subcontinent, Spanish was also the colonisers' language, much earlier than English. Indigenous communities spread around South America experienced suppression of their own languages and dialects, thus parts of their own native culture. To have their voices heard, they had to learn and adopt the language of the colonial power, be it either Spain or, later, England.

Nevertheless, mastering the language of the coloniser does not mean one is culturally disenfranchised (Freire, 2000). Otherwise, dominating the oppressor's language might be a central tool to question the social and political order (Freire, 2000). Therefore, the question that remains is: How can one speak the language of the coloniser—as we do in this book—and simultaneously contest its colonial powers?

It is argued that the body language manifested on a football pitch needs to be understood as one of the most powerful means that Latin Americans possess to express themselves. Playing the game with official rules, or more informally amid a chaotic urban space, certainly contains the main elements of local identity. By using the body language in a special manner in a football match, South Americans suppress time and space and may create a new, liberated social order.

This order, however, has been constrained, for several decades, by a rigid and binary colonial gender order (Oxford, 2019). According to this author, gender order manifests itself not only through the traditional binary gender order that opposes male versus female, men versus women, boys versus girls; but also colonial gender order creates binary hierarchies in the women's game—namely, the 'neoliberal empowered players' versus 'the victimized players' who have no access to any resources (Oxford, 2019). Within women's football, this has been the norm that endures and keeps bodies imprisoned, stealing their potentialities to produce the new language of the oppressed.

Therefore, as Oxford (2019) argued, a decolonial footballing feminist perspective must break this traditional gender order that was imposed onto South American women. It needs to create several new social orders that challenge the geopolitical status quo of knowledge (Radcliffe, 2017); a new order that brings genuine opportunities for participation in the civic spheres that football can produce across the continent. This new order must ensure that women's football and its participants do not become another neoliberal token, but become the owners of their destinies (Cusicanqui, 2012) and destroy coloniality in micro-, meso- but also macro-social and political spaces (Garton et al., 2021). Moreover, an order that ensures that the decolonial feminist perspective can be perceived across bodies and minds of the continent. Therefore, this perspective must include all bodies, and guarantee that 'everyone belongs'.

Freeing the Diverse Footballing Bodies

Maranhão and Knijnik (2011) discuss how Gilberto Freyre, a key South American twentieth-century sociologist, has drawn an interesting parallel between South American football, and European football, at the beginning of the twentieth century. They identify that Freyre uses the metaphor of poetry versus prose to conceptualise the visible styling differences between the bodies that play football on various continents; whereas Europeans had a more mechanised playing style, like robots. South Americans had a dancing footballing elegance, with plenty of creativity that made their bodies dance on the football pitches.

The authors claim that Freyre's metaphor is still relevant in today's football. Even though nowadays the European clubs and countries are dominant in the sport, Latin Americans have always displayed a dancing culture that most of the time pervades their football endeavours. As a post-pandemic agenda, the authors believe that the dancing bodies need to return to the fields to demonstrate all their powerful eroticism within the game and beyond (Iannotta & Kane, 2002).

Nevertheless, as women's football experiences a never seen before growth (Williams, 2019), one needs to reconceptualise what bodies individuals believe will be acceptable in the football discipline. As open and public spaces (Branz, 2012), should the pitches be open to everyone, or is there a need to block 'certain' bodies from the women's fields and relegate them to other 'non-spaces'? This topic deserves more attention, and the chapters in this book are evidence of that. Women have historically been excluded from football across the whole continent because of a series of factors, from misogyny to open homophobia (Dennie, 2019; Cunningham, 2019). Thus, at a moment when they have been conquering their spaces across the football arena, from pitches to management, from broadcasting to sponsors (Williams, 2003), there is the necessity to further the concept of women's footballers and to address transgender issues in the sport (Travers, 2018).

Transgender women are currently promoting a 'new gender revolution' within the sports realm, in particular within football (Love, 2014). Although major international bodies, such as the International Olympic Committee, after years of deliberations and strict regulations, have now accepted the inclusion of transgender people in their competitions, there are persistent 'myths' about transgender women that need to be fought against; for example, the idea that transgender women would 'steal' the space of 'real' women to play sports (Kamasz, 2018) after decades of hard-fought battles to win the right to play sports and football on the continent.

Nevertheless, transgender bodies have been transforming the way one sees sports; they bring a new dimension to the will to include everyone who wants to play football. Transgender people, and women, challenge the ways one discusses inclusion and equity within football, and pushes for new boundaries that, rather than being restricted, can become porous and opened to anyone who wants to join and enjoy the pleasures of a dancing body on a football field (Scharagrodsky, 2019). Transgender bodies certainly will bring back the needed dancing and poetry to the football fields, and women's football needs to be the first to include them in any capacity.

Is Social Media the New Space for Feminist Footballing's Revolution?

For many underrepresented groups, social media has become their 'lost paradise'. Many groups who have been traditionally ignored or marginalised by mainstream media, have found their space in a range of social media channels to manage and amplify their visibility, and to put forward their messages. Simultaneously, they can also profit from this exposure, by advertising products or services or branding their sponsors.

Women footballers have embraced this process in recent years and increased their social media presence and profiles. Although this movement might have been seen as positive for them, many questions remain, specifically from a feminist perspective. Is social media involvement a liberating development for women's footballers? Have they put forward a more collective approach to support sustainable change within the game? Have players manifested their will for social and gender justice in football and beyond?

Recent research has shown that in many cases, what women athletes display in social media is a neoliberal profile (Toffoletti & Thorpe, 2018). Rather than looking at the key issues and social struggles that their game faces, the authors argue that women athletes' social media profiles emphasise their individual achievements. Exposing themselves as 'winners' in the sports entertainment capitalist market, these profiles, instead of advancing the feminist cause within the game, demonstrate how these athletes have been absorbed by this market and want to be seen as 'empowered and entrepreneurial' individuals, not as leaders of a social movement (Toffoletti & Thorpe, 2018).

Rather than criticising this 'neoliberal' approach that the players take on social media, one needs to understand these tensions. Football researchers with a feminist agenda must look at all the players' perspectives and see how distinct feminist perspectives are in place when they go public on the Internet (Thorpe et al., 2017). Although there is no single response to the challenges and constraints presented by social media to the women's football context in Latin America, the authors believe that researchers and activities must increase feminist education around all football fields and spaces so that players enhance their *conscientização* (Freire, 2000) of the oppressive social contexts in which they still live. *Conscientização* brings action for transformation, and this is the key for a better usage of all social media channels that can be occupied by women's football in Latin America and around the world.

'Si nos permiten jugar': For a Feminist Football That Changes the World

This chapter started by bringing in the powerful voice of Domitilia Barros de Chungara, a woman Bolivian mining worker who was also a trailblazer of a different feminism. Domitilia's feminist struggle disturbed the white middle-class mainstream feminism of her time. She demonstrated that among the exploration and subtraction of her continent's underground treasures by large mining companies, there were voices and demands that needed to be listened to. She shocked the mainstream feminist world by showing that their social justice struggle would only be completed if they considered not only individual demands from certain groups, but also the needs and hardships of other women and communities who were suffering unequal and corresponding layers of oppression.

The metaphor could not be clearer. As Domitilia wanted her voice to be heard, here the authors claim that Latin American women must be allowed to freely play football, without any more legal, economic or social constraints. Like Domitilia's feminism, what can be seen here is a footballing feminism that is concerned with its communities and people. Rather than another piece of the whole neoliberal sporting entertainment industry, it is possible to see this football as a tool to advance social justice for all women across the continent, with its rich and diverse cultures.

The authors are not naïve to claim that football is a panacea for all social issues. It is evident that football can become, as it was in the past, a tool for colonisation and commodification of bodies and minds. One can see how a neoliberal ideology has become relevant within players' social media profiles—for example, backing the notion of individual success rather than community development. Nevertheless, the same game, if understood as a collective tool for conscientização, can be the means for achieving a better life for several communities.

Therefore, *Let Us Play!* is not an empty demand, but a struggle for collective rights that goes far beyond the football pitch. It embraces the tensions and paradoxes of the new footballing gender order; it understands the neoliberal forces that want to commodify the game, but at the same time it brings a communal dimension that cannot be ignored. Whereas Domitilia was asking for her right to talk ('let *me* talk'), the motto here asks for the rights of the collective (i.e., *nossotras*, we, *us*) and of every single girl and woman; this should be regardless of their social and ethnic background, or gender orientation so that they can be part of this key element of their cultural and political life. In this sense, a community-led feminist football will be revolutionary and show the actual Latin American capabilities to the world.

References

Abbassi, D. (2009). Le sport dans l'empire français: Un instrument de domination? *Outre-Mers. Revue D'Histoire, 96*(364), 5–15.

Añorve Añorve, D. (2021). Gender social change, international influence and sensemaking in the launch and evolution of the Mexican professional women's football league. *Sport in Society, 24*(7), 1122–1140.

Biram, M. D., & Martinez-Mina, C. Y. (2021). Football in the time of COVID-19: Reflections on the implications for the women's professional league in Colombia. *Soccer & Society, 22*(1–2), 35–42.

Branz, J. (2012). Fútbol, mujeres y espacio público. In G. Cachorro (Comp.) (Ed.), *Ciudad y Prácticas Corporales* (pp. 339–352). Faculty of Humanities and Education Sciences (UNLP).

Bravo, G., de D'Amico, R. L., & Parrish, C. (2016). Football in Argentina and its institutions, 1980–2014: Changes and traditions. In *Sport in Latin America* (pp. 253–267). Routledge.

Burki, T. (2020). COVID-19 in Latin America. *The Lancet Infectious Diseases, 20*(5), 547–548.

Colombo, S. (2021). Agravada pela pandemia, pobreza na Argentina afeta quase 6 de cada 10 crianças. *Folha de S. Paulo.* https://www1.folha.uol.com.br/mundo/2021/05/agravada-pela-pandemia-pobreza-na-argentina-afeta-quase-6-de-cada-10-criancas.shtml

Cunningham, G. B. (2019). Understanding the experiences of LGBT athletes in sport: A multilevel model. In M. H. Anshel, T. A. Petrie, & J. A. Steinfeldt (Eds.), *APA handbook of sport and exercise psychology, vol. 1. Sport psychology* (pp. 367–383). American Psychological Association.

Cusicanqui, S. R. (2012). Ch'ixinakax utxiwa: A reflection on the practices and discourses of decolonization. *South Atlantic Quarterly, 111*(1), 95–109.

Darder, A. (2016). Latinos, education, and the church: Toward a culturally democratic future. *Journal of Catholic Education, 19*(2), n 2.

de D'Amico, R. L. (2019). Socio-political context in which the business of women's sport takes place in Latin America. In *Routledge handbook of the business of women's sport* (pp. 280–291). Routledge.

Dennie, A. (2019). *The effects of homophobia, biphobia and transphobia in high school physical education classes, school sports and community sports on future sports and physical activity participation: A retrospective study.* Doctoral dissertation, Laurentian University of Sudbury.

Dine, P. (2002). France, Algeria and sport: From colonisation to globalisation. *Modern & Contemporary France, 10*(4), 495–505.

Elsey, B., & Nadel, J. (2019). *Futbolera: A history of women and sports in Latin America*. University of Texas Press.

Everbach, T., Nisbett, G. S., & Weiller-Abels, K. (2021). Rebel, rebel! How Megan Rapinoe's celebrity activism forges new paths for athletes. In *2019 FIFA women's world cup* (pp. 267–289). Palgrave Macmillan.

Franco, J. (1992). 'Si me permiten hablar': La lucha por el poder interpretativo. *Revista de Crítica Literaria Latinoamericana, 18*(36), 111–118.

Freire, P. (1996). *Pedagogia da autonomia: Saberes necessários a prática educativa [Pedagogy of freedom: Ethics, democracy and civic courage]*. Paz e Terra..

Freire, P. (2000). *Pedagogy of the oppressed* (30th Anniversary ed.). Continuum.

Garton, G. (2019). *Guerreras: Fútbol, Mujeres y Poder*. Capital Intelectual.

Garton, G., Hijós, N., & Alabarces, P. (2021). Playing for change: (Semi-) professionalization, social policy, and power struggles in Argentine women's football. *Soccer & Society, 22*(6), 626–640.

Hancock, A. M. (2016). *Intersectionality: An intellectual history*. Oxford University Press.

Hang, J. (2020). Feministas y triperas. Mujeres y política en el área de género del club gimnasia y esgrima La Plata. *Debates en Sociología, 50*, 67–90.

Iannotta, J. G., & Kane, M. J. (2002). Sexual stories as resistance narratives in women's sports: Reconceptualizing identity performance. *Sociology of Sport Journal, 19*(4), 347–369.

Kamasz, E. (2018). Transgender people and sports. *Journal of Education, Health and Sport, 8*(11), 572–582.

Knijnik, J. (2013). Visions of gender justice: Untested feasibility on the football fields of Brazil. *Journal of Sport and Social Issues, 37*(1), 8–30.

Knijnik, J. (2018). *The World Cup Chronicles: 31 Days that Rocked Brazil*. Fair Play Publishing.

Lin, C. Y., & Lee, P. C. (2007). Sport as a medium of national resistance: Politics and baseball in Taiwan during Japanese colonialism, 1895–1945. *The International Journal of the History of Sport, 24*(3), 319–337.

Litke, M. A. (2020). 'Me paro en la cancha como en la vida': Un análisis del fútbol feminista en la Villa 31 desde las teorías de género. *Zona Franca, 28*, 79–104.

Love, A. (2014). Transgender exclusion and inclusion in sport. In *Routledge handbook of sport, gender and sexuality* (pp. 376–383)). Routledge.

Maranhão, T. F., & Knijnik, J. (2011). Futebol mulato: Racial constructs in Brazilian football. *Cosmopolitan Civil Societies: An Interdisciplinary Journal, 3*(2), 55–71.

Nadel, J. (2015). The antinational game? An exploration of women's soccer in Latin America. In *Sports and Nationalism in Latin/o America* (pp. 45–65). Palgrave Macmillan.

Oxford, S. (2019). 'You look like a machito!': A decolonial analysis of the social in/exclusion of female participants in a Colombian sport for development and peace organization. *Sport in Society, 22*(6), 1025–1042.

Radcliffe, S. A. (2017). Decolonising geographical knowledges. *Transactions of the Institute of British Geographers, 42*(3), 329–333.

Scharagrodsky, P. A. (2019). Trans-formando el espacio educativo y deportivo. El caso de la comunidad trans en la capital Argentina. *Investiga+, 2*(2), 15–35.

Singer, M. (1996). A dose of drugs, a touch of violence, a case of AIDS: Conceptualizing the SAVA syndemic. *Free Inquiry in Creative Sociology, 24*(2), 99–110.

Thorpe, H., Toffoletti, K., & Bruce, T. (2017). Sportswomen and social media: Bringing third-wave feminism, postfeminism, and neoliberal feminism into conversation. *Journal of Sport and Social Issues, 41*(5), 359–383.

Toffoletti, K., & Thorpe, H. (2018). Female athletes' self-representation on social media: A feminist analysis of neoliberal marketing strategies in 'economies of visibility'. *Feminism & Psychology, 28*(1), 11–31.

Travers, A. (2018). Transgender issues in sport and leisure. In *The Palgrave handbook of feminism and sport, leisure and physical education* (pp. 649–665). Palgrave Macmillan.

Viezzer, M. (2013). *'Si me permiten hablar…': Testimonio de Domitila, una mujer de las minas de Bolivia*. Siglo XXI Editores.

Williams, J. (2003). The fastest growing sport? Women's football in England. *Soccer & Society, 4*(2–3), 112–127.

Williams, J. (2019). 'We're the lassies from Lancashire': Manchester Corinthians Ladies FC and the use of overseas tours to defy the FA ban on women's football. *Sport in History, 39*(4), 395–417.

Index[1]

---

[1] Note: Page numbers followed by 'n' refer to notes.

Ingram Content Group UK Ltd.
Milton Keynes UK
UKHW021911290323
419374UK00004B/49